RESTORATION ROAD

The Master Key to a New and Satisfied Life of Authenticity

MITCH KRUSE
with DEREK WILLIAMS

"I recommend Mitch's book for the same reason that I chose him to auction my restored Norton Spirit Penske/Cosworth that I drove to my third Indy win: he has a passion for excellence in everything he does. Mitch is a winner in my book, and by reading Restoration Road, you will discover the key to victory in your life."

—Bobby Unser, world champion Indy car driver
and three-time Indianapolis 500 winner

"My friend Mitch creatively tells his story of restoration while teaching what the Bible communicates on the subject. I watched a business renovated to new heights and a life restored to authenticity because he discovered the Master Key that unlocked the gate to Restoration Road. Whether in marketplace or ministry, this book is a must read for anyone who desires to lead. I highly recommend it."

—Truett Cathy, Founder of Chick-fil-A

"Mitch Kruse has written a fascinating account of his world of auctioning classic cars. More importantly, he shares with us his practical insights and biblical wisdom on living life to the maximum level."

—Pat Williams, Sr. Vice President, Orlando Magic
author of *Extreme Dreams Depend on Teams*

"My friend Mitch Kruse has had a life of extreme experiences, from the taste of great wealth to the degradation of serious business setbacks. It is from this school of hard knocks knowledge, combined with formal education in theology and psychology, that he is able to teach and write with depth, vulnerability, and solid insights."

—Dr. Dennis E. Hensley,
author of *The Power of Positive Productivity*

"It's all here: the glitzy world of classic automobiles, the thrill of the deal, the fall from grace, and a new beginning. With a personal story made for Hollywood, from auctioneer to stardom Mitch Kruse takes a surprisingly frank look at how life, apart from God, can never be enough. Here's your invitation to ride shotgun on one man's drive down Restoration Road. It's a trip I'll never forget."
—Clint Kelly, author of *Scent, Echo, and Delicacy*

"While reading *Restoration Road,* something familiar happened to me. I was transported to another day and another masterpiece: Robert Boyd Munger's *My Heart Christ's Home.* Just as Munger walks us through the restoration of an old home to illustrate the renovation of a battered heart, Mitch Kruse uses the restoration of a classic old car to probe the miracle of God's 'inside out' work in our lives. This work has depth and drama."
—Keith Potter, pastor, author and renewal agent

"Mitch shares his story as he traveled a traversing mountain top journey toward success that ended in a valley of total loss. Little did he know that his road would become a speedway filled with risk-taking and innovative leadership that culminated with not only the revitalization of an international corporation but the restoration of one man with his Creator. Each chapter guides the reader toward the destination of Restoration Road filled with biblical truths packaged in years of marketplace experiences."
—Guy S. Higashi, President, Pacific Rim Christian College

"What a surprising, engaging, and wise book! *Restoration Road* combines perspectives that have never been joined before (antique car restoration and the parable we call "The Prodigal Son") to help us be renewed by the master Restorer, Jesus Christ. Wonderfully written, this book is full of biblical insights, real-life connections, and delightful illustrations. I am happy to commend it to all who seek to advance further on the road to living fully as restored people."

—Dr. Mark D. Roberts, Senior Director, Laity Lodge

"*Restoration Road* is a fascinating read, full of wonder and wisdom. The author weaves the vastly rich experiences of his life with proven and eternal precepts, creating short stories that both intrigue and encourage the reader. Mitch Kruse skillfully uncrates age-old truths many of us thought were antiquated. He blows the dust off and gives us fresh perspectives on how to live authentic lives with purpose and joy."

—Dwayne Moore, President of Next Level Worship,
www.nextlevelworship.com

I dedicate this book to Uncle Derald.
I don't see how I could have written it without you
guiding me to the wisdom of the Restorer.

CONTENTS

ACKNOWLEDGMENTS

Susan, thank you for modeling the Restorer to me. Your commitment draws me to the unique expression of the Restorer in you. I'm so thankful that we have each other.

Megan, thank you for demonstrating your contagious heart for people. It's no wonder why so many of your classmates and teammates seek your guidance. You are God's first gift to us. It has been such an honor to have a front row seat in your incredible story.

Kelsey, I love your desire for excellence. Thank you for your insights beyond your years. I love hanging out with you to watch games or to rebound shots. You are a portrait of grace. I can't wait for your first book.

Lilly, thank you for asking us deep questions and for living out your faith. I love your desire for harmony and reconciliation. You are a picture of the embodiment of the Restorer's heart for relationships. I'm so eager to see what God has in store for your gifts.

Haley, thank you for being our joy. You are a beautiful package of abundant energy that helps me forget about all perfectionist tendencies. You brighten up each day in a way that makes me lighten up.

Mom, thank you for modeling a clay heart to me and for forgiving me for the shiny metal box incident.

Dad, thank you for teaching me your leadership skills and how to auctioneer. You are truly one of a kind.

Curtis Smith, the best meteorologist on the planet, thank you for teaching me about weather.

Derek, thank you for encouraging me to follow the Restorer's prompting to connect the culture with Him through writing this book.

David Sanford, Tim Beals, Mike Vander Klipp and the entire team at Credo House Publishers, thank you for your investment to bring this project to completion.

Kruse Automotive and Carriage Museum, thank you for providing the restored 1930 Duesenberg J Murphy Torpedo Roadster donated by Richard Losee for the cover photograph.

Jon Bill, Director of Education and Archives, Auburn Cord Duesenberg Automobile Museum, thank you for providing the original factory photographs from the legendary Auburn Automobile Company.

Laura Brinkman, Executive Director and CEO, Auburn Cord Duesenberg Automobile Museum, thank you for providing the ideal setting to communicate the message of restoration as the backdrop to film the companion DVD.

Kruse Automotive and Carriage Museum — www.kacmuseum.org

Auburn Cord Duesenberg Automobile Museum — www.automobilemuseum.org

"Stone is heavy and sand a burden, but provocation by a fool is heavier than both." Proverbs 27:3

Chapter One

SAND, STONE, AND CLAY

In the small French town of Molsheim, a mystery remained un-
earthed inside the estate of famed automobile designer Ettore
Bugatti. A vision, first shaped in a clay mold, was later transformed into seven of the most magnificent vehicles ever crafted—
the Bugatti Royales.

These breathtaking vehicles were launched just as the world
economy began to sour on the verge of the Great Depression.
All seven had been built by 1933. They were enormous, with
a 169.3 inch wheelbase and an overall length up to twenty-one
feet—five feet longer than today's average car length of sixteen
feet. They sported the first true "bling," with twenty-four inch
rims to support their 7,000 pound body. The 12.7 L "straight 8"
engine produced up to 300 horsepower, with cylinders bored 5.1
inches, each discharging more horsepower than the entire engine
of a contemporary Type 40 touring car of its day.

The Bugattis were rolling sculptures. And one man, now driving through Molsheim's Nouveau Quartier, was nearing the end
of his quest to uncover these works of art.

Briggs knew that four of the Bugattis had already been sold,
and the seventh one made had been destroyed by fire. But the re-

maining two were still missing. He slowed the truck along a dirt road as two refrigerators bounced back and forth in the back, and stopped at a wrought iron gate just outside of Bugatti's estate.

Ten minutes later Briggs stood in the main hall, surrounded by paintings and photos of Ettore's grand accomplishments. One piece of sculpture struck Briggs as unique. It was a statue of a boy kneeling before his father. Etched into the stone were the words, *The Prodigal Son Returns*. It was a beautiful work of art by Rembrandt himself—Rembrandt Bugatti, that is. Ettore's brother was a world-renowned sculptor who had added his considerable talent to the designs of the famed Bugatti Royales.

A woman's voice echoed through the hall.

"Good afternoon, Mr. Cunningham."

"Therese, it's so good to see you again," Briggs replied.

Therese was all business.

"As I mentioned to you yesterday, I'm not sure how much help I can be. However, you are welcome to take a look around."

"Great! I'd like to start in your father's study."

"Very well."

Briggs followed Therese down several corridors. He glanced into the rooms as they passed by and noticed all of them were empty. It seemed that the cost of the war had wounded even those whom society had previously deemed untouchable.

Therese stopped at a mahogany door and reached for a key. Years had passed since anyone had entered this forgotten place— until now. As she swung the door open, Briggs noticed that this room was still fully furnished. Inside was a beautiful wooden desk and two leather chairs facing an old, red-brick fireplace. In the far corner, a sledgehammer stood propped next to a gas lantern.

Therese waited in the doorway as Briggs stepped inside. It had been years since her father had passed, and this unexpected visit had flooded her with forgotten memories, none of which had occurred in this room.

"Mr. Cunningham, what is it you do?"

"I build race cars," Briggs replied. "And I've been captivated by the beautiful automobiles your father built for quite some time."

He ran his fingers over the aged brick and wondered if he was about to unlock a piece of history. Could the stories he'd heard possibly be true?

"Whether I find what I'm looking for or not," Briggs said as he reached into his pocket and handed Therese an envelope, "this is for you. And, as promised, the refrigerators are outside."

"Thank you," she replied.

Briggs' eyes gleamed with excitement as he glanced back toward the brick wall at the south corner. He was here to find an authentic original. Without another word, he picked up the sledgehammer and pounded into the center of the wall. As he did so, pieces of brick scattered in all directions.

Therese was stunned by this sudden burst of destructive energy, but she continued to watch, a bit bewildered by what unfolded before her. Even though reluctant to admit it, she was captivated by what this American might find hidden after all these years. All the while she told herself that her memories of her father and the legacy he had left behind were greater than any artifact that might now be uncovered.

Sweat poured down Briggs' face as he swung the hammer again and again. Thirty minutes later, Briggs and Therese stood in front of a small black hole. With one final grunt, he pulled a pile of bricks out of the opening. As the bricks tumbled at his feet, he grinned and turned toward Therese.

The moment of truth.

She lit a flame and handed the lantern to Briggs. Now she stood by his side and followed the glow that illuminated what was behind the wall. What they unveiled was a forgotten garage, built to protect two pieces of art that no one believed still existed. Briggs had found a lost treasure—Ettore's personal Bugattis, one of which was the prized Bugatti Royale Kellner.

"I knew you'd keep them close," he whispered.

"*Fou d'Amérique*" Therese muttered. *Crazy American.*

What a day this had been! Briggs Cunningham had passed through a gate to Ettore Bugatti's estate, traveled up an unassuming dirt road, and arrived at a destination where he discovered two of the most sought-after, most valuable automobiles in the world—the rarest of Ettore Bugatti's priceless works of art. It had cost him a mere fifty thousand dollars and two refrigerators. Now that he had found them, he knew he *must* restore the automobiles to their original, authentic condition.

Briggs Cunningham was an American adventurer, a risk taker, whose heart beat to build the fastest cars on the planet. He was also a treasured acquaintance of mine who shared his love for rare automobiles with me. I remember strolling through his museum as he shared the Bugatti story. (I've taken the liberty to fill in the missing pieces as I imagined them.)

What always remained true about Mr. Cunningham was his heart's desire to find the rarest pieces of Bugatti's collection and restore them to their authentic, original condition. It was a dream that he believed one day would come true. He never gave up, using every resource at his disposal to fuel his treasure hunt until he found what was needed to complete the authentic restoration.

Maybe you too are an adventurer, a risk taker, in search of your heart's desire; someone who is searching for a hidden treasure to restore your authentic life. Perhaps you have repeatedly asked yourself, "How can I make what's old in my life shine like new again? How can I restore the truest desires of my heart?"

Whether we are CEO's, blue collar workers, stay-at-home moms, college graduates or freshmen in high school, we all have old patterns in our lives that we would like to change so that we can be restored to new. The challenge we face is answering the question, "How do we restore what's old in our lives—the rust that has formed on our purer motivations, the dings that have appeared in our passion for the good, the faded paint of our resolve to love God with all our hearts—to its authentic, original state?"

By definition, something that is *authentic* reflects the design of the designer. As in the case of Ettore Bugatti and his magnificent creations, an authentic collector car reflects the design of its designer. This is the design that Briggs Cunningham worked so tirelessly to restore, the same design that the Designer desires to restore in us.

The Desire of the Designer

Each collector vehicle begins life as a clay mold that carries the handprints of the designer who fashioned it. That design flows from the heart of its creator. Later, the design comes to life through a community of engineers, manufacturers, and executives who work together to carry out the *inspiration*, or the "breath," of the designer. When it comes to automotive restoration, there is no greater value than a restoration that is carried out by a car's original designer.

Like a collector car, we also began as clay molds in the hands of the Designer who breathed life into us (Genesis 2:7), the same Designer who desires to restore us to the original creation that He intended. Our deep, inborn desire for authenticity originates from the One who designed us from the inside out.

Authenticity, one of the highest values in our postmodern culture, aligns our lives from the *inside out*. As postmoderns we deconstruct the layers of every person we encounter to discover whether he or she is someone who is the same, someone who is truly "authentic," all the way through to the core of his or her being.

Pretense, the opposite of authenticity, misaligns our lives from the *outside in*. Pretense focuses on the outside at the expense of the inside. In the collector car world, we call this a cosmetic restoration—a vehicle is spruced up on the outside just enough to fool others that it is restored. It is only a matter of time before the concealed truth about the vehicle's cancerous undercarriage is revealed, followed by another *outside in* attempt at restoration. This process never satisfies.

When we are uninformed, unaware, or unbelieving, we often pretend that *we* are the ultimate designers in our lives. Consequently, we pretend with ourselves, with God, and with others that we do not need inside out restoration. Those of us who continue on this path live our lives trapped in continual, progressive pretense that leaves us dissatisfied.

In life, our desire to be restored comes as a result of the damage, the dings, the rust and the corrosion that comes from trying to live lives our own way. And such a desire is not new to us today—we find the desire to be restored to authenticity scattered in writings throughout history, in religious texts, in those we love, and even in today's news headlines. And when we're honest, we also find it hidden in the darkest places within ourselves. We hear it in the countless whispers of anyone who longs to be brought back to a life that restores him from the pride-filled addictions that leave him destroyed. Restoration is truly humanity's deepest desire.

The Restoration Process

A life of pretense keeps us unrestored; therefore, a life of authenticity is impossible without restoration.

To be *restored* means "to be made new again." When an auto enthusiast finds the car of his dreams buried under tarps in an old barn or chicken coop, he has a vision of what the car was and what the car could be again. He has a firm belief that this dusty, rusty, dinged-up old crate can be remade to the specifications of the designer.

This optimist, this visionary, surrenders his old basket-case of a car to a restorer so that the restoration process can begin. During the process, the car is disassembled and the individual parts are restored, piece by piece. After each part of the car is restored, it is carefully reassembled. After all the work is done, it's finally time for a test drive.

As the owner displays his pride and joy, others learn from his experience and dedication. However, even the most detailed, correct restorations lose their luster over time. The car gets dinged again, the paint fades, the interior tears, the tires wear, the engine grows tired and the metal rusts. But the true restorer's passion is to make these things new again.

The same is true for our lives.

First, *the old is surrendered*. Like a classic car that needs restoration, each one of us must surrender our old basket case of a life to the Restorer. Second, *the pieces are surrendered*. The Restorer begins to disassemble and renovate the components of our lives, piece by piece, whether they be unrestored or self-restored. Third, *the new is surrendered*. As the restoration process unfolds, we learn that we are designed to bring authentic restoration to others. We surrender the new for this purpose and continue to surrender any old parts that corrode again over time.

On our restoration journey our resolve can fade, tear, wear, grow tired, and become rusty as we occasionally turn from the Restorer in an attempt to restore the individual pieces ourselves. Pride deceives us into either believing that our self-restoration attempts are working, or thinking that we cannot bring a particular piece to the Restorer more than once. Consequently, pride leaves us questioning how we are supposed to surrender that one last piece of our lives.

Pride is the Lock on the Human Heart; Humility is the Key

Imagine the inner workings of a lock fashioned with two concentric cylinders that are held together by four spring-loaded pins. A key is the perfect combination for each respective lock. It pushes up the spring-loaded pins high enough so that the innermost cylinder can turn freely inside the outermost cylinder, unlocking the door. If by inserting the key we say we are surrendering the key to the lock, then partially surrendering the key into that lock will never open any door. Only fully surrendering the key will unlock it.

The same is true for our lives. In order to be restored to authenticity, we must humbly and fully surrender our hearts, desires, and lives to the Restorer.

Let's look into this metaphor a little more deeply. The inner cylinder represents our spiritual heart. The four pins are indicative of its four chambers. The outer cylinder illustrates our four primary, God-given desires (both the chambers of the heart and the four primary God-given desires are defined later in this chapter).

When the key is fully surrendered into the lock, all four pins pass through the inner cylinder, representing the heart, and the outer cylinder that encompasses our four primary desires. The lock is opened, which allows us to open the gate to the three key resources of our life: our *time*, *talent*, and *treasure*. When we unlock this gate, our lives are unlocked and opened to a restored life of authenticity. This newly surrendered life is measured on the basis of godly wisdom, not by any temporal measure of success.

Jesus spoke of similar keys when he said to his disciple Peter, "I will give you the keys of the kingdom of heaven; whatever you bind on earth will be bound in heaven, and whatever you loose on earth will be loosed in heaven" (Matthew 16:19). When paired with our current metaphor, this kingdom perspective comes into clearer view. The kingdom of heaven is God's divine reign, rule, and order in the hearts and lives of people on this earth, both now and in the future. It is one of the most profound expressions of Christ living within us. When we fully surrender the key of humility into the lock of our human heart, we open wide the gate to the kingdom of heaven in our lives. When we partially surrender the key of humility into our prideful heart, the gate to the kingdom of heaven remains locked—both in this life and the next.

The Sand and Stone of Pride

Pride is a hard heart, one that makes itself higher than others. We find it in two forms: a heart of *sand* or a heart of *stone*.

A *sand* heart partially surrenders the horizontal at the expense of the vertical. It focuses on people and tasks rather than on God. This is license. A heart of sand is loose and scattered; it requires a storm to be shaped and restored.

A *stone* heart partially surrenders the vertical at the expense of the horizontal. It focuses on God rather than on others. This is legalism—the thought that one can manipulate the deity of the universe through the actions and activities of our lives. A stone heart is hard. It requires tooling by a sharp instrument to be shaped and restored.

Ironically, both sand and stone are the same substance, just a different aggregate. In its essence, sand is just tiny pieces of crumbled up stone. However, neither a heart of sand or a heart of stone reflect the design of the Designer who is also our Restorer. Sand hearts and stone hearts break apart the vertical from the horizontal, creating four walls that form a prison. The result is the incarceration of pride.

The Master Key of Full Surrender

The Master Key that fully surrenders our hearts, desires, and lives to the Restorer is cross-shaped; this is the perfect picture of the vertical intersecting with the horizontal. The vertical axis is our relationship with God. The horizontal axis is our relationship with people. In order to fully surrender the Master Key into the lock of pride on the human heart, one must humble his heart vertically to God, and horizontally to others.

Christ the Designer (Colossians 1:16) and Restorer (Colossians 1:19) holds the restoring key of David that unlocks the kingdom of heaven. What he opens, no one can shut; what he shuts, no one can open (Revelation 3:7). He has unlocked the door to abundant and eternal restoration to those who humble their hearts, desires, and the three resources of life to Him. For those who choose to live in their pride and reject Him, the door will remain closed on this side of life and the next. In order to discover who God created us to be, we must gather the courage to travel into the mystery that God will reveal to us as He unlocks the condition of our hearts, our desires, and our three resources of life for the advancement of His kingdom.

A Clay Heart

A *clay* heart lives in the sweet spot where the vertical intersects with the horizontal—where our relationship with God intersects with our relationships with others. A heart of clay is a humble heart. The words "humility" and "humanity" come from the same Latin word, *humus*, which means "from the ground." Humility involves bending the knee. It means "to make ourselves lower than." Consequently, humility always has an object.

Whereas a sand heart is a picture of license, requiring a storm to be fashioned, and a stone heart is a picture of legalism requiring a severe tool to be shaped, a heart of clay is a picture of love. It's a heart that is malleable in the hands of its gracious Designer. While all three substances come from the ground, the heart of clay is void of meaning unless it is shaped and restored by the heart and hands of the Designer.

CLAY is an acronym that helps us remember how to live with a humble heart. First, we *confess* to God our proud sinful hearts of sand or stone. Second, we *learn* His design for our lives from the Bible. Third, we *apply* what we learn from the Scriptures to our daily tasks and relationships. Fourth, we *yield* the outcomes to God. A clay heart experiences the design of the Designer through full surrender.

The heart of the Designer, the One we desire to emulate, is clay. His deep desire is to restore all that He has designed. As the Designer, he understands the pattern that he has built into humanity—the pattern that has been damaged by sin. As the Restorer, He is the embodiment of a clay heart, of the vertical axis intersecting with the horizontal axis. He walked the earth as fully God and fully man. He is the authentic picture of a humble heart that fully surrenders everything in communion with the Father and at the same time humbly surrenders everything in community with others. He has restored the vertical (God with man) and the horizontal (man with man). He invites each of us to be restored to authenticity, to the unique expression of the Designer in us.

Outside In versus Inside Out Living

On Restoration Road, we are reminded that the Restorer is Jesus Christ. He fully surrendered His heart, His desires, and His life to the Father. His heart was humble (Matthew 11:29). All of Jesus' time, talent, and treasure were completely surrendered to the promptings of His heavenly Father. Jesus glorified the Father in coming to earth as a sacrifice for sin, and in return, the Father restored Jesus to the glory of heaven (John 17:1-4). He came to inaugurate the kingdom of heaven, the biggest restoration project in the universe, because He came to restore the unique expression of the Designer in each one of us.

But we turn away from that design. Often times, our hearts of sand and stone sign up for self–restoration—that which takes place from the *outside in*. We think that if we *go* somewhere, we can *do* something, and then we will *be* somebody. This pattern attempts to restore our three resources of life (time, talent, and treasure) without first addressing our hearts or desires.

But living restored to authenticity occurs from the *inside out*. This is the *be-do-go* of full surrender. Who we are designed to *be* determines what we are designed to *do,* which determines where we are designed to *go*. This is the individual design of the Designer in each of our lives. Consequently, Restoration Road transforms our hearts, then our desires, and finally our three resources of life for the advancement of God's kingdom.

Let's unpack this a little more thoroughly. As we established earlier, Restoration Road is the road we travel in our journey of life. Remember, Jesus is the Restorer. First, *Restoration Road transforms our hearts*, the identity of who we are designed to *be*. When a vertical line intersects with a horizontal line, four chambers result. These represent the four chambers of the spiritual heart. We can remember them with the acronym, *WISE*.

The first chamber is the *will*. This is the chamber of our choices. The second chamber is the *intellect*, or the mind. This is the chamber of our thoughts. The third chamber is the *spirit*. This is the lead chamber of our prayers. The fourth chamber is the *emotions*. This is the chamber of our feelings.

In order to be restored to authenticity, we must fully surrender each of the four chambers of our hearts to the Restorer. We must choose, think, pray, and want to make this surrender. This is the prerequisite to unlocking wisdom's gate (Proverbs 1:7; 11:2).

Second, *Restoration Road transforms our desires*, or what we are designed to *do*. This is the heartbeat that connects our hearts with our three resources of life—our time, our talent, and our treasure. As we travel the road of life, we can see the desires of our hearts in three different ways, depending on the condition of our hearts. Whereas sand hearts see desires for their *gratification*, and stone hearts see desires often in terms of *negation*, clay hearts see desires for their *transformation*. The last one is what we were designed to *do* with our desires.

God created us with at least four primary desires, each coming from his *being*, or his identity.

Desire 1: Significance from being created in God's image (Genesis 1:27).

Desire 2: Contentment from being blessed by God to be fruitful, multiply, and subdue (bring contentment to) the earth (Genesis 1:28).

Desire 3: Control from being empowered by God to rule over the earth (Genesis 1:28).

Desire 4: Security from being given every seed-bearing plant and fruit-bearing tree (Genesis 1:29-30).

These desires flow vertically from the heart of God into each one of our hearts. They flow horizontally into our relationships with others (Genesis 2:18).

So the next question is, what happened to these pure desires? How did they become corrupted? The answer to this question is summed up in one word that we focused on earlier in this chapter: pride. This original sin came into play when humans searched for the satisfaction of their desires apart from God (Genesis 3:5-6).

God had created Adam and Eve with humble hearts. In the perfected Garden, God was the object of their desires. Consequently, He satisfied their desires. However, pride made humans the object of their own desires and created the need for restoration. This is a pattern that each of us repeats both by birth and by choice (Genesis 8:21).

The first sin was followed by the world's first self-restoration program. I call it "sin's trifecta": (1) Adam and Eve were *ashamed* because they had been *swayed* (Genesis 3:7), (2) they *hid* because they were *afraid* (Genesis 3:12-13), (3) they *blamed* because they had *disobeyed* (Genesis 3:12-13). Adam and Eve ate of the forbidden tree of the knowledge of good and evil, and from that point, humans have determined for ourselves what is right and wrong (Genesis 3:1-6). This is our heritage; this is our legacy.

In essence, we take God's gift of life and continually attempt to satisfy our desires by setting ourselves up as gods in our own self-made kingdoms. We trust in our giftedness rather than our godliness. We follow our will rather than surrendering willingly. We rely on our own decisions rather than submitting them to the Decider. However, God the Designer responds by offering us the opportunity to be restored to authenticity (Genesis 3:15, 22).

Restoration Road transforms our three resources of life, or where we are designed to *go*. *Time* is fully surrendered to the

Restorer, and our calendars are transformed. *Talent* is fully surrendered to the Restorer, and our business cards are transformed. *Treasure* is fully surrendered to the Restorer, and our investments are transformed. When we surrender all three resources of our lives to the Restorer, He leads us down Restoration Road to reflect the design of the Designer.

The Pursuit of Wisdom

Money is pride's measurement of our giftedness (time, talent, and treasure). Wisdom is humility's measurement of our godliness (Christ in us). Although the Bible often comments on money, it is the latter commodity that we are advised to pursue repeatedly throughout Scripture.

Wisdom is the intersection of the vertical with the horizontal. It is God's heart (vertical) combined with street smarts (horizontal). Wisdom applies one's relationship with God to one's relationships with others, including the tasks to be achieved. We were designed to have a heart for wisdom (Proverbs 3:5-6; 22:17-18). We were designed to desire wisdom (Proverbs 3:15). We were designed to pursue wisdom with our three resources of life (Proverbs 4:7). Wisdom begins with a humble, malleable, clay-like heart toward God (Proverbs 1:7; 11:2; 22:4).

Thousands of years ago, Jewish Rabbis searched for the ultimate word to describe God. They chose "wisdom." Wisdom resides in a person in whom the vertical perfectly intersects with the horizontal. Christ the Restorer is the wisdom of God (1 Corinthians 1:24). Christ is the authenticity of God (Hebrews 1:3). He is humble in heart (Matthew 11:29). Humility toward him is the beginning of His wisdom in our lives (Proverbs 11:2).

Foolishness is the opposite of wisdom. It is derived from a proud heart. It begins as wet cement and progressively hardens like cured concrete. A stone heart is foolish. A sand heart is foolish. The two substances added together form a concrete mix that imprisons us in lives filled with pride instead of humility, and foolishness instead of wisdom. In our pride, we foolishly pretend that the satisfaction of our desires will occur through the pursuit of more time, talent, and treasure apart from God. The result is a life of pride, pretense, and foolishness that leaves us unrestored and dissatisfied.

The Gate, the Road, the Destination

So what happens as we move down Restoration Road? What are the mile markers, the signposts, the points of interest that we should be looking for? When we surrender our hearts, we know that Jesus is the voice on our GPS device directing our paths. But why are we on this road, and what is the goal?

The gate represents our hearts. On Restoration Road, we learn to shift the gates of our hearts, or who we were designed to be, from us to the Restorer. We move from a heart for our position to passion for His grace and His provision in our lives. We transition from a heart for our purpose to a passion for His vision. We change from a heart for our contentment to a passion for His peace. We journey from a heart for our competence to a passion for His character of wisdom. We travel from a heart for our control to a passion for trusting His power relationally manifested in our lives. We leave a heart for our security for a passion for His authentic truth. We give up a heart for our significance in exchange for a passion for His love. We let go of a heart for false liberty apart from the Restorer in lieu of a passion for the freedom found in the Restorer.

The road is imagery for our desires. Restoration Road leads us to change our perspective, or what we were designed to do for our satisfaction, from us to the Restorer. As Jesus leads us away from what was done in the Garden of Eden, we move from a desire that is closed to open. We go from a desire of hiding to seeking. We travel from a desire of protecting our pride and disobeying to praying and obeying. We change from a desire that is stubborn to one that is teachable. We cease our desire to trust ourselves and begin trusting the Restorer. We transition from our desire of denying truth to recognizing and acknowledging truth. We leave a desire of rejecting others and begin to accept others. We stop our sand-and stone-hearted desires of resisting and withholding forgiveness to surrendering to receiving and offering forgiveness.

The destination is where we go with our three resources of life (time, talent, and treasure). Restoration Road is a dirt-road journey into the secret places of our lives, places still filled with sand and stone, to a place that brings us to authenticity. As we travel this road, we gain the wisdom needed to live restored. Our time, talent, and treasure moves from the lock of death to the key of life. We go from the darkness of detouring from God to the light of His vision for our lives. We transition from living off-line, deaf to God, to living on-line, listening to Him. We travel from damming His river of wisdom to opening the flow of His wisdom in our lives, learning from Him. We no longer go through life as slaves, dividing ourselves from God, but now we live as sons and daughters, leaning into Him. We give up going through this journey with a heart of stone or sand that is deceived and have it replaced with a heart of clay that can lead others to the Restorer. We stop building walls in relationships where we are detached, and build bridges through love. We no longer live in the dungeon of unforgiveness for our wrongs and those of others, but we live waving the white flag of full surrender to freedom in Christ that allows us to let Jesus take the wheel of our lives. This is the goal of our journey down Restoration Road.

Briggs Cunningham unlocked the key to restoring the Bugattis when he broke through that brick wall. What brick wall in your life needs to be torn down so that you can travel Restoration Road? Will you allow the Restorer to unlock the chambers of your heart, your desires, and the three resources of your life?

Imagine how your life might be different than it is today if you traveled Restoration Road. As you surrender your life to Jesus, every activity, every relationship, every task, every decision in your life will come down to this: have you unlocked the door to a restored life with the Master Key that guides your journey? Are you working with the Restorer to help you choose between humility and pride, authenticity and pretense, wisdom and foolishness? As you travel Restoration Road, do you do so with a teachable, moldable heart of clay rather than one of sand or stone? If so, then you're venturing, with the help of the Holy Spirit, toward a life that is truly priceless.

Chapter Two

SOMETHING OF VALUE IS LOST

A s he stood in front of a circle of people, I watched as tears streamed down this man's face. He stood ready to confess his darkest secret, one that held him captive and kept him from the life of freedom that he longed to live.

By most accounts, this man was a loser, not worthy of being saved from the train wreck his life had become. At least that's what he had been told. Now, here he stood before a group of people as one who still struggled with his demons—the pipe in his back pocket was proof of that. He was not a loving husband; he had lost count of the one-night stands a long time ago. He was not a model father; he had ignored the ringing of his phone when his daughter had called six months earlier. He was not even a reliable friend. Rather, because he had used those who loved him, he had become a loner. One by one, his family left him alone in his chosen prison.

Yet here he was, standing amid a group of people who were anxious to hear what he might say. In this moment, he took a deep breath and let go: "I'm hooked on cocaine."

His own words shocked him.

Confessing his addiction did not take the craving away. Even in that moment, it ate away at him like a burning hunger. However, strangely enough, his confession revealed a deceptive, broken, and pain-filled life searching for a glimpse of hope. He could almost sense that something old was searching to be made new.

It was a courageous act. He knew in that moment that it was one of the most authentic moments he had ever experienced. In this nondescript place, he was surrounded by some who still struggled, but also by others who had discovered a life restored to authenticity that led them to a freedom they had once believed was impossible.

So there it was; the truth was finally out. For years his pride had convinced him that relationships were not the answer, yet here he stood with others who were just like him. In the past he had believed religion was just a band-aid, but now he realized that the bravest discoveries about faith were about to unfold. As this child of God (and addict) stood before the group, he was ready to risk everything if it meant that the Restorer would transform his addiction.

Two Audiences

Similarly, some two thousand years ago, a woman who felt the sharp pain of her past mistakes worked her way through a crowd. She was desperate to hear the words of one man—one whom others had told her about in excited whispers. With her head lowered, she quietly slid among an audience that was sharply polarized along two lines. The tax collectors represented licentious living. Their sand hearts shifted with each breeze that blew by. On the other side, the stone-hearted Pharisees stood stiffly, secure in the assurance of their superiority over these obviously sinful people.

Shocked that one whom the public considered a Rabbi would mingle with such people, the Pharisees haughtily announced, "This man welcomes 'sinners' and eats with them" (Luke 15:1).

The Pharisees lived their lives couched in the assurance that their system of belief was lock-tight. The 1,500 regulations their tradition had added to the Torah's 613 laws virtually guaranteed the justifiability of their judgment. Their growing list of *rules* and *regulations* prevented them from understanding what Jesus was about to communicate regarding a *relationship*. Threatened by the wave of turbulence His presence had created and offended by His penchant for mingling with sand-hearted people, they refused to listen to what He had to say.

After only a few seconds with these Pharisees, the woman knew where she belonged: with the other people in the crowd. Here she found people like her, licentious misfits who were viewed as "less than" by the religious elite because they were indeed sand-hearted sinners. Many in this crowd were well-known and hated tax collectors, while others were also known for their reputations for sin. At any rate, this woman knew instinctively where she belonged. Along with all the other sand-hearted people, she was as drawn in by the words of Jesus as she was repulsed by the rules of the Pharisees.

Jesus' Family Tree: Five Women's Stories

Jesus understood both sand and stone hearts, yet the Gospels show us that He related more closely with sand-hearted sinners than with stone-hearted legalists. Why? Scholars have written volumes in answer to that question. But perhaps a glimpse at genealogy of Jesus' life will give us an indication of part of the answer. In it we see the stories of five women who had histories that were disreputable in the eyes of society: Tamar, Rahab, Ruth, Bathsheba, and Mary.

Tamar was the daughter-in-law of Judah. She was a childless widow who had been given to different brothers-in-law after her husband's death, in obedience to Levitical law. After her second husband's death, Tamar disguised herself as a prostitute and tricked her father-in-law into sleeping with her—he who had been unwilling to give her to another one of his sons for fear of death (Genesis 38:6-30). After her deception, Tamar conceived and gave birth to twins, Perez and Zerah. Perez continued the family tree of Jesus.

Rahab was a prostitute who lived in Jericho. She hid Joshua's spies from the townspeople and was spared by the Israelite army when they conquered Jericho (Joshua 2:1-24). Later, her faith would be commended with these words: "By faith the prostitute Rahab, because she welcomed the spies, was not killed with those who were disobedient" (Hebrews 11:31).

Ruth, a Gentile foreigner from the land of Moab, was the widow of a Hebrew. Her mother-in-law, Naomi, also lived in Moab. After her husband and sons died, Naomi journeyed back to Israel, to the town of her youth. In an extraordinary act of devotion, Ruth left her own country to follow Naomi. While in Israel, Ruth met and married Boaz, one of Naomi's relatives. This union allowed Ruth to become the mother of Obed, the grandfather of David, who would become Israel's greatest King (Ruth 1:1-4:22).

Bathsheba was the wife of Uriah the Hittite, a soldier in the army of King David, the man with whom she would have an adulterous affair. When David discovered that Bathsheba was pregnant, he tried to cover up his misdeeds by summoning home Uriah from battle, hoping that Uriah would have intercourse with his wife and that her pregnancy would be assumed legitimate. However, upon his arrival from the front lines, Uriah refused to sleep with his wife out of dedication to his comrades in the field. So David sent Uriah back into battle carrying concealed orders that would seal Uriah's own fate. Uriah was killed, and David took Bathsheba as his wife. God punished them for this by taking their first child (2 Samuel 11:1-27), but Bathsheba later gave birth to Solomon, who became Israel's king after David and is widely regarded as the wisest man to ever walk the earth.

The fifth woman, and the most well-known, was Mary the mother of Jesus. She was a virgin when "the power of the Most High overshadow[ed]" her and Jesus was conceived (Luke 1:35). One can imagine the controversy that surrounded Mary, an apparently unwed mother-to-be. How the townspeople in her small village must have talked, even after Jesus was born. In the eyes of both the Pharisees and the community at large, she was likely seen as a sand-hearted woman, even though history would prove her malleable clay heart.

Jesus' family tree is proof that it is never too late for a sand or stone heart to be transformed into a heart of clay. No religious, stone-hearted formula will magically restore us. Rather, the gate to Restoration Road is unlocked when we humble our hearts, our desires, and our lives.

Why else would Jesus gather a crowd like this? He lived in a world that had lost sight of God. Popular culture, whether rooted in sand or stone hearts, could not find the way to true restoration. They were on Desperation Road instead of Restoration Road.

Traveling Companions

Which road are you traveling? An indicator lies in the description of your traveling companions.

Are you walking with the stone-hearted religious of society who compare the heart of God with the hard heart of a chief Pharisee? Do you find yourself associating with those who follow lists and rules, yet fail to connect with the message God communicates in a society filled with Ivy League capitalists, blue-collar workers, working poor, Republicans, Democrats, conservatives, liberals, chosen, condemned, and a multitude of other social cliques?

In your crowd you might find stone hearts that foster and promote religious prejudices, happy to keep their feet rooted in the cement of their rules and regulations, secure in the justification of their prejudices. They are oblivious to the reality that today, in their own communities and all around the world, lives are still being transformed as people turn away from lists and rules toward deeply rooted beliefs and compassion for God and others. Such stone-hearted legalists are filled with judgment instead of grace. Their subsequent self-restoration program leaves them unrestored.

Are you walking with loose sand-hearted types who lower the moral bar, acting as if God has turned His back on society? What started as acceptance has turned into license. Few boundaries seem to exist. However, they still have lists: narrow versus open-minded, uncool versus cool, spoiled versus hard working. They even have rules: drink this, but not that. Smoke that, but not this. Be seen with this crowd, but not that one. Go here, but not there.

Strange as it may seem, some similarities exist between these two groups. Stone hearts and sand hearts make lists that discriminate. Stone hearted people discriminate with prejudice from the top down. Sand hearted people discriminate with jealousy from the bottom up. Both compare and label, and these are two characteristics of failed self-restoration programs.

Three Stories of Loss, Restoration and Celebration: Luke 15

In at least this one aspect, culture is consistent: there were as many sand hearts and stone hearts in Jesus' day as there are today. Luke helps to prove this point when he provides the backdrop to the three stories we're about to examine: "Now the tax collectors and 'sinners' were all gathering around to hear him. But the Pharisees and the teachers of the law muttered, 'This man welcomes sinners and eats with them'" (Luke 15:1-2).

However, Jesus stood among them as a picture of the heart of the Father—a heart of clay without lists, prejudices, or judgment.

The stories that He was about to share were a trilogy of word pictures that would reveal how lists and rules could never be enough for anyone who wanted to pursue authentic restoration. His word pictures shared a common theme in three parts: (1) something of value was locked outside its gate, (2) the lost treasure warranted an all-out search on Restoration Road, and (3) the destination was life-giving restoration that called for an all-out celebration.

In the first act of His trilogy, Jesus told His audience about a shepherd who was looking over his flock at the end of the day. He counted ninety-nine. After recounting, he panicked that one of his sheep had wandered away. In this culture, a shepherd would not leave the other ninety-nine sheep unattended; typically there was more than one shepherd in the field. Consequently, he did not abandon them when he left to journey down Restoration Road for his lost sheep. But he did set out on an all-out search, and when he found the missing sheep, he put it on his shoulders and carried it safely to its destination. The shepherd's actions brought about life-saving restoration that resulted in celebration.

Jesus concluded act one with these words: "In the same way, I tell you, there will be more rejoicing in heaven over one sinner who repents than over ninety-nine righteous persons who do not need to repent" (Luke 15:7).

Jesus: 1. Pharisees: 0.

The second act in the trilogy describes a woman who had lost one of ten coins. She grabbed a broom, swept her house, and searched in every crevice until she heard a familiar sound — the rolling of a coin across the floor. She had found her missing coin! So she did what any of us would do: she called her friends over and ordered delivery from the Falafel House. The coin had been lost outside its gate, so she traveled down Restoration Road where she restored the coin to its destination. The woman's actions brought about life-giving restoration that resulted in celebration: *Hey, rejoice with me! I found my lost coin! Something of value was lost, and I found it after an all-out search. Let's party!*

As the second act ended, Jesus showed once again the value of restoration. His statement echoed again, "In the same way, I tell you, there is rejoicing in the presence of the angels of God over one sinner who repents" (Luke 15:10).

Jesus: 2. Pharisees: 0.

Imagine how the blood must have boiled within the stone–hearted Pharisees as tax collectors and prostitutes were drawn in by Jesus' words and stories. The Pharisees, frozen in their self-imposed wisdom, reached one conclusion: Jesus was officially never going to be in their club; therefore, he was a false prophet who must be stopped at all costs. He was out of control and dangerous.

Jesus finished the trilogy with the final act. This story, passed down through generations, has been popularly known as the Parable of the Prodigal Son. But Jesus didn't single out just one of the sons. He simply started his story with, "There was a man who had two sons" (Luke 15:11).

Notice how the stakes had increased in each of the stories Jesus told. The shepherd's dilemma: one lost among one hundred. The woman with the lost coin: one lost among ten. And now this story; one lost among two sons. Those who listened understood that Jesus was increasing the stakes as he amplified the value of that which was lost in each story. In this third story, Jesus wanted to demonstrate to his listeners that both sand and stone hearts matter to God because He created them.

As the final act began, the younger son made an outrageous request to his father: He wanted to receive his inheritance. The son believed that he deserved it. To Jesus' audience, the suggestion was scandalous; it was as if the younger son, the one who was not in line for the bulk of the inheritance due to his birth order, was saying to his father, "I wish you were dead." The young son, his heart filled with sand, saw his connection with his father as loose. "I can do whatever I want! And I'm sure you'll go along with it. You can't stop me. Nobody's looking. We don't even care about customs and formalities anymore. We're all sinners."

Jesus showed the Pharisees, tax collectors, and prostitutes that this son had a heart of sand, and that a storm would be needed to shape it.

Even though cultural ridicule was imminent, the father replied to his son's request with an unequally outrageous act, uncharacteristic of a patriarch in that culture. Instead of refusing the request, he "divided his property between them" (Luke 15:12b). Since the father had two sons, he transferred to the younger son his customary one-third of the property's title, giving him the uncustomary right to sell it. Again to his hearers, this situation would have been an affront to their Middle Eastern sensibilities.

Jesus was painting a picture of God's heart through the heart of this wounded father. The father in the story reached out to his young son with unconditional love, but the son refused to accept it. So the father granted the one thing his youngest son desired—freedom from him.

The younger son planned to satisfy his desires for security, contentment, significance, and control apart from his father. The pursuit of a deeply rooted relationship with his father didn't figure into his plans to pursue satisfaction.

The younger son trusted in his giftedness rather than his godliness. He trusted in the gifts rather than the giver. He wanted to leave home with cash in hand to pursue life away from his father's love. He wanted to search out new territory and experience new things. He wanted the freedom to interpret life any way he desired.

The younger son became a "prodigal"—bent on spending all he had. He gathered all his time, talent, and treasure after he turned his deed into cash, and he left the homestead. This act would have also shamed the family, whose identity and livelihood had been in their land.

After he had spent everything, famine struck, and he began to be in need. All the friends who had partied with him were gone; they left as soon as the money dried up. Every possession he had purchased had been pawned to support his lavish lifestyle. Destitute, he decided to hire himself out to a citizen who sent him into his fields to feed pigs. Being with pigs was not a good place for a young Hebrew to be.

This was the younger son's self-restoration program: "He longed to fill his stomach with the pods that the pigs were eating, but no one gave him anything" (Luke 15:16). This longing was a picture of his dissatisfied desires. Consequently, the younger son was left insecure, discontent, insignificant, and out of control. Finally the young man came to his senses and thought, "How many of my father's hired men have food to spare, and here I am starving to death. I will set out and go back to my father and say to him, 'Father I have sinned against heaven and against you. I am no longer worthy to be called your son. Make me like one of your hired men'" (Luke 15:17-19).

Let's look at this speech line by line.

"How many of my father's hired men have food to spare, and here I am starving to death." This statement reveals that the younger son's pursuit of security apart from the father had left him insecure. He lacked the resources that he had needed to survive. "I will set out and go back to my father and say to him, 'Father I have sinned against heaven and against you.'" This phrase points out that his search for contentment apart from the father had left him filled with discontentment. He now saw his search as sin. "I am no longer worthy to be called your son." This statement specifies that his desire for significance apart from the father had resulted in insignificance. He no longer saw himself as worthy enough to be a son. "Make me like one of your hired men." In this he shows that his desire for control apart from the father had left him feeling out of control. However, he still had vestiges of a self-restoration program. He was prepared to continue in his illusion of control by taking charge of earning his way back to the father as one of his hired hands.

He was almost out of *time*; he was fading away in *talent*; and his *treasure* had dissipated. The makings of a clay heart would be the Master Key to unlock the gate to Restoration Road. With his speech well rehearsed, the young man returned home.

Unlike a sheep or a coin, a lost son was created with a spiritual heart comprised of four chambers that beat with four primary desires connecting his heart with his three resources of life. The son's *will, intellect, spirit,* and *emotions* swirled in to find something new, an authentic restored heart of clay. He was nearing the point of choosing, thinking, praying and wanting it. He realized that his four primary desires had been dissatisfied on his dirt road journey apart from the father. The result was his *insecurity, discontentment, insignificance*, and a life that had been *out of control*. He was spent. His three resources of life had blown away in the wind.

Outside the city gates, the father waited. Contemporary culture dictated what would happen should the younger son return: he would undergo a ceremony called *qatatsa* for losing all his wealth to Gentiles. A funeral would be held for him even though he was still alive. He would be kicked out of the community, his children would not be educated in it, and he would not enjoy the provision and protection that it offered.

The son would be cast out unless the father chose to spare the son from this humiliating act by reconciling with him outside the city gates.

One day, the father recognized his son far away on the horizon. He was filled with compassion for his lost son. Uncharacteristic of a patriarch of that era, he ran to his son. When he reached this young man whom he had not seen in so many months, he threw his arms around him and kissed him.

Without hesitation, the son blurted out, "Father I have sinned against heaven and against you. I am no longer worthy to be called your son" (Luke 15:21). He was getting ready to add, "Make me like one of your men so that I can earn my way back into this deal. Show me a little mercy." But before he could continue, the father interrupted him, commanding his servants to gather four specific items that symbolized restoration to authenticity:

"'Quick! Bring the best robe and put it on him. Put a ring on his finger and sandals on his feet. Bring the fattened calf and kill it. Let's have a feast and celebrate. For this son of mine was dead and is alive again; He was lost and is found.' So they began to celebrate" (Luke 15:22-24).

The servants scattered to find the father's robe and found the best one. This symbolized the father satisfying the younger son's desire for security in the truth that everything he owned had belonged to the son. They placed the ring on his son's finger to restore his ability to make business deals, an act that committed the father's resources to his son. This demonstrated the father satisfying the younger son's desire for control in the power that he had transferred. The sandals were placed on the son's feet, which transformed him from a slave back into a son. This illustrated the father satisfying the younger son's desire for significance in the love of the patriarch. A calf, rather than a goat, implied that everyone in the community was invited to the feast of celebration, not just the family. This signified that the father was satisfying the younger son's desire for contentment, and with this act the father was reconciling his son with the community.

In all these ways, Jesus demonstrated what has been addressed in this book. The son's trip down Restoration Road, fueled by his failure to be able to control his own circumstances, ended in the arms of his father, who restored his son to authenticity. His son knew he deserved justice, so he asked for mercy but instead received his father's grace. He gave his son the gift of being restored to the original design of the Designer.

Meanwhile, the older son finished his day of hard work in the fields and returned home to the sounds of celebration and dancing. He called one of the servants over and asked, "What's going on?"

"'Your brother has come home,' he replied. 'And your father has killed the fattened calf because he has him back safe and sound'" (Luke 15:26).

The older son was furious because he knew that the father had restored his younger brother, this punk kid who had broken all the rules and had seemingly gotten away with it. So he responded in a way that culturally would have been as much an affront as the younger son's original request: he refused to celebrate with his father. Jesus reached the climax of the third act to show how equally proud both brothers had been toward their father. While the sand-hearted crowd was relieved with the younger son's restoration, the Pharisees reacted in the exact opposite manner. In their self-righteous anger, they related to the older brother's reaction. They wanted justice against the injustice caused by this sand-hearted son. They agreed with the older brother's refusal to enter into the celebration, even though this was unacceptable in Middle Eastern culture.

The father chose not to respond in anger rooted in pride, but rather in humility as he stooped down to find yet another lost son. He pleaded with the older son, which was another act that opposed their cultural norm. A father would never plead with someone, especially a son who refused to celebrate with him. The response of the older son cut deeply into his father's heart: "Look! All these years I've been slaving for you and never disobeyed your orders. Yet you never gave me even a young goat so I could celebrate with my friends. But when this son of yours who has squandered your property with prostitutes comes home, you kill the fattened calf for him" (Luke 15:29-30). The older son's stone-hearted pursuit of the satisfaction of his desires apart from the father had left him dissatisfied.

Again, let's break down this son's response. "Look! All these years I've been slaving for you." This phrase indicates that the older son sees himself as a slave, not a son, a mark of significance turned into insignificance. "And never disobeyed your orders." This phrase demonstrates that he had attempted to control the father with his non-heartfelt, mechanical obedience, which left him feeling out of control. "Yet you never gave me even a young goat so I could celebrate with my friends." This shows that the older son was filled with discontentment. "But when this son of yours who has squandered your property with prostitutes comes home, you kill the fattened calf for him." This angry statement proves how the older son had equated property with security. Following the customary practice, the older brother had received his inheritance too—two-thirds of his father's estate, twice as much as his younger brother (Deuteronomy 21:17). The possibility that his inheritance was about to be usurped again by the restoration of his younger brother increased his insecurity.

Can you almost see the Pharisees nudge one another as they sense that vindication for the older son is near?

While the younger son viewed his relationship with his father as loose, the older viewed his relationship with his father as legalistic, not one between a gracious father and a loving son.

Stone hearts nodded in approval. Sand hearts wondered what the father would do next.

The father responded with another act of radical grace. He called his elder son over and said, "My son, you are always with me and everything I have is yours. But we had to celebrate and be glad, because this brother of yours was dead and is alive again; he was lost and is found" (Luke 15:31-32).

The father offered the same satisfaction of the elder son's desires that he had provided in the four images he used to restore his younger son. The phrase "My son" demonstrates significance in the love of the father for his son; this is reflected in the sandals that covered his elder son's feet. "You are always with me" reveals control in the power of the father noted in the ring that would always be on his elder son's finger. "Everything I have is yours" illustrates security in the truth of the father providing all that his son had needed, evidenced in the father's robe draping over his elder heir. "But we had to celebrate and be glad, because this brother of yours was dead and is alive again; he was lost and is found" points to contentment in the father's peace symbolized by the killing of the calf for the feast. In this way, the father reconciled both of his lost sons to the larger community, and all at his own personal expense.

Jesus' words grabbed the Pharisees and included them as older brothers into the climax of the parable with one defining poetic question that haunted them from the inside out. This same question had to be considered by the tax collectors and prostitutes. In effect, Jesus said, "Are you going to surrender your sand and stone hearts for the father's loving heart of clay?"

Shock rippled through the sand-hearted because of the father's response.

A wall of silence arose from the stone-hearted who were unable to answer.

Jesus: 3. Pharisees: 0.

Game. Set. Match.

Our Response to the Rule-Breaking Father

Jesus' question still echoes today for all of us. What are you going to do with the radical, limitless, undeserved love of the One who wants to restore you to authenticity?

The father, as an archetype of God the Father, committed four acts atypical of a Middle Eastern patriarch. (1) He gave, (2) he ran, (3) he restored, and (4) he pleaded.

First, the father gave an inheritance when he did not have to. He even gave the younger son the property complete with the right to sell it when he did not have to. Second, he ran to a younger son outside the city gates. Running would have been considered very inappropriate for a man of his age and position. Third, he restored him to authenticity when he did not have to. Fourth, he pleaded with an older son who attempted to shame him in front of the whole community when he did not have to. He even offered the older son the same opportunity to be restored to authenticity as well.

In the same way, even though He never had to, God gives us life: hearts, desires, and three resources, complete with the freedom to resell them. God runs toward us in spite of our attempts to satisfy our desires apart from Him. God restores us to authenticity to reflect the original design of the Designer when we humble our hearts to Him. God pleads with us to not only be restored, but to joyfully help others to do the same.

With these stories, Jesus in effect asked both the sand- and the stone-hearted, "Will you allow the Restorer to unlock the gate of your heart with the Master Key of full surrender? Do you desire to travel down Restoration Road where the Spirit of the Restorer intersects the vertical with the horizontal? Will you arrive at His destination of life-giving restoration and celebrate it with others?"

———————

Hanging in my office is a replica of Rembrandt's painting, *"The Prodigal Son Returns."* It was a gift from a friend of mine who purchased it at the museum in St. Petersburg, Russia, where Rembrandt's original hangs. The story did not merely influence my life, it is one that I have lived. I too was once lost, unrestored, locked out from the life that reflected the design of the Designer. Happily, the Restorer found me at just the right moment to restore me to authenticity.

I had been searching for something to transform my heart because something of value was lost. I was a slave to the life I had created for myself. Journeying through both a heart of sand and stone left me dissatisfied, and I longed to find that "something" that would satisfy the desires of my heart.

That something was in fact Someone. He was the Restorer. I would later learn that satisfaction could only be unlocked in the gate of my heart with the Master Key of full surrender reflected in a heart of clay. My journey along Restoration Road has reached the hallowed halls of the rich and famous and has also led me to the forgotten alleys of the poor. The pages ahead are filled with stories of tragedy, triumph, and what I have discovered about the destination of living restored to authenticity as I helped others celebrate the same.

I believe God wants each of us to trade our dilapidated heart of sand or stone for a heart of clay. In the moment, we might not immediately comprehend the value of being restored to authenticity, but the Restorer does. He promises to restore anyone who comes to Him with a heart of clay.

Everyone's invited, including you.

Which substance from the earth dominates the contents of your heart: sand, stone, or clay? Are you prepared to unlock the gate of your heart to travel Restoration Road where the vertical intersects with the horizontal leading to the destination of living restored to authenticity? Are you ready to exchange your sand or stone heart for one of clay?

Whether you are in the midst of a storm or see one looming on the horizon, whether you feel the pressures of an invisible and severe tool pounding your heart, whether you feel as though you have life all figured out, or whether you humbly receive the shaping of the Restorer's hands, join me in order to discover the clay in your dirt-road journey.

Are there things hidden within your heart that need restoration? Choices? Thoughts? Prayers? Feelings?

Do you feel insecure, discontent, insignificant or out of control?

Whether you have a lot or a little, do you feel like your time, talent, and treasure are never enough?

If something of value has been lost, something deep within, let today be the day that you begin to consider surrendering your life to the Restorer. If you surrender yourself to Him in humility, He will unlock your gate to Restoration Road.

With each page you turn, may the Restorer reveal to you authentic wisdom that is embedded deep within His heart. He promises to guide you and unlock the life that you were designed to live. If you humble your heart to Him, He will align your heart, desires, and three resources of life to the authentic design He created for you.

Chapter Three

THE DIRT ROAD

At nine years old I stood on a dirt road that had been originally used as a carriage path. This road of sand and stone had crunched beneath the hooves and wheels of horse-and-buggies that carried people to County Line Church of God, a church my great-great grandfather had co-founded a century earlier in response to a traveling evangelist. I was on somewhat of a mission, a quest to get an answer from God. This was a day that I would vividly remember for the rest of my life.

Not far from County Line, my great-grandfather, Fred Kruse, owned 13.5 acres of what appeared to be worthless property. My Dad had an eye on that acreage because he wanted to dig a pond on it.

In vintage Dad fashion, he persuaded my great-grandfather to sell him the land and subsequently agreed on a handshake with a general contractor to build a new house. Not long afterward, we moved into a beautiful new home that overlooked a 3.5 acre pond stocked with bluegill, bass, and catfish. I still remember the countless days I walked from our house down this dirt road to County Line. Although I didn't know it at the time, the sand, stone, and clay beneath my feet would provide three unique images of the future journey of my heart.

On this particular day, I embarked on the half-mile walk to County Line Church of God, walking some 900 steps down that dirt road to arrive at my destination. I approached the church's double doors to tug on one. I had learned over the years that it was always unlocked. As I crept in, I noticed that no one else was in the building—it was just God and me. I walked a few more steps and opened one of the doors to the sanctuary. I remember that the interior was dark due to the dim sunlight that struggled to shine through the stained-glass windows. I slowly walked up the aisle to the altar at the front of the church, and I could not recall a time when I had ever been that close. Now that I was there, I figured I had God's undivided attention, so I thought I would ask Him a question that had been on my heart for quite some time. I knelt down at that wood railing and asked, "God, what do you want me to do with my life?"

When I look back at that moment, I reflect on the condition of my nine-year-old heart. Perhaps that was my first glimpse at a heart of clay, but for whatever reason, I walked away with a heart of stone. Even though I was young, my stone heart was hard, rigid, and legalistic, the result of my misguided interpretation of my family's religious beliefs. I always wanted to *be* right, *do* right, and *go* in the right direction. My heart of stone fueled my pride, for I trusted in me, rather than God or others. I wondered why others could not keep the rules as rigidly as I did. My self-restoration program led to an internal battle that would rage for many years.

Later in my life there would be times when my heart scattered like sand: loose and licentious. When I grew older, I would want to get rid of the rules that tied me to my circumstances, while still feeling compelled to act in a certain way to earn God's forgiveness. For almost three decades, the steps of my dirt-road journey would leave imprints of stone or sand until I stood at a crossroads with only one place left to turn. However, as a young boy, I was years away from this discovery.

Those dirt road walks to County Line marked only the beginning of my quest.

Indy Storm

A couple months prior, I had found myself riding one of three chartered buses with about 150 of Dad's employees, friends, and customers, headed for the Indianapolis 500. This Memorial Day extravaganza has been billed as the "Greatest Spectacle in Racing." Originally built in 1909, the track now known as "The Brickyard" hosts one of the world's oldest motorsport events and is considered one of the three most significant racing events in the world.

On this trip, 400,000 fans had gathered and were electrified by Fast Friday, Bump Day, and Carb Day. A military trumpeter played Taps, there was a military fly-by, and the Purdue Marching Band led up to the legendary Tony Hullman's historic words, "Gentlemen, start your engines!"

It was a wonderful weekend, one I always looked forward to as a child. I loved this place along with its legends: The Unsers, Andrettis, and Foyts. This was my third trip to the Brickyard, and once the race got underway, I started to get distracted. Before long, I was thinking of the gift shop and my desire to purchase an awesome blue tie-dyed T-shirt in remembrance of this historic day. To me, that gift shop was the greatest place in the world. I wanted every single thing they sold, and I wanted to keep every piece of clothing I bought there looking brand new. These were the early warning signs that I was indeed a perfectionist.

Like the sand-hearted son in Jesus' trilogy, I pestered my parents for hours to let me walk over alone but they refused. Finally, my gift of persuasion convinced them, and I was on my way across the half-mile stretch behind the grandstands that lined the straightaway. What I had not anticipated was the thunderstorm that would strike the track only minutes later.

I had barely reached the shop and purchased my coveted piece of Indy 500 clothing when race officials called off the race due to the bad weather. Bobby Unser won this weather-shortened race, as he was leading when conditions were deemed too dangerous for the drivers.

The storm presented me with two problems. First, the obvious, I was lost with no way to communicate with my parents. Second, 400,000 people now stood between my parents and me. I faced a human wall, including the drunken and half-naked, as I swam upstream against a myriad of people in the pouring rain. The sky flashed, followed by rolling thunder that I can still vividly remember—it shook the ground underneath me. Frozen in place, I did what any other nine year old would have done: I cried. Fortunately, a woman noticed me drowning in my tears and came to my rescue.

"Are you lost?" She asked.

I nodded affirmatively.

I headed toward the grandstands, but she stopped me.

"I don't think your parents are up there," she said.

I was convinced this woman was wrong. My parents would not leave without me. To my surprise, the woman was right. Track officials had already cleared out the stands, so she and I walked together toward the track offices. Along the way, I recognized one of Dad's employees—150 in 400,000 odds. Minutes later, I was reunited with Mom and Dad at the Kruse entourage's luxury buses. Even though I was relieved that I would not be lost in the hallowed grounds of the Brickyard, I still had a few words for my parents: "What were you thinking? Why did you leave the grandstands?" I wondered how could the people who loved me the most be so untrustworthy?

When I look in the rearview mirror of my life, I am often reminded of the day I got lost at Indy. I realize how the storm reflected what would later shape the sand in my heart.

Our family attended County Line Church of God religiously. It is where I learned what it meant to be a Christian. Dad attended whenever he was home, maybe ten times a year, but Mom instilled in us the discipline of near-perfect attendance. We went to church three times a week—Sunday morning, Sunday night, and Wednesday night. We never thought about not going.

As a child, I watched Sunday-school teachers place Bible characters against a green felt board to capture our attention as they told Bible stories. However, I remember thinking that some of them were a bit over the top, and hard to relate to for a kid living in the rural Midwest in the twentieth century. I mean, what did Samson ripping a jawbone from a wild beast or Moses raising his staff to part the Red Sea have to do with me or my life? The topper for me was David disrobing and dancing before God. Would you want God to see you naked? Neither did David. That's why he wore a linen ephod.

There came a day when I decided that I needed to be saved because I could not perfectly follow the treasured Ten Commandments (the event that brought me to this conviction is explained later in this chapter). I had grown up in the church, but it was time for me to submit to this simple act of confessing my faith in God, not fully realizing the implications of my actions as I did so. I did not fully comprehend how my life would later be transformed, my priorities altered, and how this act would bring me face-to-face with my God-given destiny.

At this time I was a kid, and kids don't have these kinds of mind-blowing, life-altering thoughts. I simply believed with a childlike faith that God was the real deal and would do what He promised. As the years passed, life became more complex as I felt a longing within me to return to this simple faith. Childlike faith is authentic, yet as life evolves we pretend to make faith either about following all the rules, or about making our own rules. In either case, we often lose the relationship with God we once held so closely.

At any rate, my failure to live up to God's Top Ten rules weighed heavily on me. Let's briefly review these rules that are so foundational to our Christian faith.

The first four commandments are vertical, between God and man: (1) you shall have no other gods before me, (2) you shall not make yourself an idol in the form of anything in heaven above or on the earth beneath or in the waters below, (3) you shall not misuse the name of the Lord your God, and (4) remember the Sabbath day by keeping it holy.

The last six commandments are horizontal, between man and man: (5) honor your father and mother, (6) you shall not murder, (7) you shall not commit adultery, (8) you shall not steal, (9) you shall not give false testimony against your neighbor, and (10) you shall not covet your neighbor's house, wife, donkey, or anything that belongs to your neighbor.

While I had understood the Ten Commandments as the church's rules for success, I had an internal desire to pursue something else to define my success—a belief that I could restore myself to authenticity. Unfortunately, what began as a childlike response to Him evolved into a checklist of *do's* and *don'ts* that I followed consistently in an effort to earn my way into heaven. This was the beginning of my stone-hearted self-restoration program.

God's Response to List-Makers

What rules, regulations, and stipulations have you added to or subtracted from the Restorer's message of heart transformation? They probably fall into two categories: *do's* and *dont's*. *Do* go to church, *do* fast, *do* vote Republican or Democratic, *do* have it all together, *do* serve in church programs, *do* dress for success, *do* go to public Christian gatherings, *do* listen only to Christian radio, and the list goes on and on. Then we add in the *don'ts*. *Don't* drink, *don't* smoke, *don't* chew, *don't* go with girls who do, *don't* cuss, *don't* go to rock concerts, *don't* watch prime-time television, *don't* go to R-rated movies, *don't* listen to country music, *don't* dance, and this list also goes on and on. The result of this endless list-making is our attempt at either the gratification or the negation of our desires apart from the Restorer. Consequently, we miss Restoration Road, thereby hampering the transformation of the kingdom of God in our lives. In reality, this is faith in our faith. And when I was young, this was my life. Two thousand years ago, God's plan for heart transformation was hijacked by the Pharisees with their added rules, regulations, and stipulations to the Old Testament laws. When they encountered Jesus, they could not handle the posse He rolled with—disciples who included tax collectors like Matthew who flaunted the rules that they so cherished.

Jesus responded to sand and stone hearts with parables, like the lost sheep, the lost coin, and the father who had two sons. The word *parable* means "to throw alongside." A parable throws an earthly truth alongside a spiritual truth. They are allegorical, but they are not meant to be allegorized—neatly fitting each earthly character or object into a convenient spiritual box.

About forty parables are recorded in the Gospels. One in particular categorized Jesus' intention to bring the manifest kingdom of God within the lives of his people. When challenged about rules, regulations, and stipulations, Jesus answered with this word picture: "No one sews a patch of unshrunk cloth on an old garment, for the patch will pull away from the garment, making the tear worse. Neither do men pour new wine into old wineskins. If they do, the skins will burst, the wine will run out and the wineskins will be ruined. No, they pour new wine into new wineskins, and both are preserved" (Matthew 9:16-17).

The new patch and the new wine Jesus described alluded to Jesus' message of heart transformation, an ushering in of what he called "the kingdom of heaven"—God's divine reign, rule, and order in the hearts and lives of people on earth now and in the future. The old garment and the old wineskin illustrated the

Pharisees' dogged adherence to religious traditions that accentuated their hearts of stone. Jesus was saying that He did not come to patch up the Pharisees' religious system. He came to start a revolution. Consequently, Jesus' message of heart transformation was not going to fit into the Pharisee's religious framework.

Jesus' point was that His kingdom of heaven would not be contained by the Pharisees' rules, regulations, and stipulations. Nor can it be contained by religion today. No denomination, whether Baptist, Catholic, Presbyterian, Methodist, Orthodox, Lutheran, or any other has an exclusive lock on the kingdom of heaven. Those who simply follow the rules while neglecting a relationship with the Restorer are only fueling their stone hearts. Jesus unlocked the gates to anyone who humbles his heart to Him.

Have you tried to contain the advancement of the kingdom of heaven to a place (a church building), a time (one hour a week on Sunday morning), or a style (of worship or rules)? Have you found that your childhood relational encounters with God have disappeared? Are you still searching for something or someone to restore you to your authentic condition?

Just like that new cloth and new wine, the revolution within a heart that longs to be restored to authenticity cannot be contained. He invites all to live a life restored to authenticity instead of remaining imprisoned in hearts of sand or stone.

The Love Factor

The proof test of rules, regulations, and stipulations is love. Jesus said, "So in everything, do to others what you would have them do to you, for this sums up the Law and the Prophets (Matthew 7:12). Love toward others is a defining characteristic of a life headed in the right direction down Restoration Road.

Jesus also spoke of love when He was asked to bottom-line the commandments: "Teacher, which is the greatest commandment in the Law?' Jesus replied: 'Love the Lord your God with all your heart and with all your soul and with all your mind. This is the first and greatest commandment. And the second is like it: Love your neighbor as yourself. All the Law and the Prophets hang on these two commandments" (Matthew 22:36-40). Here Jesus described a love that flowed vertically with God and horizontally with others.

This was God's original idea, to love vertically and horizontally. A vertical love causes us to "Love the Lord your God with all your heart and with all your soul and with all your strength" (Deuteronomy 6:5). A horizontal love says, "Do not seek revenge or bear a grudge against one of your people, but love your neighbor as yourself. I am the Lord" (Leviticus 19:18). This is what Jesus had quoted in The Gospel of Matthew. Paul said it in this way: "The commandments, 'Do not commit adultery,' 'Do not murder,' 'Do not steal,' 'Do not covet,' and whatever other commandments there may be, are summed up in this one rule: 'Love your neighbor as yourself.' Love does no harm to its neighbor. Therefore love is the fulfillment of the law" (Romans 13:9-10; Galatians 5:14). James, the half-brother of Jesus, said it in these words: "If you really keep the royal law found in Scripture, 'Love your neighbor as yourself,' you are doing right" (James 2:8).

The Restorer's message of heart transformation cannot be contained regardless of our transgressions, even if we have been told otherwise by the contemporary religious Pharisees in our lives. Love can break through in a hospital, a bar, a concert hall, a business deal, or a dance club. It can break through in our work, play, and family. Wherever there is a humble heart surrendered to the Restorer, there the kingdom of heaven breaks through. Where we find the heart of the Father in the trilogy, we find a heart of clay that is willing to be molded in God's image, moved by His love to show grace, mercy and love to others.

You Shall Not Steal

So what event triggered my sudden interest in and conviction toward the Ten Commandments? I stole a shiny metal box. I know, it's not exactly earth-shattering news. Ironically, I thought I had kept the commands on the tablets with my stone heart; however, trust in my faith led me to commit a sand-hearted act.

I stood in my Dad's office supply room in the half-light (how many of our sins happen in the dark?), in my mind risking eternal salvation for a metal box to hold my rock collection. I hesitated and hedged, but I eventually decided it was worth the risk. I took it.

Now, you understand how guilt can swallow up a youngster. In the days after I stole the box, I tried to justify my actions by claiming that Dad owned the office and therefore everything in it, including this box. Technically, I thought taking the box should not be considered stealing. However, just in case and perhaps out of conviction for breaking the rules, I tearfully approached my Junior Church teacher after a Sunday morning service. He had just taught on Jesus' parable of the two sons, and I began to shake as I approached him to ask if God would understand if I had knowingly done something wrong. I mean, I had just heard the story of the father letting the younger son off the hook, so I figured there was no time like the present.

Still, I wondered if I was covered by all the times I had kept the rules, like the older son. But I didn't know for sure, so I felt like I needed to find out if some way I'd be covered in case I had earned myself a potential one-way ticket to hell. Thankfully, my teacher spoke words of comfort to me, recognizing my sorrow for sin and desire to be forgiven.

I will never forget the dichotomy of my parents' response during that Sunday lunch when I shared my confession about the shiny metal box. Mom was appalled. I was sure the wrath of God was going to explode from her mouth and pulverize me into dust, cutting short my final day on planet earth. However, in the other corner sat my favorite politician, boxing legend, and the Dean of Auctioneering that I admired so much, ready to set the record straight. He came through like a champ, saying, "I *do* own the office and everything in it. So, you're entitled to take whatever you need, including the shiny metal box."

I was young, but I wasn't stupid. For my own safety I remained silent, even though I wanted to jump across the table and give Dad a high five. The look in Mom's eyes spoke volumes, even though she never uttered another word about it.

From where Dad sat, I hadn't broken any commandments. So when the conversation ended, I left the table liking Dad's sand theology a lot more than Mom's stone theology. The lens through which Dad saw things was less convicting. Once again, it opened the door for me to believe that reconciliation with God solely depended upon me. If I committed sand-hearted sins, I could cover them with stone-hearted acts. This resulted in a self-reliance that would slowly harden my heart condition seemingly beyond repair.

Nevertheless, I asked to be baptized in water as evidence of my commitment to God. Afterward, I felt another item was checked off my stone-hearted list of *do's* in order to walk in my new-found faith toward my limited definition of authenticity. It was a decision I would fight both for and against countless times in the years ahead.

Deep down, like the younger son in Jesus' trilogy, I believed that one day I deserved to cash out of the family business. Unlike the younger son, yet indicative of his older brother, I would earn it and not inherit it. I would earn it through stone-hearted hard work—the same way I adhered to the rules of my religious faith. After all, in my mind, I believed the rules supported my right as the son of my father to rule the Kruse empire.

My definition of wisdom walked a tightrope between both stone and sand. On the one hand, I believed that I had been accepted into the kingdom of God because I had confessed my sins, been baptized in water, and attended church every Sunday. I'd done what I needed to cover my bases. On the other hand, I struggled because deep down in my heart I wanted to make my own decisions, to run my own life, to do whatever I wanted as long as it remained within the boundaries of those ancient tablets. I thought that my sand-hearted sins could be covered by my stone-hearted acts. I did not realize that my ultimate desire, even from the time I was a nine-year-old standing alone in the front of that church, was for God to grant my unspoken request to give me what I believed I deserved. I was convinced from a young age that my destiny would only be fulfilled when I stood alone at the top of the business world.

My stone heart revolved around a customized faith in God driven by rules instead of a relationship. I believed that my stone-hearted rules protected me from any future transgressions, but they left me rigid and legalistic in my faith. However, as I reached my teenage years, I saw the supposed benefits of a sand heart for the very first time. I wanted to pursue an inheritance filled with greatness and overabundant success. I had everything I needed: a shiny metal box, a legend for a father, and a new-found belief in God. I was relieved that I didn't, like David, have to take off all my clothes (yes, that story about David really did get to me), or like Samson, kill a wild beast to make it happen. Unknowingly, I was simply starting the journey through both stone and sand that we all travel in order to discover a heart of clay. Still, I was continually reminded of Jesus' word picture, the parable of the lost sons, that would reveal itself in the most unexpected places throughout my life and lead me toward Restoration Road.

Chapter Four

"IF I CAN GET YOU CONVINCED, I CAN GET THEM CONVINCED!"

1983 was a year of novelty:

- Tom Sneva won the Indy 500 after three previous runner-up finishes.
- The Nintendo entertainment system was released for the first time in Japan.
- The tennis world waved goodbye to Bjorn Borg, whose passion for the sport earned him five consecutive Wimbledon Championships.
- The 55th Academy Awards concluded with *Gandhi* winning best picture.
- Michael Jackson debuted the world famous $1.1 million, 14-minute video, *Thriller,* at the Metro Theater in Westwood, California.

- The Mile High City clashed with the Motor City as the Nuggets and Pistons faced off in an NBA-record 370 point, triple-overtime scoring frenzy.
- *Flashdance* and *Return of the Jedi* became box-office hits.
- Thousands stood in line at McDonald's to get a taste of the new menu item, the McNugget. "Barbeque sauce or sweet and sour?"
- The world bid farewell to American heavyweight champion boxer Jack Dempsey, and welcomed the birth of future American Idol winner, Carrie Underwood.
- President Ronald Wilson Reagan signed a bill to honor freedom fighter, Martin Luther King, Jr.

Amidst all of its change and innovation, the early 1980's was also a time of trial and strife.

- President Reagan called out the Soviet Union as an "evil empire."
- Congress reviewed a proposal to develop a new defensive technology against intercontinental ballistic missiles that would later come to be known as "Star Wars" missile defense.
- A communal riot broke out in Sri Lanka that came to be called "Black July."
- Benigno Aquino Jr., former President to the Philippines, returned from exile only to be assassinated.
- Pope John Paul II visited his would-be assassin Mehmet Ali Agca in prison to forgive him.
- Israel and the United States signed an agreement for the Israeli withdrawal from Lebanon.

Do you remember where you were in 1983?

College? High School? Junior High? Elementary? Pre-School? Still in diapers? Married? Divorced? Single? Or were you "looking for love in all the wrong places"?

Was life filled with success? Financial ruin? Fame? Infamy?

Were you even alive?

My life in 1983 was a galaxy away from these major world events. Except for the McNuggets, the NBA scoring frenzy, MTV and, of course, the Indy 500. I grew up in the house Dad built in Auburn, Indiana, fishing in the pond that no one had believed could be dug on our property. I was firmly planted in the American heartland. It was nothing like growing up on the East or West Coast. I was not a celebrity, a world leader, a legendary athlete, an inventor, or even someone who fought for world peace. At the age of seventeen, I was a diehard Hoosier at heart.

My list of priorities was significantly different from larger world events as I entered my senior year at DeKalb High School. My top priority was reaching the state finals in basketball (single class — as God intended). Not far behind was running for student-council president and being in love with my high school sweetheart, Susan. Oh yes, and then there was my dream of auctioning.

Kruse International: The Early Years

Since I had been a young boy, I had auctioned jars stored in cellars of farmhouses with Grandpa Russell. During my first auctioneering opportunity at five years old, I hid behind a cellar corner, microphone in hand, and auctioned while the crowd placed their bids. "Russell" — as he liked to be called by his children and grandsons — coached me along the way.

I admired my grandfather for what he had achieved. After his farm flooded in 1952, he graduated from the Reppert School of Auctioneering and began a local auction business at the suggestion of his father-in-law, my great grandfather, Lester Boger, who had clerked auctions since 1929.

My dad and Russell pioneered the selling of multiple parcels of real estate in a single auction during the 1960's, but an unforeseen opportunity that presented itself in 1971 changed the family business forever.

When the Auburn Chamber of Commerce tried to raise money to celebrate its automotive history in 1971, the organizers approached Russell to help auction some old classic cars: Auburns, Cords, and Duesenbergs. In those days, no one expected a crowd of 15,000 to flock to an auction of about seventy-five old cars in a muddy field at the west edge of town. When a bidder's $61,000 offer for a locally made Duesenberg was turned down, the press picked up the story, and—quite literally *overnight*—a whole new industry was born. NBC's national news closed its television broadcast with a story proclaiming that, "Two fools had met in Auburn, Indiana"— the one who made the offer, and the one who turned it down. It was after this event that the term "collector car" first came into use.

At the age of twenty-five, Dad added to his busy life when he was elected State Senator of Indiana, where he served for the next six years. He gained national attention as the youngest state senator in the nation. He worked to maintain the autonomy of Amish schools, introduced a bill for Auctioneer license law, and helped champion the construction of Indiana University and Purdue University campuses in satellite cities throughout Indiana.

When Dad's term ended, he focused on the family business with a renewed tenacity. In 1972, he auctioned a Duesenberg once owned by Greta Garbo for $90,000—at that time a world-record price for an automobile. Charles Wood, founder of the world's first theme park in Lake George, New York, purchased the car on a last-second final bid. This automotive work of art featured a body designed to fit Greta Garbo's reclusive personality. She would hide behind a three-position top fixed in the landau position as her chauffeur was exposed to the elements. In the rear of the vehicle were secret compartments strategically placed so that Ms. Garbo could hide her expensive jewels. It was a vehicle with an interesting story—vital to bring high-dollar bids at auction.

Dad quickly garnered a reputation for having sold more vintage and collector cars than all other auction firms combined. He became the youngest man to call 5,000 auctions in 48 states and 11 foreign countries as he broke more than 250 world-record prices in the collector car industry alone. He claimed the title, "Dean of Auctioneering."

Not only did Dad auction cars, but he also auctioned islands, zoos, rare oil paintings, airports, vintage aircraft, race tracks, high rises, ranches, marinas, an open mine shaft, the Acapulco home of movie legend John Wayne, and even three entire towns. He traveled more than 200,000 miles per year and became a sought-after personality on television, appearing on programs such as CBS's 60 Minutes, the Morning Show, and CNBC's Power Lunch. If you ever had a chance to hear him share his legendary story, he would also tell you about his amateur boxing record of sixty fights, with one draw and zero losses. (I'm still trying to find out if this is legend or reality.)

He was a powerful politician, a savvy marketer, a true survivor. In the fast pace of his business and personal life he acted as my coach, oftentimes calling from a different city, to fuel my dream of one day becoming an auctioneer like him. He was priming me for the big show; and the truth was, I wanted it.

In the years that followed, Grandpa Russell was inducted into the Indiana Auctioneer's Association Hall of Fame along with his two sons, Dad and Uncle Dennis. They, along with charismatic Uncle Daniel, had managed to build an innovative company that popularized the antique-car auction business. My family was living the American dream, and I remained convinced that one day it would all belong to me.

Troubled Times

However, by the late 1970's, the business crashed due to cash-flow problems that resulted from growing too quickly and unadvisedly attempting to act as a bank in order to finance collector cars. My eternally optimistic dad, who never dreamed that his borrowers wouldn't pay for their purchases, found it difficult to repossess cars not paid for, especially when they were scattered throughout the world. All the while, the auction company had paid numerous sellers the purchase price for their collector cars. This problem was exacerbated when the proceeds from a Las Vegas sale, which had been checked as luggage on an airline, was stolen.

The Kruse Classic Car Auction Company had amassed millions of dollars in debt, both to sellers who had not been paid and to banks who had underwritten much of the financing because Dad had signed on recourse for each loan. Additionally, corporate vendors were postponing payment for months beyond the agreed-upon terms. The result was more than 1,400 creditors knocking on Dad's door, nearly each one filing a lawsuit.

Our home telephone rang off the hook from sellers and finance companies who demanded their money. I fielded many of those calls at the beginning of my ninth grade year. The headlines in newspapers, on television stations, and in newly blossoming collector car trade publications communicated that the Kruse Empire had officially crumbled. The unflattering, accusatory stories flooded the press for nearly eighteen months. In an attempt to resolve the situation, Dad bought out his two brothers and Grandpa Russell for one dollar each, and personally set out to resurrect the company. Against the advice of many business associates, he refused to file for bankruptcy protection.

The dream that I'd felt destined to live since I was five years old was now on hold due to someone pressing the newly invented pause button on my life's movie. I had to consider what would become my life's Plan B.

My Path to Prosperity: Dreams Fulfilled

During high school, I passed my real estate salesperson's course and awaited my eighteenth birthday after graduation. I soon became the youngest licensed Realtor in the nation. I planned to syndicate real estate and possibly become a motivational speaker, earning thousands of dollars per speech. One of my idols at the time was Zig Ziglar; he transformed my perspective through his book, *See You At The Top*. Dad had persuaded me to read it the summer before my senior year. All of this activity and these new goals meant forgoing my highly anticipated future as an auctioneer, that is until the auction of an antique piece of furniture wrecked my Plan B for good.

During that summer of '83, amidst all the accolades and achievements mixed with the failures, my life was permanently altered when Grandpa Russell became my teacher. On one hot and humid day, in some podunk Hoosier town that sat along a back-road two-lane highway, I stood before a crowd of several hundred people with a beautiful antique curio cabinet on one side and Russell on the other.

Russell waited patiently for me to step up to the mic and shout out my first bid. My heart pounded. My hands were sweaty. For some reason, I was more nervous that day than when I had stepped on the basketball court to play for the semi-state finals in front of 10,000 Hoosier hoop fanatics, or when I spoke at my high school graduation in front of 4,000 people. I had a sense of expectation—of what, I was unsure. However, I knew for certain that I was about to call my first auction as the youngest licensed auctioneer in the world.

––––––––––

A couple of years before, I had traveled to the nation's premier collector car auction. It was smack-dab in the middle of an oil patch during its boom of the early 1980's, and the clientele reflected that newfound wealth. We attended a cocktail party to celebrate the opening of this annual auction, and I remember Gold Rolexes glittering in abundance on the wrists of collectors who jammed Tulsa's 11.5-acre exposition hall, which on this day housed 550 of the world's greatest classic cars.

Why their watches struck me I'm not sure, but I remember one Piaget watch laced with diamonds in each link valued at $80,000. One comedian said for that kind of money the owner could pay someone to follow him around and sense when he wanted to know what time it was, then shout, "Hey Boss! It's 5 o'clock!" Diamonds dripped from the women as they were dressed to the nines for Oklahoma's largest social extravaganza of the year.

It was straight out of an episode of *Lifestyles of the Rich and Famous*, full of "champagne wishes and caviar dreams." (In fact, I recall that the producers of this show were among the media elite who filmed at the event over the years.) For anyone too young to remember Robin Leach's signature tagline, imagine an episode of *Cribs* featuring legendary skateboarder Tony Hawk or Shaun White, "the Flying Tomato," or catch a behind-the-scenes glimpse into an MTV world in *The Hills*.

As a teenager, the world of auctioning looked like the fulfillment of the dream I had always envisioned. My heart searched for a common thread that intertwined the tapestry of the wealthy with my taste for success. Some of the wealthiest people I knew had worked hard for it, while others had inherited wealth from generations before. Both had led to a lifestyle of exclusive elegance and notoriety. I knew that I could not base my future on a family inheritance, due to Dad's mountain of debt; however, if I could figure out a formula for success by observing those around me, maybe I too would become rich and satisfy the deep desires of my heart.

In fact, the thought of an inheritance repulsed me. I wanted to earn my success and prove my abilities to the world. In some ways, this was the beginning of my life as a workaholic, money addict, and materialist. Like a junkie who attempts to satisfy his desire with his drug of choice, my veins popped, ready for the gold needle that would infuse the obsession of money straight to my heart. When I stood on the farmhouse steps two years later, next to this curio cabinet and Russell, I believed this was my chance to satisfy my addiction.

I had watched Dad and Russell auctioneer more times than I could count, so I knew that I needed to move the auction quickly in order to sell the final items at a decent hour—one mark of a seasoned auctioneer. Additionally, I needed to know market values.

I thought back to a story Dad had shared about when he was twelve years old and began his first steps onto the auction block at a grocery store closeout. Russell was right beside Dad, as he was beside me today, and instructed him to begin selling jars of currant jelly with a starting bid of fifteen cents each. When Dad started the bidding at ten cents, Russell demanded to know why he lowered the price. Dad responded, "I don't like currant jelly." One of the bidders shouted out, "Neither do I. Ten cents!" It was the first time Dad's intrinsic ability to determine values had surfaced. The question of whether or not that knack had passed on to me remained unanswered.

Russell had placed me right in the center of the action in this little town as cars passing through pulled over on the two-lane highway. My deep sense was that what they were about to witness was a master class. I stepped up to the invisible podium, and my voice cut through the public address system, echoing into the air.

"One hundred dollars. Now one-fifty."

I paused and awaited the crowd's reaction. Nothing.

"Anybody else want to bid?"

More silence. I was not sure how to respond, so I rushed to close the sale. That's when Russell abruptly stopped me. I didn't know it at the time, but this was all part of the show. Two hundred bidders watched as he shouted, "Wait, Mitchell! Is there anything else you can say about this curio that might enhance the bid?"

I stood there stunned; I never suspected that Russell would step in.

"It has beautiful woodwork," I replied.

I waited for a response. Nothing happened. So I continued.

"It would probably cost thousands of dollars to build today?" I said sheepishly.

Russell leaned forward and loudly communicated, "Don't tell me. Tell them."

In that instant, it was as if a switch turned on inside, a light so bright that it illuminated my soul. It resembled the flash of lightning that struck overhead at the Indy 500. My voice grew stronger. Much like a preacher, I became the curio cabinet evangelist.

"This curio cabinet has beautiful woodwork! It would cost thousands of dollars to handcraft today."

As the seconds passed and I saw the crowd responding to me, my confidence level jumped. "One-fifty, now two hundred! Two hundred, now two-fifty."

My words shot out in rapid succession like an announcer yelling at a horse race on the final turn. The response of the crowd made my adrenaline flow like a tidal wave. I had arrived! Or so I thought. Before I continued, Russell interrupted me for the second time.

"Mitchell, wait! Is there anything else you can say about this cabinet that might encourage them to bid higher?"

In a split second, he sent my mojo into the depths of an unknown abyss. My moment of glory was gone, and my confidence was replaced by a tight knot in my stomach. What else was I supposed to say? Russell leaned in closely and crooned, "If I can get you convinced, I can get them convinced." He stepped back and waited patiently.

"The beveled glass is quite incredible," I replied. "Really, I have not seen anything like it." With Russell's nod of approval, I knew I was back in the game. I stepped closer to the crowd and boldly proclaimed, "The beveled glass is incredible! I've never seen anything like it!"

The crowd came alive again as hands were raised. "Two-fifty, now three hundred! Three hundred, now three-fifty."

Numbers fired from my lips like an automatic weapon. In a matter of minutes, Russell had made me believe that I could be the world's greatest auctioneer! Okay, maybe in retrospect not the greatest, seeing as we were only selling a single cabinet. Regardless, I was ready to bring down the hammer with such force that the crowd would erupt in celebration! I could already picture myself on the front page of my local newspaper, *The Evening Star*. I gripped the gavel in anticipation, eyes ablaze, waiting for just the right moment.

I glanced toward Russell and watched him raise his hand for the third time. "Mitchell, wait, wait!" Isn't there something else you can say to increase the bid?"

I was frustrated, angry, and bewildered. I was seconds away from victory, yet now I had grown to hate the curio cabinet as much as Dad hated currant jelly. It was the one thing that stood between failure and my future as an auctioneer. Russell was not making it any easier. Why was he doing this? I pulled myself together, stepped back, and this time, caught him by surprise.

"Wow, look at the feet. I never noticed them before. They're hand carved. No one does that today, it's too expensive."

This time I did not wait for his response. I waved my hand high above my head and cried, "Four-fifty, five hundred, now five-fifty. I have five-fifty, now six hundred! Six hundred, thank you! Who'll give me seven?"

Then I went in for the altar call.

"Eight hundred, eight-fifty, now nine hundred, nine-fifty! Who'll give a thousand dollars?" A man standing near the front of the crowd raised his hand.

I pretended not to see Russell, waited a few seconds, and finally turned to him and asked over the public address system, "Can I sell it now?"

"Yes!" he shouted, satisfied that the infamous curio cabinet was about to trade hands for one thousand dollars.

The crowd waited for me to close the sale.

I was officially being introduced into the family business by the pioneer himself, Grandpa Russell. It was a business that had unleashed a novelty industry that had exploded into a new market. The days of auctioning on the porches of farmhouses soon catapulted into events that showcased some of the rarest classic cars in the world. In earlier years, owners of antique or classic cars had to basically sell them on their own by placing ads in newspapers or magazines, or simply had to rely on word of mouth. No one actually knew the true market value for these rolling sculptures. For instance, Duesenbergs were bringing in $12,000 to $15,000. The Kruse family business took these unlisted commodities and made standardized values for them, defining a market price for each collector car, anywhere in the world.

The Auburn automobile company in Auburn, Indiana, achieved its fame by building Duesenbergs, America's greatest luxury cars. My family sold the exact same cars for 10 to 100 times their original prices. Even with the financial struggles of the company, Dad had managed to keep it alive.

In the 1920s and '30s, the Auburn Automobile Company put its hometown on the world and national map. A half-century later, Kruse International would repeat the same feat.

My first licensed auction selling a curio cabinet was simply a warm-up for the main event. Russell always taught me, "Auction each item like it is your own, and you are three months behind on your mortgage payment with the bank ready to foreclose." And, at this moment, I was ready to enter that world.

Like Briggs Cunningham who found the lost Bugattis, in the summer of '83, I had caught a glimpse of my destiny as I stood on that front porch, seconds away from closing out my first sale as the world's youngest licensed auctioneer. Unaware if it was fate, ordained, predestined, or simply meant to happen, I believed it was my chance for self-restoration. What I discovered in the years ahead was a never-ending roller coaster as I sacrificed everything for a family business in my pursuit of wealth and fame. I did not realize it at the time, but it also marked a new direction on the dirt road that led me further away from living as one who had been restored to authenticity.

On this day I looked out on to the crowd, glanced at the curio cabinet one final time, and smiled at Russell. Then I shouted with authority a word that would become not only my favorite four-letter word, but also my addiction:

"SOLD!"

Chapter Five

THE DEAL MAKER

I wish I could say that when I was seventeen I did not relate to the younger son in Jesus' trilogy. But the truth is I entered a family business, encountered early victories like the curio cabinet, and even in the midst of Dad's insurmountable debt my stone heart continued to loosen. I chose to keep control of my life because I refused to allow my dream to be taken away.

Ironically, the *Indianapolis Star* wrote an article about my future when I was the youngest Realtor in the nation. My stated goal was to become a billionaire by the age of forty, proving that a good Christian person could do it. The newspaper writer made me furious when in the headlines he changed the "b" in billionaire to an "m," subtracting three zeroes from my ambitious goal. This only fueled my desire to prove to everyone that I would achieve greatness. Failure was not an option. With Dad, I believed I had the best mentor in the business.

He rented an office in Auburn and carved out a small space for me to set up a desk and chairs as I began to work my way up the auction ladder. I have never been employed. Consequently, I never received a steady paycheck. Dad's plan for me was to be a person who could employ others, so from the beginning of my career I had to learn to generate commissions through auctions, private sales, and brokering real estate transactions. I was hungry for instant gratification. I often walked into his office yelling, "I need a deal!" He understood, because he was as addicted to the deal as I was becoming. Life quickly became about earning the almighty dollar and achieving my goals. None of them would be reached without first uttering the word, "Sold!" For me, cash was king.

The greater my success, the more I refused to remain under the shadow of Dad or Grandpa Russell. I did not want to play by the same list of rules. I wanted to achieve affluence, wealth, riches, and triumph on my own terms. Even though I was often reminded of Jesus' trilogy, I was not going to let a parable about a sheep, a coin, or two brothers who fought with their old man stop me from accomplishing my dreams of success.

The pursuit of my desires apart from God caused me to neglect my faith because I loved the elusive satisfaction of money too much. Like the younger son who had separated himself from his earthly father, my journey separated me from the full benefits of the love of my spiritual Father. My stone heart crumbled into a heart of sand that overflowed in particles of pride. I was about to learn that whether I had a stone heart or a sand heart, I was still trusting in my giftedness rather than my godliness—the Spirit of the Restorer in me.

———————

I met Susan on the first day of seventh grade. We sat next to each other in Mrs. Bard's English class. We were instant friends, but it took four years before I mustered up enough courage to ask her out on a date. I guess I thought that I had to earn my driver's license first. With sweaty palms, I had all the best lines rehearsed as I battled an internal voice that whispered, *"You don't have a chance."* But I did. One of my best friends was dating her best friend, and without my permission, he had requested that she ask Susan if she would agree to go out with me. He conveniently forgot that merely one class period earlier I had sworn him to secrecy.

After laying the groundwork, he told me, "Dude, she'll go out with you." I was in shock. No turning back now.

With no voicemail, no e-mail, no text messaging, and no Facebook, I did it the old fashioned way. I asked Susan the million-dollar question while we stood next to her locker. I almost dropped to my knees when she replied, "Yes."

See? There is a God!

Susan was my first true love. We got along so well that it took two years before we had our first argument.

During our freshman year in college, I got down on one knee and asked her to marry me. Again, she said, "Yes." In the whirlwind of our romance, we boarded a plane for Maui to enjoy ten days of paradise on our honeymoon.

We didn't have a care in the world. All that mattered was that we were together. We started out in the seclusion of a private resort villa on the beach, but soon traded that for the cheapest room at the Hyatt after a night of fighting a native island bug that landed on my underwear. Susan was ready to come to the rescue by smashing it with her tennis racquet. *Did I mention I was wearing the underwear at the time?* I am still thankful that I survived the night without permanent injury.

We were in love. I was living life the way I wanted, and everything seemed to be working out as planned. I refused to look back or allow myself to be distracted by anything that did not equate into money or wealth. Life was great! The fight to hold on to my stone heart, with all the rules I had obeyed as a child, all but disappeared as I embraced what seemed to be an easier dirt road in a heart of sand. Looking back, I understand that the chase was almost more satisfying than the achievement.

One morning in Maui, I sat down and mapped out our entire financial future, centered around investing in real estate. For each of the next fifty years, I projected asset values, gross rental income, debt, and net worth along with estimated cash flow with modest annual increases. I was determined to plan out how I would succeed where others in my family had fallen short. After all, as Zig Ziglar said, "Failing to plan means planning to fail."

Like the younger son in the parable, I had my own plan for life. While I did not go to my earthly father with an outrageous request, I did go to my Heavenly Father with a sand heart weighed down in pride. I asked for what I had believed I deserved. I thought that if I followed steps one through ten, my financial future would direct everything else, including my faith in Him.

I interpreted love and acceptance solely on my growing accomplishments in business, not on deeper relationships. Even though I didn't wish that anyone would die, as had the younger son, sometimes I treated people as if I didn't care if they were alive. At times I even lived like I didn't care if God was alive. My faith was placed in a shiny metal box and stored away in a dark place, hidden while I breathed in the aroma of success. It was becoming sweeter by the minute. Life revolved around my choices, thoughts, prayers (or lack of them), and feelings, all directed toward satisfying my desires. This selfishness added grains of sand to my increasingly licentious heart. I was unaware of how quickly the hourglass of life could be turned upside down.

Rock-Star Auctioneer

My notoriety in the classic car auction business reached rock-star status in 1985 when I sold a beautifully restored, one-of-a-kind, 1934 Duesenberg SJ LaGrande supercharged dual-cowl phaeton. This piece of art was built with front opening doors, originally designed for the extremely wealthy who required a chauffeur to lift the heavy rear windshield in order for a passenger to sit in the back seat.

This rolling sculpture's new owner was a man by the name of Tom Monaghan. He was raised in St. Joseph's Home for Children in Michigan, expelled from seminary, and accidently enlisted in the U.S. Marines instead of the Army. He was honorably discharged in 1959 and returned to Ann Arbor, Michigan, where he bought a small pizza store called DomiNick's with his brother James. Tom would later trade his brother a Volkswagen Beetle for his half of the business. That was a wise trade, for today that business is recognized around the world as Domino's Pizza. I would meet Mr. Monaghan years later after he had acquired the Detroit Tigers who won the World Series in 1984.

The day I met him, he landed his helicopter on the grounds of our Labor Day Weekend auction in Auburn. I met him as he disembarked from his chopper. Within seconds, I found myself describing the Duesenberg to Mr. Monaghan, along with a record asking price of one million dollars. I had located this vehicle for another collector who was not prepared to fund the purchase.

After a subsequent meeting in Mr. Monaghan's office, we flew together in his private jet to view the vehicle. While in the air, we received word that his good friend, the previous owner of the Tigers, had suffered a heart attack. Tom was stunned. I was too. His security staff asked if he wanted to turn the plane around. Seconds passed, but for me it seemed like an eternity. I watched in suspense as Mr. Monaghan pondered this question, because I was worried that I might never see my commission from the deal if he decided to turn back. When the word came that his friend was stable, he decided to stay on course. I remember him saying, "I want to buy that car."

We arrived at the private collection where the Duesenberg was displayed. Three of us—Mr. Monaghan, the potential seller, and I as the broker—examined every inch of the vehicle together. Judges gave the car 100 points, which is a perfect rating in the Classic Car Club of America competition. I was anxious when we thought we found a scratch on the car. Imagine a tiny scratch standing between you and a million-dollar sale! We were all relieved when we discovered that it was only a piece of lint protruding from the trunk.

The owner turned the key in the ignition and the car roared to life. The original supercharger kicked in and goosebumps rose on my arms, partly because I loved cars and partly because I was one step closer to sealing the deal.

Mr. Monaghan agreed to purchase the car, and I later watched him write the first check I had ever seen in the amount of $1,000,000. To add to the excitement, he decided to take delivery of the car, soon to be marketed as Domino's Doozy, at home plate in Tiger Stadium. (The phrase, "It's a Doozy!" comes directly from the Duesenberg era.) Not long afterward I stood with Mr. Monaghan at home plate in Tiger Stadium on a sunny day in Detroit, surrounded by eight thousand Domino's employees who filled the stands. Everyone was eager for the car to make its way from center field to home plate. The driver hit the supercharger, and the unfamiliar roar echoed throughout this historic ballpark. The crowd erupted in celebration.

Photographers snapped portraits of the million-dollar piece of art that would grace the covers of most newspapers and automotive publications. With the transfer of the title, the transaction was almost complete. The one remaining exercise that needed to happen, as with every purchase, was for the seller to hand Mr. Monaghan the keys to the most expensive vehicle in the world.

My heart overflowed with joy because I had officially closed not only the biggest deal of my life, but at the time the single largest sale of a vehicle in the history of the world—the first car to ever change hands for a documented million-dollars cash! Standing at home plate in Tiger Stadium, I had just hit a grand slam.

Less than a year after the Monaghan sale, I was consumed with working around the clock because I believed that I could auction anything, and in my world everything was for sale. I earned more money in one auction than I would in fifteen years of paying off my newly developed 12-unit apartment complex's mortgage. So much for my Maui plan!

I sold great collector cars in private transactions like that of Mr. Monaghan, including an entire muscle car collection for $2,000,000 to baseball's Mr. October, Reggie Jackson, winner of five world series championships with the Oakland A's and the pinstriped New York Yankees.

I traveled with Reggie in our private aircraft from our Labor Day Weekend Auburn Auction to a collector's warehouse in the beautiful southern United States. The seller even had someone string up lights for the big reveal. Rows of muscle cars, including a 1970 Chevelle 454 LS6, glistened in the shadows of the night. I will never forget the collection's ZL1 Camaro rumbling to life, its deep *"ram pop pop pop"* pulsing through my chest. Once I saw Reggie's reaction, I knew I had sealed another deal.

Rumors in the collector car world circulated that Reggie had paid for this collection with insurance checks secured after his previous collection had been destroyed in a fire. We all but closed the transaction in a Denny's, and then flew to Chicago's O'Hare Airport where I dropped Reggie off at 5:00 a.m. By mid-morning, our private plane landed at the DeKalb County Airport in Auburn, and I drove to our twenty-five-year-old, eight-hundred-square-foot ranch where I went to bed. The juxtaposition of the deal I had just landed against my tiny house was almost laughable.

Before I closed my eyes, I mentally moved on to another deal that I had in the works—a one-of-a-kind Duesenberg that I knew would be ideal to add to one particular collector's stable. The question was whether or not I could get the buyer and seller to come together, since neither of them knew that either one wanted to buy or sell. Throughout all this, I sensed a pulse of invincibility. I refused to admit that my outward appearance of authenticity merely masked the pretense I lived with as I battled my fractured heart, which I had placed for sale to the highest bidder.

Regardless of my internal struggle, the auction business continued to skyrocket. We created the first auction broadcasted live via satellite and the first such event broadcasted live on cable television. I traveled all over the country to auction cars for buyers and sellers, including Wayne Newton, Burt Reynolds, Mark Miller of Sawyer Brown, The Oak Ridge Boys' Duane Allen, Jay Leno, Hank Williams Jr., Zsa Zsa Gabor (her Rolls Royce complete with scratches from her jewelry caused during her much-publicized arrest), as well as Tommy Hearns, Mike Ditka, Lou Holtz, Rodney Crowl, Wynona, Lauren Hutton, Larry Hagman and a growing list of rock stars.

I had conquered what many in the press deemed an impossibility. I believed I had managed to resurrect the Kruse legacy, and the public vindication fueled my passion for more. While Dad was known as the "Dean of Auctioneering," some said that I was the "Deal Maker." I was like an evangelist who convinced buyers and sellers to raise their hands and come forward to an altar call of fulfillment, satisfaction, and notoriety discovered in the value of a rare piece of art. Anyone who has ever sat behind the wheel of an original '69 Shelby Cobra with the beat of the engine vibrating under their seats understands how spiritual an experience this really is. All I had to do was convince potential buyers that the return was worth the risk.

The media devoured my next press release. To reinforce the value of the collector car investment, I had created an historical price pro forma of the ideal collector car portfolio. I valued what the greatest cars in the world had been worth in the mid-1960's, prior to the first consignment collector car auction. Then based on recorded sales, I demonstrated that this ideal collector car portfolio's performance actually *exceeded* that of the stock and bond markets through 1987. I said to the press, "You can't peel away from the stoplight in your stock certificate or wave to your friends in a parade from your bond." This information and my quote was carried by numerous publications throughout the world. The collector car market was officially *en fuego*!

The Younger Son and Me

To fuel my addiction, I acquired elaborate cars, bronze statues, jewelry, collectibles, and took expensive trips as appetizers to the main course. I fraternized with the super-rich; on the outside everything looked good, but on the inside my heart of sand was becoming ever more dependent on the next fix. My legalistic heart of stone had crumbled, and in its place I had built countless sand castles to represent my kingdom. I now realize that this was my attempt to contain the kingdom of God in me. I traded intimate relationships with others and with God for a belief that my success would fix my waning friendships and repair my repressed longing for a restored heart.

I relied on my self-restoration program to bring me back to the Restorer's authentic condition. And true to form I was left dissatisfied. My pursuit for even more riches was relentless. I was in the office from 6 a.m. to 6 p.m. when in town, and then traveled Friday through Monday about forty-five weekends per year. In doing so, I had squeezed in another day each week to generate more business. My self-ambitious pride convinced me that I was bulletproof.

I was disillusioned and often times disconnected from marriage and family. Even after Susan and I had our first daughter, Megan, I still prioritized work first at the expense of a relationship with my family. Money became an end product instead of a byproduct. At best, my faith in God remained an outward appearance instead of an inward pursuit of intimacy. I was too busy turning assets into cash. I was willing to go to the ends of the earth to find the rarest automobiles to finance my lifestyle and add to my treasure chest, but I had neglected to stop for a few minutes to pray let alone read my Bible. I had chosen the same path as the younger son: "Not long after that, the younger son got together all he had, set off for a distant country" (Luke 15:13a).

I had used my life in the auction world as an escape from my relationship with God. While the younger son was on a search for something to fill the void in his heart, I had searched for everything except for what God promised to give: *love* that offers *significance*, *truth* that provides *security*, *peace* that blesses with *contentment*, and *power* that brings *control*. All of these are rooted in humility which leads to restoration and authenticity, and humility was a characteristic in which I was severely lacking.

Both the younger son and I were willing to gamble the love of our fathers with a false promise of *significance*, *security*, *contentment*, and *control*—the four primary desires placed in our hearts by our Creator. We both searched for a missing piece to restore the center of our love and affection, to fill an eternal void deep within our hearts. We chose to do life outside our father's loving design. We were motivated by greed, a form of idolatry that we had woven into a pattern of sin that camouflaged our longing for intimate relationships. We would both pay a heavy price for our choices.

The Tradition of the Ring

God designed a different solution for the satisfaction of our desires. In the third commandment God said to Moses, "You shall not make for yourself an idol in the form of anything in heaven above or on the earth beneath or in the waters below. You shall not bow down to them or worship them; for I, the LORD your God, am a jealous God, punishing the children for the sin of the fathers to the third and fourth generation of those who hate me, but showing love to a thousand generations of those who love me and keep my commandments" (Exodus 20:4-6).

We can relate this command to the younger son in the trilogy. After he ran away from his father, he ended up pawning his sandals, his robe, his standing in the community, and his right to be a member of a family to pursue the idols he had created in his life. He even sold his ring, the one outward symbol that represented his ability to carry out his father's business.

Families often pass down heirlooms from one generation to the next as a symbol of their patriarchal lineage. This was true in my family as well. On his deathbed, my great-great grandfather, William Kruse, passed down his wedding ring to his sixteen-year-old grandson, Russell. Grandpa Russell wore this ring until I purchased the family farm that my great-great-great grandfather, James Kruse, homesteaded from the government. Russell included it with the purchase price of the farm and told me what his grandfather told him: "Keep it, and pass it on to future generations."

Russell's words to me included another message that would later become a mantra for my life: "Restore the ring to authenticity." This century-old ring, crafted from rose gold with a rectangular black onyx setting that includes a gold English "K," is still a significant piece of my family's history. I would never consider this heirloom for sale.

When I placed this ring on my finger, I accepted a priceless generational treasure. Interestingly, the Hebrew word for "generations" is the same word used for "circle"—*dor*, the shape of a ring. Made from precious metal, a ring is symbolic of the abundant value of love. Being circular, a ring is also symbolic of the eternal value of love. It illustrates God's love that is both overflowingly abundant and eternal.

"Abundant" is the same as "more than enough." "Eternal" translates into "our satisfaction in the Restorer will never end." I had spent so much of my life attempting to satisfy my desires apart from God in idolatry, that I was always left dissatisfied without intimacy.

We will either live in God's circle of intimacy or we will live outside in idolatry. God made this clear when He gave Moses the Ten Commandments. God is jealous *for* us, not *of* us. He desires that we live in His circle of intimacy. The important question to ask is whether we are inside or outside of His circle.

Another tradition passed down through the Kruse generations was praying on our knees. I still remember, when I was about five years old, walking down the hall outside my mom and dad's bedroom late at night. I saw in my peripheral vision that someone was kneeling beside the bed. It was my dad. I stopped and watched. When he had finished, I asked what he had been doing. He said that he had been praying on his knees, just like his grandfather Fred had done. He then said, "Mitchell, always pray on your knees at night. It is a picture of what should be going on inside your heart. Keep it, and pass it on to future generations."

Little did I know then that this intimate connection of my heart with God's, where he shaped my desires to be like His, was the ultimate heirloom that would be passed down through my grandfathers and father. Unfortunately, like the younger son, I had mortgaged my prayers beyond what I was able to repay.

In the explosive insanity of our auction business, I did not understand the freedom found in a life of authenticity and wisdom. Like the younger son, I had relied solely on my street smarts. I had never connected the significance of God's wisdom with the condition of my sand-hearted ways. I had traveled far from my stone-hearted upbringing toward the things I believed would bring fulfillment. All I was left with was a sandcastle kingdom. I had not yet learned that my heart of sand would always leave me feeling like I needed more.

I didn't equate the focus on the vertical at the expense of the horizontal that came with having a stone heart, or the focus on the horizontal at the expense of the vertical that came with having a sand heart. What I needed to discover was the wisdom found only in the sweet spot where the vertical and the horizontal intersected.

Like the younger son, it took time and a life-changing moment before I made a decision to rediscover a God who promised to reveal a life-altering transformation—a chance to be restored to authenticity. If I had surrendered and fallen on my knees before the Restorer during this time, perhaps my life would have taken a different path.

Unfortunately, I did not surrender. I was too busy pursuing the next deal, one bigger than the deal before. With my rise to success, I remained unconvinced that I needed to face this reality. The sand in my heart had spread to my desires, my eyes blinded by pride's ambition. The hourglass of my life of sand was turning upside down, and I would soon stand face-to-face with the addict that I had become.

Chapter Six

THE GREATEST AUCTION

A 1931 Bugatti Royale Type 41 Cabriolet surfaced in a New York junkyard in the early 1940's and was later restored. The owner later gave it to the Henry Ford Museum, where it still stands on display today. The placard reads that it had an original selling price of $43,000. Today, a Bugatti Royale is still considered the ultimate status symbol, one of the biggest, most rare, and most desirable cars in the world.

Bugatti Royale Berline de Voyage

In 1986, our company was about to auction a Bugatti Royale Berline de Voyage. It was considered to be one of the most original of the six remaining Royales. It featured a locomotive engine, fixed in a one-of-a-kind body crafted with wood coachwork. It also featured a three-position top that could remain fully closed, folded partially to form a town car, or completely lowered to form a convertible sedan. I didn't realize it at the time, but we were about to auction both of Briggs Cunningham's European discoveries from Ettore Bugatti's personal collection.

No Royale had ever been offered at a public auction. The first of these two rare automobiles was placed on the auction block with no reserve, selling regardless of price to the highest bidder.

I convinced Red McCombs, then-owner of the San Antonio Spurs, to join the auction. Although he was one of the wealthiest men in Texas, he had not jumped through all the credit approval hoops to enter the auction. On my recommendation, the corporation that owned the cars agreed to accept Red, and on the day of the auction he was approved to bid.

The event was an evening gala, the third and final segment of the sale of the William F. Harrah collection which had spanned three auctions in three years. The owner of the collection, the Holiday Inn Corporation, had purchased Harrah's after Mr. Harrah passed away on the operating table in Houston during open-heart surgery. He had left no estate planning. Consequently, his heirs could not pay the estate taxes without liquidating the assets, so they were forced to sell his casinos along with the automobile collection—1,500 of the finest cars ever built.

Among his collection were two Bugatti Royales and several of the lowest mileage, most-coveted Duesenbergs and Mercedes Benzes ever manufactured. Mr. Harrah used to bring an entourage to the Hershey Swap Meet in Pennsylvania each year to comb through the inventories of thousands of vendors scattered throughout hundreds of acres, all carefully organized in an effort to locate the parts he needed to complete the restoration of his automobiles. He was a true purist.

The executives of Holiday Inn Corporation feared that the market might flood if they sold the entire collection at once. They were wrong. The market escalated to never-before seen heights. Our company sold 1,000 cars in three auctions held in three separate calendar years (1984, 1985, and 1986). At the time, the $44 million sale total was the largest personal property auction ever conducted. Amidst pressure to keep the collection intact, the

Holiday Inn Corporation even donated several of the cars to a new non-profit that formed a museum in Nevada. The remaining vehicles were sold in a private transaction for an estimated $25 million on December 31, 1986, minutes before midnight, when President Reagan's new tax law went into effect.

The offering of the first Bugatti Royale was made possible at a dinner with Tom Monaghan and the executive of Harrah's Corporation overseeing the auction. At that dinner, I asked Tom to make an offer of $5,000,000 each for either one or both of the Royales. He wrote the offer to purchase in one sentence on the back of a square paper napkin that sat beside his soft drink. As I handed the old-school contract to the Harrah's executive, I was praying that I was about to do a $10,000,000 deal over dinner. He picked up the napkin, read it and said, "We will auction one of the Royales."

We sold the first Bugatti Royale Berline de Voyage—one of the two cars that Ettore Bugatti had kept hidden for himself—in the Reno/Sparks Convention Center with Dad as the auctioneer. I worked directly with the eventual buyer during the auction at his request. He outbid General William Lyon from Newport Beach, California, after a hard-fought battle. The second runner-up bidder was Ken Behring who had built Blackhawk, an upscale development in Danville, California. Ken would later donate his car collection, one of the finest ever assembled, to the University of California at Berkley.

I had spoken personally with all of the registered bidders months before the auction. I worked the phones incessantly, trying to convince collectors to register to bid for the most valuable car in the world. I believed it would bring $10 million, and I still believe it would have if Mr. Monaghan had been able to bid. His company had taken a new direction that involved cutting expenses, and he was not prepared to once again set a record price for purchasing a collector car. When the gavel fell at $6.5 million, it was still the third-highest price ever paid for a piece of art at the time. But we weren't finished. We had one more Bugatti Royale to auction.

In 1987 during my last semester of earning my B.S. in Business Administration from Indiana University, I established a new corporation called Kruse, Inc. Along with this new business entity and a refurbished brand, I drafted a personal services contract with Dad because he could no longer own anything due to his continued problems with creditors. I was finally running the business my way, and I loved it. This auction was a great forum in which to demonstrate my knowledge and expertise.

Bugatti Royale Kellner

The Bugatti Royale Kellner coupe was the second Bugatti up for auction. For years it had resided in the Briggs Cunningham collection after he had found it hidden in Europe. Mr. Monaghan and I had previously flown in his private jet with an offer to purchase Briggs' entire collection, a group of automobiles that included one of the finest Duesenbergs in the world: Gary Cooper's SSJ. Briggs declined the offer, but years later sold the cars to Miles Collier of Naples, Florida. Being a vintage racer at heart, Miles elected not to keep the Royale so he sold it to another collector who offered the Bugatti at *"The Auction"* in 1989 at the Imperial Palace Hotel and Casino in Las Vegas.

We collaborated with Don Williams and Richie Clyne to conduct the sale of an amazing array of vehicles. By this time, Mr. Monaghan had rearranged his finances and quietly purchased the Berline de Voyage for $8.1 million. Rumors swirled that a Ferrari GTO had traded hands for more. The prices for these rare and beautiful works of art were reaching stratospheric levels.

The owner of the Imperial Palace was interested in the Bugatti, but did he did not end up with it. Although the Bugatti Royale Kellner did not sell that night for the high bid of $ 11.5 million, it later changed hands for an undisclosed amount.

In the final analysis we had auctioned two of the rarest cars in history, but like the younger son in Jesus' trilogy, I wondered if I was really any closer to Restoration Road.

In Luke 15, we see that the younger son set off for a distant land, "and there squandered his wealth in wild living" (Luke 15:13b).

These words do not necessarily imply that his squandering included immoral acts; rather, it meant that he simply lost the money. This is based on the definition of the Greek word for "wild living" which is *asotos*. It essentially means that one day the cash flowed, and the next day the younger son could not find two coins to buy a falafel and hummus. In those days, the idea of a Jew losing money to Gentiles was utterly unthinkable—akin to billionaire Warren Buffet handing over a blank check to Paris Hilton.

Imagine what kind of wild or riotous living the younger son experienced. Maybe he bought a room filled with wine skins, or maybe he bought dozens of sandals that he never wore. He might have even purchased a mule or a camel—one hump or two? He might have thrown a few coins at the lepers who begged on the street to show others how he really was compassionate deep down inside. Whatever he did, he did it at a cost.

Over time, this kind of living caught up with him. His heart of sand became even looser as he faced one storm after another. It was a natural consequence for the foolish way he had abused his resources. What had appeared to be a stable, luxurious life fueled by a significant inheritance slowly disintegrated into nothing more than a struggle for survival. Once again, riotous living captured a prideful sand heart, leaving it destroyed and in desperate need of restoration.

I had also learned to spend with the best of them, and like the younger son, I chose to do this at the expense of sound business practices. Over the years I fought to overcome my desire for short-term pleasure because it threatened to outweigh my long-term business goals. In a matter of time, I would discover that a life of riotous living offered only short-term gain accompanied by long-term pain. After the Bugatti auction, my sand heart drifted toward a looser state.

After I spent years living the riotous life from 1987 to 1990, the business quadrupled. However, on July 1, 1990, the beginning of an economic recession, my business fortunes began to plummet, dropping like an eagle nose-diving toward its prey. And this time, I was the prey. In my relentless pursuit of success, my heart of sand quickly slipped through my fingers. I began to face one storm after another, both financially and relationally.

Problems Mount

One of our biggest customers, a legendary collector, took off in his private plane at his personal airstrip after a party with three hundred of his staff watching. Aboard the plane were his three top executives. Tragically, the plane crashed on takeoff in full view of the entire staff and their families. All of the passengers died.

Shortly after this accident the executors called us to secure short-term financing for the car collection to maintain positive cash flow in the business. I arranged it through a new collaborative relationship I had developed with a finance company, and we signed an auction agreement to offer the 150 vehicles without reserve.

In Uncertain, Texas, population 120, we stood amazed as nearly ten thousand people descended on the ranch for the auction. One of the finest collections of MG Motor Cars in the world was housed only minutes away from the ranch, and I asked the owner to also consider selling his collection at this event. He decided to take advantage of the opportunity created by the international exposure generated by the auction. We put both collections together and sold them to the highest bidder. Nearly ten million dollars changed hands that day as international news media covered the bittersweet event.

By the end of the year I realized that without this auction, our business would have been dealt an enormous financial loss. Dad's eternally optimistic response was to not worry because the market would bounce back. The only question was when.

In the midst of realizing the state of our business, we survived in the short run by the initial supply of collectors who had to sell their cars to keep their businesses intact. At the same time, new problems were developing. We continued to attract bidders who bought cars and then did not pay for them.

To make things really sporty, we also had received a random death threat against Dad during an auction that put us all on edge. We hired armed, secret service-type security to ensure our safety—they came with a bill that totaled nearly $30,000. The first step that these security guards took was to escort my wife, mom, and daughter Megan to the gate of the airplane that would take them home.

Like the younger son in the trilogy, my life was spiraling out of control. *"After he had spent everything, there was a severe famine in that whole country, and he began to be in need"* (Luke 15:14).

Pride Blocks the Way to Restoration

The younger son jumped at the chance to live free from the rules of his father; his pride fueled his decision. He survived for a while by his own giftedness and survival skills, but again he found himself in a predicament as a result of his pride. We see that this son was reminded of a problem. His choices created a tug of war between pride and humility, and now his heart was scattered like grains of sand on a beach. The farther he traveled away from home, the more compact his heart became. This kind of heart requires a storm to shape it, and this young man was standing on the verge of a tsunami. It was the natural consequence of the foolish way he had abused his resources from his lack of humility, especially toward his father. Perhaps the younger son would have reflected on Solomon's warning, "An inheritance quickly gained at the beginning will not be blessed at the end" (Proverbs 20:21).

Remember, the younger son saw his connection with his father as loose. His connection with others was the same way. He had defined horizontal wisdom as doing whatever had served his own selfish interests, basically living by his own street smarts. When this severe famine hit, his proverbial storm touched down. He had already spent everything, and was now destitute. He needed a way out, and his street smarts told him there were two options: (1) try to work his way out of his situation, or (2) swallow his pride and return home.

If he chose door number two, he would experience the *qetsatsah*. We introduced this term earlier in the book; this is essentially a funeral service that is held, even though the individual is still living. After this ritual he would be treated as if he were dead, and then kicked out from the community for shaming his family. At that point, door number one looked like a clear winner.

His street smarts said, "I'm choosing door number one. Sure I'll stay unchanged on the inside, but if I pull myself together on the outside, then it will all be fine. I can work my way out of this. I don't need anyone else's help."

This was his self-restoration plan.

In each choice there was a clear downside.

In choosing door number one to fix his problem, he would leverage his three resources of life just to keep himself alive. Looking through the clouded lens of his misdirected wisdom, the younger son believed it was worth the risk. Pride won out yet again as he plotted to fool his family and himself into believing that he had truly changed. Sandy pride stood in the way of the realization that a full surrender of his heart, desires, and the three resources of life to God would lead to authenticity and wisdom (Proverbs 1:7; 9:10).

Like the younger son, I too continued to pretend that I could engage in my own self-restoration program because I trusted in my giftedness rather than my godliness.

While my business was imploding, I kept an outward appearance of control amid all the adversity in my life. I held it together on the outside, a survival instinct rooted in me from an early age. People looked at the beautiful cars I auctioned, the wealthy people in my circle of influence, a family legacy, a loving wife, an adorable daughter, and they came to one conclusion: "Mitch has it all!" And in my pretense, I let them believe just that.

Like the younger son who lived with a sand heart, I too experienced the result of my sand-heartedness as my downward spiral picked up momentum. I chased after what I believed would bring satisfaction and comfort, only to discover that none of it would ever repair the damage I had done to my spiritual heart. My pursuit satisfied a proud heart for a while, but it would never provide an eternal satisfaction found in living restored to authenticity. I had to accept my need for God, because everything else always left me dissatisfied.

I had interpreted Christianity as merely a set of moral values instead of as a deep well of wisdom that could be applied to my marketplace life. I did not think God cared much about how a collector car auction was operated. I left my stone heart behind and replaced it with a heart of sand scattered in countless directions because of my attempt to be the designer of my own kingdom. I struggled to hang on as a tidal wave of uncertainty rose on the horizon. I was unsure how to stop it. I read the Bible. I even prayed. However, I did these things while in the midst of my deepest sin, darkening my heart toward God.

Desperation Road, Second Generation

Instead of searching for the wisdom found in an intimate relationship with the Restorer, my self-restoration plan was to work longer and harder, even if it meant getting up at 4:00 a.m. I struggled with the foolish decisions I had made in the past that had allowed everything to get out of control. In the end, I believed my only option was to dig my way out of the debris alone.

Instead of planning for family time, I traveled further and more frequently to visit every person who might want to buy or sell a significant dollar amount of collector cars. I stayed late at the office because there was literally no end to what I could do each day in my effort to earn enough money to stay one step ahead of disaster.

Regardless of what I tried, my heart of sand slipped through my fingers as my business and personal life continued to free fall. By 1992, even though my credentials were seemingly impressive as the owner of Kruse International, my reality told a much different story. The company represented millions of dollars in accounts payable without enough resources to pay them. I sat down with each one of our vendors in order to work out a solution. I found myself in the same position as Dad had found himself years earlier. Somehow, I was repeating the identical journey on Desperation Road that the generation before me had traveled. Still, I had no idea that a storm was on the horizon, a storm that would crush my riotous living into a million little pieces.

Chapter Seven

THE RAID

I nhale.

Wednesday, July 1, 1992.

I exited my car in the office parking lot, already dreading the pressure of my multi-tasked life. Sure, I was trying to live out my dream, but dealing daily with an unstoppable downward spiral as the fearless leader of Kruse International left me fighting a battle that I was no longer convinced I could win. As I walked across the parking lot, I struggled to generate enough motivation to prevent circumstances from escalating further. That wouldn't be an issue for long; what happened next proved to be the symbolic straw that broke the proverbial camel's back.

Change Agents

For the first time since I had instituted monthly meetings with our employees, I was late. I hurried to unlock the first of two glass exterior doors to my office suite. When I stepped into the breezeway that came before the second door, something strange happened. I noticed that the door was already unlocked. To my surprise, two members of the Criminal Investigation Division of the Internal Revenue Service greeted me. That's right—the *IRS,* every businessman's worst nightmare!

At first I thought that this was a joke, masterminded by a few employees. Many of them were friends with local police officers who performed traffic control and security duty during our Labor Day weekend event. Very quickly, I realized I was not on an episode of "Punk'd," (which didn't even exist yet on MTV). I hoped the purpose of their visit was to investigate records for one of our 450,000 customers. However, within a matter of seconds, my hope was dashed like a bug smashing into a windshield at ninety miles per hour. And I felt like that bug.

I guess you could say all four chambers of my heart imploded simultaneously. As my eyes locked on their badges and the sight of their holstered guns, I realized that this would be a defining moment in my life. I had grown used to my inner heart struggle to keep my business intact, attempting to avoid the inevitable financial storm. Well, the inevitable had just paid me a house call wearing the uniform of Uncle Sam, saying, "Kruse, I want you!"

My heart was out of alignment. My will and efforts were forced to reside in the present, as I was faced with unreasonable expectations that were rarely met. My intellect focused on the future, afraid that I wouldn't achieve success. My spirit was breaking from the vertical relationship with God as each minute passed. My emotions still cycled back to the past as I relived former hurts. With the swell of choices, thoughts, prayers, and feelings that rifled through the four chambers of my heart, I tried desperately to keep my wits about me. Hurriedly, I canvassed my memory for anything that might have triggered a reason for this unexpected and unwanted visit.

My employees were already gathered in the conference room at the end of the hall as the agents busily combed through the rest of the facility. Their activity symbolized the fact that I was no longer in control of my future.

Partly because I absolutely detested anyone controlling me and partly because I had seen it in the movies, I asked the IRS agents for permission to make one telephone call. They obliged, saying, "We appreciate you remaining calm during our raid." *RAID!* Chills rippled down my spine.

I picked up the receiver and dialed the one person who I knew could help. Shortly before the raid, I had initiated weekly meetings with Uncle Derald to help guide me through the business challenges and ride the relational roller coaster with my bulldozer business partner: his brother, my Dad. Derald immediately jumped in his car and drove the six-minute route from his office to mine, praying the entire way. In less than an hour of communicating with the agents he discovered two crucial facts: first, the IRS had orchestrated a sting operation against our company; second, we needed to pull together expert legal counsel to mount a white-collar criminal defense. I knew right away the legal fees alone would eventually put us out of business. Then I learned the disturbing details behind the sting.

Prelude to a Sting

In October 1990, two years earlier, Dad approached me right before an auction in the eastern United States. He insisted that I avoid speaking to a tall, but unassuming, man he pointed out to me. Dad believed he was an IRS agent because he had been asking the "stupidest questions he'd ever heard."

Dad had an ability to convince anyone of nearly anything, and his seasoned street savvy had saved him on more than one occasion. He had traveled to the mountaintop more times than most, and had also sunk to the depths of despair and failure. Through it all, his determination to succeed made him fearless as well as extremely observant. So I listened to him. He wanted to know what the government was doing at one of *his* auctions. Due to his past political battles, he linked the presence of this supposed undercover agent to his recent support of Oliver North's legal defense fund.

For those readers who aren't history buffs, let me summarize the situation by saying that Lieutenant Colonel Oliver North was considered largely responsible for the establishment of a covert network that was used to sell weapons that indirectly aided the Contras, an opposition and anti-Communist force to the standing government in Nicaragua, even though U.S. funding of the Contras was prohibited by the Boland Amendment. The sale of these weapons served both to encourage the release of U.S. hostages in Iran and to generate proceeds to support the Contra rebel group. In November 1986, the press ran the story of his involvement, and North was fired by President Reagan. Less than a year later he was summoned to testify before televised hearings of a joint Congressional committee formed to investigate what came to be known as the Iran-Contra scandal. The image of North taking the oath became iconic, and similar photographs made the cover of *Time* and *Newsweek*. During the hearings, North admitted that he had lied to Congress, a crime for which he was later charged, among other charges. He defended his actions by stating that he believed in the goal of aiding the Contras, whom he saw as freedom fighters.

He was indicted on sixteen felony counts. On May 4, 1989, he was initially convicted of three: accepting an illegal gratuity, aiding and abetting in the obstruction of a congressional inquiry, and directing his secretary to destroy documents. He was sentenced to a three-year suspended prison term, two years probation, $150,000 in fines and 1,200 hours of community service. However, on July 20, 1990, with the help of the American Civil Liberties Union, North's convictions were vacated after an appeals court found that witnesses in his trial might have been impermissibly affected by his congressional testimony. The Supreme Court declined to review the case. On September 15, 1991, all charges against North were dismissed.

Lieutenant Colonel North was one of the warmest human beings I had ever met, though his eyes told a colder story. Despite his warm human side, I knew that Oliver North was also a marked man. After his legal defense fundraiser on our grounds, he sat between Dad and me for about an hour and a half as we auctioned classic cars in Auburn, the Mecca for car collectors. During this time we exchanged small talk about the vehicles being auctioned. When he was ready to leave, he stood up and gave me a big hug, thanking me for the day. As I embraced him, I felt his bulletproof vest underneath his suit coat. I thought, *"Thanks Ollie! I was in danger for ninety minutes and you were the only one who was wearing Kevlar!"*

Because he was curious to find out more, Dad made an appointment with the undercover agent whose eventual testimony would haunt us for the next ten years.

This meeting was taped.

Our director of operations sat in on the meeting as a witness as Dad learned the mystery man's story. He was an alleged sports bookie who wanted us to discretionarily invest his $250,000 of cash in collector cars. By this time, we were auctioning 15,000 collector cars at forty events each year. (I know, it's crazy to think that we auctioned this much volume, yet struggled to keep the company out of financial ruin. A sign of sand-hearted foolishness.) This was the first time anyone had made this kind of request. Discussions ranged from the man becoming a licensed car dealer to depositing the dollars in his bank account in Luxembourg, where we also conducted an annual auction. Dad never agreed to take the man's money, and even asked the man if he was an IRS agent, surmising that the agent's lie had just undermined his mission and provided Dad with an infallible defense.

The tape, combined with examination of both large and small cash deposits made in our corporate accounts from gate admission receipts and from car sale transactions, allowed the IRS to obtain Federal approval to raid our business under suspicion of money laundering. To compound the suspicion, we had not filed any 8300 Forms when receiving cash payments from any one purchaser in the amount of $10,000, though we could prove that we had implemented both the policy and procedure to do so about a month prior to the raid. By the time the agents left our corporate offices on July 1, they had carried out boxes and boxes filled with innumerable documents and records of cash transactions that occurred at our auctions.

While the word *sold* had always been my favorite four-letter word, I can honestly say that on this day I thought of a few others. The IRS was seeking jail time for Dad plus millions of dollars in fines levied against the corporation. As this horrific day turned into night, I was finally willing to admit for the first time that the circumstances of my life were far beyond my control.

Turning Point

Just like the younger son in Jesus' trilogy, the tsunami had officially hit my life. The sand castles that I had constructed were flattened, and I had nothing left in reserve. God was bringing me one step closer to living a life restored to authenticity. As I locked the door of our corporate office, my heart was officially empty; four-letter words were no longer enough. I finally admitted to myself that I needed to find the Restorer.

With my stomach in knots and my muscles numb from a day that defined the total disarray that my life had become, I arrived home that evening in time to see the television broadcast of our raid. Someone had tipped off the media prior to the agents' arrival. Wire services carried the story as it reached the nation's newspapers and most collector car trade publications. Our attorney, an old political friend of Dad's, gave us strict instructions not to discuss the details of this case with anyone but him. Kruse International was a high-profile business that would be presumed guilty until proven innocent—and that included me.

I entered my bedroom and knelt beside my bed for an overdue conversation with God. To tell you the truth, I was afraid of what He might say. In my brokenness and pain, I confessed all that I had held back from Him: my heart of stone and sand, my desires, and my three resources of life, including my business. Ironically, now that my enterprise was worth nothing, I was willing to surrender it.

As I prayed, memories flooded my heart: the day I was baptized, walking to County Line when no one else was around, kneeling at the altar, the Kruse ring and the legacy that it represented. I remember thinking that I was no longer the same person whom my mother had reared. I reflected back to childhood images of my church, then leaped forward to realize that my Sundays, once so focused on being in God's house, had been spent more often than not in an auction house in my adult years. I realized that my busy weekend schedule kept me from pursuing a closer walk with God. Saturday sand and Sunday stone had hardened into weekend concrete in my foolish life.

With a sand and stone heart, I had experienced my share of tragedies. Some were unexpected, and others came about as a result of my own foolish pursuits. The latter hindered my authentic vertical communion with God and authentic horizontal community with others. The most painful tragedies in my life occurred when I stopped pursuing these relationships and traded them in to spend more time on business pursuits.

I also experienced my share of triumphs—again, some unexpected, some expected. Success came when I worked hard and smart, yet there were times when I felt as if some invisible force was moving through individuals around me to orchestrate circumstances that I could have never created on my own. I failed to give credit to God for His obvious provision in these times; I also failed to give credit to others around me whom God had used in these situations. Whether in tragedy or triumph, I foolishly disconnected the vertical from the horizontal. I was imprisoned in my own pride and pretense.

I finally understood that I needed to submit and surrender my heart to the Restorer. My foolish choices had led to a spiritual darkness in my life that robbed me of the life God had intended for me. Even though I was physically alive, I had become spiritually dead. Could my faith be restored? Was that even possible? I didn't know.

For so many years I had tried to restore myself. I chose to give my time, talent, and treasure to something other than God in the vain hope that it would heal my brokenness. Like Cunningham's Bugattis, I realized that my heart had been sealed behind a thick brick wall, and I needed to grab that sledgehammer and break out. I was ready to move from a proud heart of stone and sand to a humble heart of clay. I realized that I needed the Restorer to transform my unrestored heart.

I was ready to fully surrender my desires to the Restorer, to submit myself to the design of the Designer, and to fully surrender my three resources of life to the Him. Alone in my room, I was reminded that the Restorer was right there with me, as He'd always been, even though I chose many times not to see Him.

That night, on my knees before God, I was grateful that I knew that there was still hope that my faith could be restored. However, the tragic events of this day continued to remind me of my sin.

Tragedy blinds us to the work of the Restorer. Ironically, when our circumstances are at their worst, we often want to hold on the tightest, ashamed of our actions and wanting to affect some change to alleviate the problem. In such situations we say to God, "I can fix this, You can't." This is the sin of the younger son. In the same way, success produces the same response toward God: "I can handle this situation. See how well I'm doing? You can't." This is the sin of the older son. But the heart of clay says to the Restorer, Jesus, "I can't. Only You can," whether in success or failure.

Since the raid had been broadcasted on countless media channels, I was left in a position where everyone who mattered in my business life knew what had happened. There was no hiding this event and the mistakes of my past. God's wisdom called me to stop pretending and fully surrender the old patterns of my life. I had to choose to put my pride aside and allow myself to be humbled in the midst of this situation.

I was reminded of my years in high school. Outwardly, I had it all together. I was top ten in my class, student council president, a decorated athlete, and chosen to speak at our graduation commencement. I was the youngest Realtor and licensed auctioneer in the nation. I crossed racial and social boundaries and was friends with everybody. My reputation centered on my academic and athletic achievements. In the eyes of our local newspaper, I was a shining star on a solid path to eventually lead my legendary auctioneer family.

Yet despite this outward appearance, there were times when I struggled to comprehend how I could possibly live up to the bar I had established for myself. My self-induced pride threatened to put a permanent end to the pressure I placed myself under. At one point in my young life, the pressure was serious enough that I contemplated suicide.

Thankfully, I had struck up a friendship with a Youth For Christ staffer who brought me through this time of crisis. He did not measure my success by external results, but instead focused on my interior being. As we talked, those worldly pressures seemed to fade as I moved toward an entirely new level of authenticity that I had not previously experienced. Through our conversations, he showed me that God could take my old life, my inner turmoil, and make it new again—a process that could take place every day for the balance of my life. I remembered the hope I felt during those talks on that dark night as I knelt beside my bed, pouring out my heart to the Restorer, I was finally ready to say, "I can't. You can."

Prior to the raid, sin's trifecta had surrounded me. Like Adam and Eve in the Garden of Eden, I was *ashamed* that I had been *swayed* by my own evil desires. I *hid* because I was *afraid* of my sin's consequences. I *blamed* because I had *disobeyed*. I felt like something inside me was dying that night. While I did not die physically, I struggled with my shame for the years that I had been dying spiritually. I had filed a spiritual Chapter 11, bankrupt of wisdom, demonstrated by the shambles of my business and personal life.

Facing an uncertain future, I imagined getting out of the pilot seat of my life and moving to the co-pilot chair. For the first time since I auctioned the curio cabinet on that sunny day in 1983, I did not want to be in control of my own destiny. As I finished my prayer, I asked God to take the tragedy of my life and turn it into His triumph.

Exhale.

Chapter Eight

A FOOL'S SIN AND THE RESTORER'S GRACE

All the hard work I had done to establish *SOLD!* as my favorite four-letter word led to another four-letter word being virtually tattooed on my heart. That word was *fool*. Through all of my years pursuing wealth and status, I had played the fool, traveling from gullible to godless. My pursuit had led me to the dead end of sin.

As I peer into in the rearview mirror of my life I have been able to define mile markers that led to my downward spiral. It is amazing to me what the Bible says about the foolishness of sin in a heart of sand and a heart of stone. However, it does not stop there—from cover to cover it tells the story of God's grace. My desire is that by sharing these experiences while teaching the following truths, you will have an opportunity to do the same as you reflect on your own life.

We are reminded in Jesus' trilogy, the younger son embodied a heart of *sand,* the older son embodied a heart of *stone*, and the father embodied a heart of *clay*. Each heart condition can be framed in terms of the word "give." The two sons loved the four-letter word "give," as in "give to me." They were foolish. The father loved the word "give" as well, but from a different perspective, as in "give to you." He pursued wisdom, understanding that giving without expecting anything in return was the only path to restoration of the relationship between him and his sons.

In Jesus' trilogy, each son's heart demonstrated a foolish perspective of the word "give," a progression of hardness of heart in both sand and stone that led to demanding the gift and a rupturing of the relationship.

King Solomon was the wisest mortal to ever live. Many of his wise statements and observations are captured in the biblical book of Proverbs, which is attributed to him. In it, he has much to say about the destructiveness of being a fool. Solomon's work focused more on the fool than, say, the liar, the cheat, or the murderer. He taught that the fool is the broader category because it represents the condition of a proud heart, the antithesis to humility and wisdom, which is to be prized above all else. Consequently, we want to avoid the role of the fool at all costs. Solomon warned, "Before his downfall a man's heart is proud, but humility comes before honor" (Proverbs 18:12).

A study of Proverbs shows us five stages of foolish behavior from the Hebrew language. Just like the sand heart of the younger son and the stone heart of the older son, this list represents a cycle of increasing hardness of heart, from gullible to godless. A good analogy of this pride is cement. When it is poured, it is wet and formable, but afterward it begins a hardening process that cures and turns to stone—cold, immoveable, fixed, and unchanging. The gullible fool is still formable, but the godless fool has no hope unless he fully surrenders his foolish heart to the Restorer.

Let's examine the five progressive stages of being a fool.

The Simple Fool

The first stage is the simple fool (*peti*) (Proverbs 14:15).

The simple fool is gullible. Solomon advised, "A simple man believes anything, but a prudent man gives thought to his steps" (Proverbs 14:15). The simple fool is naïve, but still teachable. He can still learn from his circumstances, leaving hope that wisdom can be learned (Proverbs 19:25; 21:11). If we are ever going to play the fool, we want to do it in stage one so that we will respond to the consequences of our foolishness with repentance and wisdom. For example, King David's foolishness with Bathsheba might have been simple, but it carried significant consequences. When the prophet Nathan pointed out his sin and rebuked him, David responded with repentance and wisdom.

Proverbs says that this kind of fool loves simplemindedness and waywardness. He lacks common sense. He is undiscerning of evil, yet his heart is still wet cement. He has hope for returning to the wisdom of the Restorer.

I was a simple fool. I believed whatever I wanted to hear, and anything that would advance my own selfish agenda. I was simple-minded when I listened to individuals who advised me to build my auction business by paying sellers of cars without collecting from buyers, while sending the vehicles and titles home with them. Had I taken the time to learn from the consequences of my actions or the experience of my Dad in the earlier years, my heart could have changed. Unfortunately, I didn't learn from my early mistakes.

How about you? Are you learning from the negative circumstances of your life? Try this little exercise: open your calendar and examine your appointments. Ask God to illuminate any gullible or naive circumstances in your life. If He does, confess the pride underneath the foolishness and humbly surrender the simple foolishness to Him. Listen to Solomon's counsel when he says, "He who conceals his sins does not prosper, but whoever confesses and renounces them finds mercy" (Proverbs 28:13), and "When pride comes, then comes disgrace, but with humility comes wisdom" (Proverbs 11:2). Ask His Spirit to lead you to wisdom, for, "The fear of the Lord is the beginning of wisdom, and knowledge of the Holy One is understanding" (Proverbs 9:10).

The Stupid Fool

The second stage is the stupid fool (*kesil*) (Proverbs 26:11).

The stupid fool repeats his negative behavior, which is folly. Solomon observed, "As a dog returns to its vomit, so a fool repeats his folly" (Proverbs 26:11). The stupid fool also repeats his patterns of lashing out in anger, leading to the disruption of family relationships. Solomon observed, "A fool gives full vent to his anger, but a wise man keeps himself under control" (Proverbs 29:11) and "A wise son brings joy to his father, but a foolish son grief to his mother" (Proverbs 10:1). Solomon also describes this individual as someone who repeats his wickedness (Proverbs 10:23), deceit (Proverbs 14:8), slander (Proverbs 10:18), and shame (Proverbs 3:35). You get the picture—this is a person who has no sense of learning from his actions, no matter how many times he falls. In this sense, he's one degree worse than the gullible fool.

Solomon also observed that the stupid fool is dangerous with money: "Of what use is money in the hand of a fool, since he has no desire to get wisdom" (Proverbs 17:16). He noticed that the stupid fool chases fantasies with his eyes (Proverbs 17:24) until he exhausts all of his resources—his time, talent, and treasure. He is complacent with his foolish behavior (Proverbs 1:32).

The reason for his stupidity is clear: The stupid fool trusts in his own heart. The book of Proverbs states, "He who trusts in himself is a fool, but he who walks in wisdom is kept safe" (Proverbs 28:26). This self-trust leads to talking rather than listening. "A fool finds no pleasure in understanding but delights in airing his own opinions" (Proverbs 18:2). The stupid self-reliant fool is hotheaded and reckless (Proverbs 14:16); he hates knowledge (Proverbs 1:22). Ironically, Solomon himself fell into this trap as his observations are recorded in the book of Ecclesiastes.

I was also a stupid fool. I repeated my gullible behavior, handling our corporation's funds foolishly time and time again. In a sense, I was that dog returning to my "vomit."

I overextended our company's resources. Consequently, I walked and talked with a very short fuse. I blew up with Dad, and others, including my wife, straining those family relationships. I exploded with employees, vendors, and customers who wanted to negotiate unreasonable deals. I chased fantasies that I thought would bring me greater wealth. They resulted in further losses to the bottom line that exhausted my time, talent, and treasure.

What I had labeled "street smarts" was actually stupidity. My repeated wickedness, deceit, slander, and shame hurt those who cared about me most, especially my mom and Susan. True to the description in Proverbs, I trusted in my own heart so much that I talked more than I listened in nearly every encounter. I delighted in airing my own opinions. All of these behaviors began to progressively harden my heart, damming the flow of wisdom into my personal and professional life.

What about you? Consider asking a close, trusted friend the following questions regarding your potential arenas of stupidity: Is folly evident in your life? Do you repeat the same destructive behavior? By biblical standards, are your time, talent, and treasure managed foolishly? Are you chasing fantasies? In relationships, do you talk more than you listen? If the answer to any of these questions is "Yes," it's time to consider that you may be trusting in yourself rather than God.

The Stubborn Fool

The third stage is the stubborn fool (*ewil*) (Proverbs 12:15).

This is the same Hebrew word translated as "evil." The stubborn fool is right in his own eyes. "The way of a fool seems right to him, but a wise man listens to advice" (Proverbs 12:15). The stubborn fool is so sure of himself that he declines sound advice. The stubborn fool despises wisdom and discipline (Proverbs 1:7). Consequently, he lacks understanding and insight into others' perspectives (Proverbs 10:21). Another aspect of this kind of fool is that he is confounded by wisdom rather than interested in pursuing it (Proverbs 24:7).

The stubborn fool is full of folly (Proverbs 16:22). This folly often displays itself in outbursts of anger, which I describe in these terms: this kind of fool is "quick to pick and stick." He is *quick* to quarrel (Proverbs 20:3). Solomon said, "A fool shows his annoyance at once, but a prudent man overlooks an insult" (Proverbs 12:16). He will *pick* a fight. "Stone is heavy and sand a burden, but provocation by a fool is heavier than both" (Proverbs 27:3). He will *stick* the blame to someone else, rather than reconcile. "Fools mock at making amends for sin, but goodwill is found among the upright" (Proverbs 14:9). This pattern destroys relationships. King Saul's heart became hardened to the point of him becoming a stubborn fool (1 Chronicles 19:13-14).

I was a stubborn fool. I was always right in my own eyes... always. I was rarely warm to sound advice, though looking back I see how the Restorer sent it to me through many different channels. If I heard wise advice that conflicted with the path that I had chosen, I saw it as the result of an out-of-touch, stone-hearted perspective. My heart grew harder. I was quick to pick and stick. I heatedly and quickly retorted to differing views. I provoked people who were in the way of my selfish agenda. When my efforts to make a deal, create an effective marketing campaign, or conduct a successful auction failed, I blamed others. As a result, I was not characterized and known by solid relationships. Instead, I insulated myself more and more from everyone except those who could advance the cause of my sandcastle kingdom.

Take Proverbs' stubborn fool test. Are you always right? Do you listen to advice, or do you resist it? Do you despise wisdom and discipline? Are you full of folly—repeating stupid behavior including outbursts of anger? Is your heart so hard that you show your annoyance immediately, refusing to overlook an insult? Is your quickness to quarrel evidenced in your provocation of more negative conflict? Are you characterized by reconciled relationships or do you mock at making amends for your sin? If the answer to any of these questions is "Yes," then it is time for a heart change.

The Scorning Fool

The fourth stage is the scorning fool (*letz*) (Proverbs 21:24).

The scorner's pride (hardness of heart) is so great that he is drunk with presumption and is often referred to in Proverbs as a mocker: "The proud and arrogant man—"Mocker" is his name; he behaves with overweening pride" (Proverbs 21:24). In moving from anger to mocking, the scorning fool is averse to wisdom. It does not flow in his life. "The mocker seeks wisdom and finds none, but knowledge comes easily to the discerning" (Proverbs 14:6).

A scorner struggles to separate wise choices from foolish ones. The scorning fool causes dissension in organizations. This is due to the fact that he ignored all previous rebukes (Proverbs 9:7-8; 13:1). Thus, he must be removed from an organization in order for it to thrive. "Drive out the mocker, and out goes strife; quarrels and insults are ended" (Proverbs 22:10). Positive relationships are fostered when the scorner leaves.

The scorning fool is also opposed by God. He is known as a scoffer who picks a fight with The Almighty, mocking at reconciliation (Proverbs 14:9) and justice (Proverbs 19:28). However, God has a pattern in His response to this level of hard-heartedness. "He mocks proud mockers but gives grace to the humble" (Proverbs 3:34). God takes direct opposition to the scorner in an effort to bring him back to wisdom. King Nebuchadnezzar was a scorning fool who eventually responded in humility to God's opposition (see Daniel 4).

I was a scorning fool. As my heart grew harder, I mocked those who were different from me, whether in business style or the underlying heart condition. Regardless of how much I attempted to garner street smarts from successful businessmen, books on business, magazine articles, or newspaper stories, I could not uncover wisdom because I was seeking the horizontal apart from the vertical. The sand in my heart clouded my eyes, hindering my ability to separate wise choices from foolish ones, which increased the amount of negative conflict in my life.

The dissension I brought to my own organization was palpable as relationships were damaged and left unrestored. Consequently, I not only felt pressure horizontally but vertically as well. I began to run into the Spirit of the Restorer who opposed my mocking heart in order to transform me. Whereas I acted out of hate and insignificance, He acted out of love. I moved in fear and insecurity; He moved in faith and authentic truth. I lived out of control; He lived in power. I walked in discontented shambles; He walked in peace and order.

Is it a challenge for you to separate wise choices from foolish ones? Would anyone at work, home, or play say that you are the cause of organizational dissension? Do you feel like you are "kicking against the goads" (Acts 26:14) with God? If so, then you are behaving like a scorner.

The Secular Fool

The fifth stage is the secular, or godless, fool (*nabal*) (Proverbs 30:32).

The secular fool exalts himself rather than God. "If you have played the fool and exalted yourself, or if you have planned evil, clap your hand over your mouth" (Proverbs 30:32). His self-exaltation perpetuates a desire for more manipulative idolatry and disappoints those who have invested in him. Proverbs communicates that the godless fool is unsatisfied by spiritual things (Proverbs 30:22). He brings no joy to his father (Proverbs 17:21). This secular fool has hardened his heart with the image of his handprint impressed solidly in his inner being. Nabal, the husband of Abigail (who later became David's wife), was a godless fool (1 Samuel 25:25). This state of mind did not work out so well for Nabal; God struck him dead.

I was a secular fool. My heart hardened to the point where I exalted myself over God as the leader of my life. Money was my idol. I manipulated others in order to grab my share of it. Ironically, the more I pursued it, the more I yearned for a bigger fix and the more I needed it just to survive. The pattern left me dissatisfied even with anything spiritual because I had ripped the vertical from the horizontal and formed a sandcastle prison that locked me up in pretense.

Unfortunately, due to my unspoken request to live apart from God, my stone heart had crumbled into a sand heart. Together, sand and stone would begin to form into wet cement, hardening my heart almost to the point of cured concrete. Nothing left in my life could bring joy to God, unless I would humble my heart to the Restorer who was about to schedule a showdown with the sand- and stone-hearted Mitch Kruse.

Carefully consider your heart. Is there any area inside you in which you have exalted yourself above God? Do you consciously refuse to seek God's heart in any of your thoughts, choices, feelings, or prayers? Are you living your life on autopilot, apart from God? Are your desires truly satisfied in Christ, or do you need more and more of your fix of choice to advance your own earthly kingdom at the expense of His? If so, you might be coming dangerously close to playing the secular fool.

It is easy to read through this list and think of someone else who fits each stage. But the list is for our own self-examination. The words of Proverbs are as applicable today as they were when Solomon's scribes wrote them down. So each of us must ask, "Is there any area of my life where I have hardened my heart to the Spirit of God?" The answer will be "Yes" more often than we think. After identifying the foolish behavior, we must (1) confess our pride to God, (2) humbly surrender it to Him, and (3) ask His Spirit to lead us to wisdom. Each is a movement that flows from a clay heart.

My sand and stone heart caused me to play the *fool*, traveling from *gullible* to *godless*, and leading to the dead end of sin.

The Gap of Sin

We've learned about the sinful nature of the foolish heart. Let's look a little more deeply into the nature of sin itself.

Sin can be defined as the pursuit of the satisfaction of our desires apart from the only One who is designed to fulfill them. Sin results in our need for restoration. As we have observed elsewhere in this book, the sin of Adam and Eve was related to their desire for *significance, contentment, control*, and *security* apart from God. They trusted in their giftedness and not His godliness. *Trust* is *faith*. Paul defined any trust apart from God as falling short of the design of the Designer: "Everything that does not come from faith is sin" (Romans 14:23).

Here is the Bible's account of the first sin: "Eve saw that the fruit of the tree was good for food, pleasing to the eye and also desirable for gaining wisdom. And so she took some and ate and she also gave some to her husband who was with her and he ate it. And then the eyes of both of them were opened and they realized they were naked, so they sewed fig leaves together and made coverings for themselves" (Genesis 3:6). Eve was tempted in the three ways that we are tempted: (1) lust of the flesh, (2) lust of the eyes, and (3) pride of life—the boasting in what man has and does (1 John 2:16).

Temptation is not sin; however, pursuing the satisfaction of our desires apart from God in the temptation is sin (1 John 2:16). In fact, it is impossible to be tempted without knowing what is right. The temptation or its subsequent sin never satisfies, but God always does (1 John 2:17). Since that first sin, man has become like god in that he has determined for himself what is right and wrong. This is the knowledge of good and evil (Genesis 3:5, 22).

Have you ever decided for yourself what was right and what was wrong? Adam and Eve's desire for life apart from God was the beginning of various dichotomies that still exist in our world today: evil and good, sin and grace, pride and humility, pretense and authenticity, partial and full surrender to the Restorer. We not only find this with Adam and Eve, but we also find this with the younger son in Jesus' trilogy who desired life apart from his father. We've discussed how his prideful self-restoration program did not produce the intended results.

Since the Garden of Eden, man has embodied a bent toward evil that manifests itself from the cradle to the grave. "The Lord saw how great man's wickedness on the earth had become, and that every inclination of the thoughts of his heart was only evil all the time" (Genesis 6:5); "The Lord smelled the pleasing aroma and said in his heart: 'Never again will I curse the ground because of man, even though every inclination of his heart is evil from childhood. And never again will I destroy all living creatures, as I have done" (Genesis 8:21). Solomon summarized this condition this way: "There is no one who does not sin" (2 Chronicles 6:36).

We see it everywhere: A toddler pushes her dish of food off her highchair while staring her warning mother in the eyes. An elementary school student fights a classmate during a game on the playground. A struggling high school student cheats on an exam. A brash college student contrives a scheme to romance an unsuspecting girl into bed. A salesman fudges on his expense account. A talkative mother gossips about a woman in her small group. A pastor clicks on a website that he knows he has no business viewing. A holier-than-thou Bible thumper condemns a fellow church attendee who exercises his liberties. A professional athlete breaks the rules in order to gain an advantage. A businessman baits and switches. A dissatisfied woman captivates her husband's best friend with a gaze of her eyes. All the while others look on, prideful that they are able to refrain from committing such sins.

No wonder over the centuries Rabbis have said, "Sin begins as thin as a spider web and ends like a cart rope." When we open the door to it, sin takes us farther than we wanted to go, keeps us longer than we wanted to stay, and costs us more than we wanted to pay. Still, God remains engaged, always wanting us to turn from that sin and to trust in Him.

The sin in our lives leaves a gap between God and us that we long to have closed (Isaiah 59:2). It is a vicious cycle. We attempt to satisfy our sinful desires apart from God through *un*righteousness, then we try to fill the resulting gap with our *self*-righteousness. The former is sand. The latter is stone. Both leave us dissatisfied.

God wants us to act righteously more than He wants us to give a tithe or an offering (Proverbs 21:3). However, even our best attempts to do right are like filthy rags in God's sight (Isaiah 64:6). Either we think that our desire to fill the gap will be satisfied by our own self-righteousness, or we just give up and continue to sin in our unrighteousness.

In the Sermon on the Mount, Jesus said "Blessed are those who hunger and thirst for righteousness, for they will be filled" (Matthew 5:6). We find a hunger and thirst for righteousness in the flawless, humble clay heart of Christ who became the payment for our sin so that in Him we might be the righteousness of God (2 Corinthians 5:21).

Just like us, Jesus was tempted in every way; however, He did not sin (Hebrews 4:15). He is the only truly righteous one. Jesus' close friend said it this way, "My dear children, I write this to you so that you will not sin. But if anybody does sin, we have one who speaks to the Father in our defense—Jesus Christ the Righteous One. He is the atoning sacrifice for our sins, and not only for ours but also for the sins of the whole world" (1 John 2:1). So, those who hunger and thirst for righteousness desire Christ, who is the righteousness of God.

The gap between God and us can only be filled by Christ, who fills everything in every way (Ephesians 1:22-23). The psalmist said that the Lord satisfies the thirsty and fills the hungry with good things (Psalm 107:9). Sin never satisfies, and its resulting gap in our hearts will never be satisfied outside of Christ.

How are we satisfied?

First, we must surrender our unrighteousness. Paul urged the self-indulged members of the Roman church to surrender their unrighteousness to Christ, clothing themselves in His righteousness. He asked them to put away any thoughts about how to gratify the desires of their sinful nature (Romans 13:14). In the same way, we must exchange our unrighteous, filthy rags for the righteousness of the Restorer. This is the pattern of the younger son who traded in his sand-hearted, filthy rags for his father's righteous clothing.

Second, we must surrender our self-righteousness—our self-restoration program to fill the gap left by sin. Jesus said that our righteousness must surpass that of the Pharisees and the teachers of the law to even enter the kingdom of heaven (Matthew 5:20). He challenged the Pharisees to acknowledge that their pretense of self-righteousness showed righteousness on the outside, while they were still unrighteous on the inside (Matthew 23:27-28).

Once again we discover that satisfaction through surrender is a heart issue. Jesus pleaded with the self-righteous to surrender to Him, but they were not willing (Matthew 23:37). Neither will we be willing to surrender if we do not first surrender our self-righteousness. This is the opportunity that the father in the parable offered to the stone-hearted older son.

Surrender says to the Restorer, "I can't. You can. I can't satisfy my desires. You can. I can't fill the gap of my sin. You can." Surrender your sin and its gap to the Restorer. You will be satisfied when you hunger and thirst for Him.

The Restoration of Grace

On the opposite side of the sin spectrum is God's grace. Grace is the kind of undeserved love and or unmerited favor exhibited in the father who ran to his son outside the city gates. God is like that father: Even though we break His law, He pursues us with His affection. Grace flows from the heart of God.

Take Moses as an example. After Moses had *literally* broken the law—the first stone tablets containing the Ten Commandments (Exodus 32:19)—Yahweh called him to a cleft in the rock on Mount Sinai where the moral law would be rewritten as Moses chiseled them out on new stone tablets. That's where God appeared to Moses.

First, God's glory passed by (Exodus 33:18-34:5). "Glory" refers to His character and presence. With the stone tablets in Moses' hand, God passed by and proclaimed, "The Lord, the Lord, the compassionate and gracious God, slow to anger, abounding in love and faithfulness" (Exodus 34:6). "Gracious," the word selected by Bible translators for God's attribute, is translated from the Hebrew root word *chanan*, meaning "to bend or stoop to one who is inferior."

In spite of our sin, the Restorer bends to us in order to engage us, the undeserving, with His love. Paul penned, "For you know the grace of our Lord Jesus Christ, that though he was rich, yet for your sakes he became poor, so that you through his poverty might become rich" (2 Corinthians 8:9).

God's radical movement toward us can be remembered in this acronym:

G: God's

R: Riches

A: At

C: Christ's

E: Expense

Moses' response to the grace of God on Mount Sinai was the only affirmative posture one could take in order to receive unmerited favor.

In an act of self-examination and surrender, he not only bent his physical knees, but also submitted to God's glory and presence: "Moses bowed to the ground at once and worshiped" (Exodus 34:8).

The Hebrew word used for "worship" is *shachah*, the term most frequently translated "worship" in the Old Testament. It means "to bow down." In order to receive grace, we like Moses must bow down and humbly receive it from the One who stooped down to us in order to extend His loving offer.

Moses' example gives us further instruction. He spoke to God in a way that showed his heart of confession, repentance and belief in God's grace: "O Lord, if I have found favor in your eyes, then let the Lord go with us. Although this is a stiff-necked people, forgive our wickedness and our sin, and take us as your inheritance" (Exodus 34:9).

The word "go" is translated from the Hebrew word *halak*, which means "walk." In spite of their sin, God graciously walked with the Israelites, just as Jesus walked with the disciples. We learn four important truths from Moses' response to grace. First, Moses examined his heart and surrendered it to God; next, he confessed his sin; third, he repented and believed in God's grace; and finally, he walked with God. All four of Moses' moves toward God were empowered by God's grace.

So we've studied an Old Testament example of moving toward God's grace extended toward us. Let's move on to a New Testament analysis, with a view, again, toward God's grace in the face of our sin.

The New Testament writers used several Greek words for sin. However, those most frequently used can be summed up in four predominant terms: (1) missing the mark (*hamartia*), (2) twisting a wrong to make it right (*adikia*), (3) missing on purpose (*anomia*), and (4) leaving good undone (*paraptoma*). Each can be illustrated using a basketball free-throw analogy.

Missing the Mark

Missing the mark is attempting to make the shot, but missing it. When a professional athlete steps up to the free throw line and averages, say, eighty-eight percent, we say that we could potentially expect that he will, when tested, usually make eighty-eight out of his next one hundred attempts. But what about the twelve shots that he misses—are those missed on purpose?

No, the basketball player doesn't miss on purpose.

And missing the mark describes one aspect of how everyone sins. Using this term for sin, the Apostle Paul said, "For all have sinned and fall short of the glory of God" (Romans 3:23). "Have sinned" is translated from the Greek root, *hamartia*. Its etymology stems from an archer who missed the mark of the target. Regardless of the level of excellence in any area of our lives, we miss the goal and fall short. No one can make every free throw. No one can place every tennis or volleyball serve within the service lines. No one can connect with every pitch. No one can hit every golf ball where he desires. Similarly, no one can get it morally right 100 percent of the time. No matter how hard we train, we will miss the mark in honoring God or others.

That is why we need grace, and God gives it freely. Paul wrote to the church in Rome, "For the wages of sin is death, but the gift of God is eternal life in Christ Jesus our Lord" (Romans 6:23). Paul juxtaposed three pairs of terms in this verse: (1) wages and gift, (2) sin and God, and (3) death and eternal life.

Let's unpack those terms further. "Wages" implies that we earn the results of sin, both by nature and by choice. Consequently, we deserve what comes our way. "Gift," in contrast, communicates that we merely receive a loving act from another. "Sin" means that we miss the mark. By contrast, God is the mark that we miss; He is holy—totally apart from sin (Habakkuk 1:13). "Death" (*thanatos*) is separation from God. "Life" on the other hand, is the abundant and uninterrupted spiritual vitality that God designed for us to have in Christ, the Restorer, who provides His Spirit to dwell in us.

Paul's teaching illustrates that, left on our own, we cannot right our every wrong. Our falling short earns us separation from a holy God. We need grace in the form of belief in and surrender to Jesus Christ, who was sinless, but who also filled in that sin-gap that we learned about earlier in this chapter. In a sense, Jesus rebounds our misses and scores for the kingdom.

When I examined my heart and life, I knew I had to surrender them to Christ—including both my makes and my misses. Sometimes, the things I got right in my stone-heartedness were bigger barriers to God than my misses in my sand-heartedness. Once again, I leaned on my giftedness rather than my godliness. If I was to believe that God's grace could restore me from my sin, I had to humbly receive the gift of eternal life in Christ (John 1:12). Like a tax collector in one of Jesus' parables, I prayed, "God, have mercy on me, a sinner" (see this story at Luke 18:13). To live in Christ, I asked God to examine my heart and reveal any offensive way in me, then I surrendered those to Him (Psalm 139:23-24).

Twisting the Shot

To return to the free throw analogy, twisting a wrong to make it right is missing the shot, then going ahead and telling everyone that we made it anyway. *Adikia* in Greek literally means "no righteousness," and that's what we're talking about here. John said that all unrighteousness is sin (1 John 5:17), and we must realize the damage that we do to the kingdom of God when we justify our unrighteous actions by calling them righteous ones, especially when our twisting is in the form of legalism or religious pride. Onlookers will see our hypocrisy much clearer than we think.

Using this term, Paul said that twisting a wrong to make it right suppresses the truth: "The wrath of God is being revealed from heaven against all the godlessness and wickedness of men who suppress the truth by their wickedness" (Romans 1:18). (Whereas the NIV translates *adikia* as wickedness, the NASB translates it as unrighteousness.) For an example of someone in Scripture who twisted a wrong to make it right, take a few moments to read the story of Simon the Sorcerer in Acts 8:9-25.

When we twist a wrong in order to make it right, we need grace. The key that unlocks the door to God's grace is confession. John said, "If we confess our sins, he is faithful and just and will forgive us our sins and purify us from all unrighteousness" (1 John 1:9). When we confess, we don't do it so that we can present God with a laundry list of our failures. No, God already knows where we've gone astray. Rather, confession allows us to see our own sin as God does. When we agree with God that we indeed missed—seeing the shortfall as God sees it—then God forgives us.

Sand-hearted individuals may confess their "sins" horizontally to each other, but rarely do they confess them vertically in prayer to God, primarily because they do not agree with God's perspective on the "sin." Stone hearts find it very easy to confess their sins to God, but find it very difficult to confess their sins horizontally to others.

Through the process that I took to get back on Restoration Road, I was learning how to confess my sins to God. I thought about how often I was held captive to sin in my life. I had been legalistic. I had twisted wrongs in an attempt to make them right. Like Simon the Sorcerer, I had justified misses into makes. It was time for me to agree with God's perspective on my sin. Even Simon the Sorcerer appeared to confess his sin to Peter and John (Acts 8:25). My short-term gain had in fact translated into long-term pain, and I was beginning to become convinced through this process that when I confessed my sin in authenticity, the Restorer bridged my resulting gap with the Father.

Perfection versus Excellence

I referred to my bent toward perfectionism in an earlier chapter. In all the years that I wandered from God, my perfectionism drove me toward a need to be right all the time. What I discovered, however, was that my need to be right all the time led to me being wrong much of the time. The more I tried to be perfect, the more imperfect

I became. I had high expectations of myself and high expectations of others. Often times those expectations were unrealistic, and my unrealistic expectations led to continual frustration.

Confessing my hard-hearted condition meant moving away from perfectionism and toward excellence. A perfectionist attempts to be flawless, but one who works with excellence does the best with what he or she has. Ironically, I could not financially afford to be a perfectionist anymore. I needed to move toward managing my money with excellence, striving toward positive outcomes and allowing myself grace in the process when my work fell short.

Excellence features two components: authenticity and wisdom. While high expectations can be beneficial at times, the perfectionist has a blind spot to the fact that everyone and everything in this life will fall short—except God. Whereas perfectionism implies flawlessness, excellence recognizes (1) authenticity: understanding the truth about one's strengths and shortcomings, and (2) wisdom: the intersection of God's righteousness with street smarts—shrewdly doing the best with what we have. Jesus encouraged his followers to strive for excellence rather than perfectionism (Luke 5:35-39).

Convicted of my failures to pursue excellence in relation to my daily walk, I made it a practice to confess to my uncle Derald the ways in which my heart of stone and sand had twisted wrongs in order to make them right. He prayed for me to be forgiven and restored, and I believed that I was.

The prophet Isaiah wrote that we all sin in our sand-hearted unrighteousness and our stone-hearted self-righteousness, "All of us have become like one who is unclean and all our righteous acts are like filthy rags. We all shrivel up like a leaf and like the wind, our sins sweep us away" (Isaiah 64:6). Isaiah continued, describing the restoration of a clay heart where God shapes us to be his authentic workmanship, "Yet, O Lord, you are our Father. We are the clay, You are the Potter. We are all the work of Your hand" (Isaiah 64:8).

When I confessed my sins vertically and horizontally, Christ restored me because I agreed with His perspective of my sins, and I surrendered my heart to be shaped like His.

Missing on Purpose

Missing on purpose is obviously shooting to miss, similar to the strategy implemented by a player at the free throw line who needs more than one point to win the game. In this situation, the player will miss the shot to give his teammates the chance to rebound the ball and score enough points to win.

Anomia literally means "no law." It is breaking the law, or committing a transgression—which is stepping over the line. John said, "Everyone who sins breaks the law; in fact, sin is lawlessness" (1 John 3:4). Lawlessness is translated from the Greek word *anomia*. This idea is not too far from the first sin in the Garden. Adam knew what was wrong, understood the consequences, and sinned anyway. *Anomia* includes a surrendering of our desires to temptation and its consequences.

In the face of our intentional sin, the need for God's grace becomes crystal clear. At the same time, God's radical love is quite possibly most visible in this situation. Quoting David who experienced God's grace when he missed on purpose, Paul wrote, "Blessed are they whose transgressions are forgiven, whose sins are covered" (Romans 4:7; cf. Psalm 32:1). The word "transgressions" is also translated from *anomia*. God forgives our purposeful misses with His boundless grace in Christ when we trust in Him (Romans 4:5). This trust leads us to a saving repentance (2 Corinthians 7:10).

I blatantly broke the laws that God had instituted for my instruction and benefit, and I needed to repent and believe the good news of God's grace found in the Restorer. In order to assimilate His grace into my life, I wrote down on one side of a note card Jesus' words in Mark 1:15, "The time has come,' he said. 'The kingdom of God is near. Repent and believe the good news!" On the other side of the card, I wrote the text of Romans 4:7, "Blessed are they whose transgressions are forgiven, whose sins are covered." I carried it with me and read each verse when I was tempted to consider any activity where I would intentionally cross the line, even though I knew the right course of action.

When I missed on purpose, I prayed these words: "God, I know that this behavior was missing the shot on purpose. I recognize that this choice has consequences, and my failure is the fact that I still chose it anyway. I can't pay for my sin. You can, and You did as Savior of my life. I can't free myself from the power of sin. You can as Lord of my life. Please free me from this prison of sin."

God's grace convinced me to turn from my sin and experience the freedom found through forgiveness, but there was still more to address.

Refusing to Take the Shot

Leaving good undone is not shooting at all. We step up to the line with the basketball in our hands, knowing what to do, and never release it toward the goal. James noted, "Anyone, then, who knows the good he ought to do and doesn't do it, sins" (James 4:17). When we operate on our own agendas apart from God, we do not execute the good we were designed to do. Paul enlightened the universal Church on this matter when he wrote, "As for you, you were dead in your transgressions and sins" (Ephesians 2:1). Dead (*nekros*) refers to a lifeless corpse, in essence doing nothing. Transgressions (translated "trespasses" in the NASB) stems from the Greek word *paraptoma*, meaning "to fall beside, or to fall away." When presented with an opportunity to do something good, we fall away from it and do nothing. Jesus gave us an example in His parable about a good Samaritan (see Luke 10:25-37).

But God's grace in our lives moves us beyond confessing and removing sin. When we experience God's grace, we are then empowered to do good works. In his letter to the Ephesians, Paul wrote, "But because of his great love for us, God, who is rich in mercy, made us alive with Christ even when we were dead in transgressions—it is by grace you have been saved" (Ephesians 2:4-5). By God's grace, through faith in Him, we are made alive in Christ to do all the good works that God prepared in advance for us to do (Ephesians 2:8-10).

After I moved toward heart-transformation and toward God's grace, I was convinced, like never before, to walk across a room, a street, a city, a state, a border or even the international dateline to respond to the grace of the Restorer. Rather than ignore or shrink away from the opportunities to reveal the heart of the Restorer that God gave to me, I chose to walk with God's grace in order to do the good works He prepared in advance for me to do. I began to poetically live out my unique expression of God's kingdom in me.

Are you missing the mark? Are you twisting a wrong in order to make it right—twisting a miss into a make? Are you missing on purpose, breaking God's law? Are you not shooting at all, leaving good undone? Examine your heart and life, and fully surrender them to God. Confess your sins. Repent and believe in God's grace. Walk with the forgiving God Who walks with you.

Prior to July 1, 1992, I missed the mark. I twisted wrongs in order to make them right. Sometimes, I missed on purpose, breaking God's law. Other times I chose not to shoot at all, leaving good undone. Like Moses, on my road to restored authenticity I examined my heart, my desires, and my three resources of life in order to fully surrender all of them to the Restorer. I confessed my sin. I repented and believed in God's grace. I walked on a road with a forgiving God who promised to always stay right by my side.

Whether you are fighting temptation as the Restorer's protection looms on the horizon or whether you are in the midst of a storm, my prayer today is that I can convince you that foolish-hearted sin is not a dead end without hope. You can walk with the Restorer against the author of evil in the midst of your hurricane. God's grace, through the Restorer, promises forgiveness and restoration from a life lived apart from Him. You will discover as I did, even when you are tempted to sin, He will always provide a way out. "No temptation has seized you except what is common to man. And God is faithful; he will not let you be tempted beyond what you can bear. But when you are tempted, he will also provide a way out so that you can stand up under it" (1 Corinthians 10:13).

When we fully surrender our hearts to the Restorer, He unlocks the gate to Restoration Road where we can travel with wisdom, the vertical intersecting with the horizontal, to our destination of life-giving restoration. The journey begins when we say to Him, "I can't. You can."

Chapter Nine

PRIDE IS THE LOCK ON THE HUMAN HEART; HUMILITY IS THE KEY

Have you ever noticed that the most valuable commodities in the world are locked in boxes? The more valuable the commodity, the more elaborate the box and the lock. For example, Fort Knox is the box that keeps the nation's gold reserve locked up. We often keep our sentimental valuables and marketable securities locked in a safety deposit box.

I will always remember the most elaborate locked box I have ever encountered. It was on the other side of the world.

I was visiting a customer of mine who lived in one of King Ludwig's castles in beautiful southern Germany. We walked through the fairy tale kitchen, kept intact as the King had left it. We continued down a series of steps that ended at a large vault door. It probably reached eight feet in height and spanned more than four feet in width. My customer described how his bombproof box had been crafted below ground, secured with an elaborate combination lock. I watched as the owner of the contents carefully entered the combination to unlock the door.

Next was that familiar noise of the locked door actually unlocking. The sound was a cross between the unlocking of a jail cell door and a hydraulic pressure release similar to the sound of a steam locomotive. As my anticipation grew, he opened the door, revealing the world's two most expensive secretary desks neatly displayed in his climate-controlled box. I immediately recognized them because they were publicized internationally years prior when they were sold at auction for nearly two million dollars each to an undisclosed bidder. I now realized that my new friend was indeed the undisclosed bidder.

God has placed a box inside each one of us that holds within it a treasure much more precious than the valuable desks I saw in Germany. Within each of us He's placed the box of the spiritual heart. The Bible tells us that God is the highest bidder for the contents of our inner boxes: our will, intellect, spirit, and emotions (1 Corinthians 6:19-20). I learned from my experience that the box of the spiritual heart is either (1) locked and unrestored, or (2) unlocked and restored. Pride is the lock on the human heart; humility is the key.

A Pride-filled, Locked Heart

When my heart was locked and unrestored, I was proud and harsh. I thought that my pride and harshness would facilitate the satisfaction of my desires. Alone in my bedroom with the Restorer on the evening of July 1, 1992, I was back to choosing between partial and full surrender. What I briefly learned in high school about humility and being restored to authenticity had gathered dust on the shelves of my past until I confessed to God, "I can't. You can."

In the Sermon on the Mount, Jesus gave us an enduring treatise on pride when He delivered the greatest speech ever given. In it,

He affirmed to the world that in the kingdom of heaven, the humble are "in" and the proud are "out." He presented the kingdom of God as very countercultural, and laid down the gauntlet, challenging His listeners to full surrender of their hearts to God. Imagine an estimated 20,000 listeners sitting along the mountainside outside Capernaum hearing the words of the Restorer outlining the *be-do-go* of full surrender. Recorded in the Gospel of Matthew (Chapters 5-7), Jesus reminded His audience that Who you are to *be* determines what you *do,* which determines where you *go.* This was indicative of God's original design. Wise King Solomon communicated that life flowed from the inside out, beginning in the heart, "Above all else, guard your heart, for it is the wellspring of life" (Proverbs 4:23). From both Jesus and Solomon, we see that God designed life to flow from the heart.

Jesus began his sermon with a Hebrew literary device called an *inclusio* featuring the Beatitudes (from *beati*, Latin for "Blessed," meaning "satisfied"). The dominant theme of the *inclusio* is evidenced in the first and last Beatitude where the following phrase is repeated, "For theirs is the kingdom of heaven," God's divine reign, rule, and order on this earth now and in the future. Thus, we find satisfaction through surrender to Christ who brings us into the kingdom of heaven.

His first words were, "Blessed are the poor in spirit" (Matthew 5:3). Restated, Jesus said, "Satisfied are the humble." Remember that humble means "to be lower than, or to bend the knee to." Humility and humanity come from the same Latin root, *humus,* meaning "from the ground." We call it being "down to earth."

The condition of one's heart is determined by the object of its desires. A humble heart desires Christ. "Pride" means "to be higher than, or to exalt." A proud heart desires *self* above all else and remains dissatisfied. Someone who is "poor in spirit" is declaring his or her moral bankruptcy before a holy God, trusting in Christ's free gift of grace as payment for sin. Humility says to

Christ, "I can't. You can." "I can't pay for my sin. You can. I can't be Lord of my life. You can." *I can't* indicates repentance. *You can* indicates faith.

Jesus, our ultimate example of a humble heart, said of the meek and humble, "For theirs is the kingdom of heaven" (Matthew 11:29). Humility is the entrance requirement to the kingdom of heaven (Matthew 18:1-4). The kingdom demonstrates fellowship with God, which is why we were created.

In order to humble our hearts, we must continue to surrender our pride. In a great story tucked in the Gospel of Luke, Jesus contrasted the temple prayer of a proud Pharisee with that of a humble tax collector. The respected Pharisee exalted himself while the disrespected tax collector stood at a distance, refused to look up to heaven, and beat his breast—three acts of humility. The tax collector finally made an attempt to put into words the condition of his heart, "God, have mercy on me, a sinner" (Luke 18:13). Jesus said that the tax collector, *not* the Pharisee, went home justified before God. He summed it up this way, "For everyone who exalts himself will be humbled, and he who humbles himself will be exalted" (Luke 18:14).

In essence, at my bedside on July 1, 1992, I was saying, "God, have mercy on me, a sinner." I did not have to pretend any longer. I did not have to allow my outward circumstances to define what was happening on the inside. I did not have to pretend that my spiritual walk was perfect. I did not have to pretend that my marriage was perfect. I did not even have to pretend that I could pull myself out of the darkest day of my business life. I could finally admit that I had fallen, and that I needed to confess my sin to God.

Every piece of my life had to be surrendered, both good and bad. God had acted to offer me restoration, and my surrender to Him would prompt restoration. My attempt to control everything around me had little to do with humility or wisdom but everything to do with suppressing addictions that skewed my pride-filled, foolish reality. Like the tree described by the psalmist in Psalm 1, I needed to be reconnected to my source of water, my source of life. My survival could no longer hinge on my self-restoration program of partial surrender; I needed to move on to full surrender to the Restorer that unlocked the gate to Restoration Road.

My pride left me dissatisfied. Only the makings of a clay heart would be the key that unlocked my spiritual box for restoration to authenticity.

Pride's *desire, determination,* and *destination* are the opposite from *be-do-go* respectively. They travel in the opposite direction, living life from the outside in. In essence they represent *been, done, gone.*

My proud heart's *desire* relegated my need for God into what resulted in a quick fix, where I attempted to earn points so that I could deem myself worthy. A quick fix flows from the outside in. I assumed that this cure would be discovered in traveling to higher positions of life by building one sand castle after another, or by adding stone monuments to my garden of life, in search of restoration. However, my efforts at self-restoration never resulted in eternal or abundant life. I needed healing from the inside out. I needed to be made new by the hands of the Restorer because I had been designed for God's transformational touch to heal my heart condition, to chisel my stone heart and shape my sand heart into a heart of clay.

My proud heart's *determination* was closed. I spoke with great conviction and pride, and was immovable on certain issues. Tasks and accomplishments far outweighed relationships. My heart, including my choices, thoughts, prayers, and feelings, as well as my desires and my three resources of life, were closed to others to advance my own personal agenda. I was so driven on my closed course that I neglected to understand anyone else.

David wrote about his enemies who had determined to remain closed to God. They chose it in their wills. They thought it in their minds. They prayed it in their spirits. They wanted it in their emotions. "They close up their callous hearts, and their mouths speak with arrogance" (Psalm 17:10). When my heart was closed, I could not be molded by God or anyone else for that matter because I believed that I could get well on my own efforts. I chose it. I thought it. I prayed it. I wanted it. Looking back, I realize that when my mind was closed, I struggled to understand inside out living. The prophet Isaiah recorded this dilemma, "They know nothing, they understand nothing; their eyes are plastered over so they cannot see, and their minds closed so they cannot understand" (Isaiah 44:1). I believed that I could be more, do more, and go more on my own—I was not interested in shifting directions. All of this was the result of my closed will, my closed mind, my closed spirit, and my closed emotions, a reflection of outside in living.

My proud heart's *destination* became a lock of death. Two Greek words are frequently translated in the Bible as *death*. The first is *thonatos*, which has four primary uses: (1) physical death (Matthew 10:21), (2) spiritual death (John 5:24), (3) plague (Matthew 24:7), and (4) eternal death (Romans 6:21, 23).

The second is frequently used to communicate that the spirit is eternally ripped from the soul and body—*nekros* (James 2:26). Pride caused me to move from *thonatos* to *nekros*, locking me out from the gracious gift of life.

Herod and Jesus: A Study in Contrasts

Pride is the lock on the human heart; humility is the key. Think back to the illustration of the lock and key and visualize how the four pins, representing the four quadrants of the heart that flow into the four primary desires, are unsurrendered. The inner cylinder (heart) and the outer cylinder (desires) are linked to the image of the ring that contrasts *intimacy* with *idolatry*, the result of either a humble or proud heart. Intimacy with God produces wisdom (Proverbs 1:7); idolatry perpetuates foolish behavior (Proverbs 17:16).

I have learned that there are three perspectives of life: (1) mine, (2) others', (3) and God's. I lived a season of my life seeing myself through my clouded perspective. It left me dissatisfied. I lived a season of my life seeing myself through the eyes of others' clouded perspectives. It left me dissatisfied. Finally, I learned to see myself through God's perspective of the inside. His is the only authentic perspective. This truth freed me from the masquerade of pretense that flowed from the outside in and satisfied my heart, my desires, and my three resources of life with healing from the inside out.

Unfortunately, sand and stone hearts crave outside in living. The apostle John described the dissatisfaction of this pretense when he said: "Do not love the world or anything in the world. If anyone loves the world, the love of the Father is not in him. For everything in the world—the cravings of sinful man, the lust of his eyes and the boasting of what he has and does—comes not from the Father but from the world. The world and its desires pass away, but the man who does the will of God lives forever" (1 John 2:15-17). When we are locked in the pride of sand or stone, we become harsh and dissatisfied. But John's statements define what happens when we move beyond the world's desires and toward God's will.

There might not have been another human being in Jesus' time whose pride imprisoned him, both figuratively and literally, and kept him apart from God than Herod the Great. In the pretense of his self-restoration program, he proudly sought to satisfy his desires of *significance*, *contentment*, *security*, and *control* apart from the design of the Designer.

Herod the Great proudly held the title of Tetrarch of Judea (a sign of his desire for *significance*) 2,000 years ago when God came to earth in Jesus Christ. Known for his great building programs, including the rebuilding of the Temple (a sign of his desire for *contentment*), Herod built his first of a series of palace fortresses three miles southeast of Bethlehem.

Herod's palace fortresses were designed to give him safe asylum in case he was forced to flee the country to his homeland of

Idumea (a sign of his desire for *security*). His largest fortress was the Herodian, 45 acres of building constructed on 200 acres of land, making it the third-largest architectural find in the ancient world. The palace featured four towers, with the highest stretching 120 feet into the air, sprawling 55 feet in diameter (a sign of his desire for *control*).

Yet, when Jesus Christ came to earth, he did not choose this physically impressive location. Instead, within eyesight of this ancient wonder, God came to earth in a feeding trough nestled in a cave, a sign of his *significance*, *contentment*, *security*, and *control* that flowed from the inside out.

Pride is the lock on the human heart; humility is the key. We find this in both the proud eyes of Herod and in the humble eyes of Jesus.

Herod the Great was proud. He was known as the "King of the Jews," a title he received from the Roman Senate (37-4 BC) —one which the Jews would not recognize because of its origin. He lived in his palaces with locked and closed doors, reflective of his heart.

Herod the Great was harsh. He killed his favorite of ten wives; he killed three sons; and he decreed to kill boys age two and younger when the Magi arrived asking, "Where is the one who has been born King of the Jews? We saw his star in the east and have come to worship him" (Matthew 2:1-2). He lived to satisfy himself. He saw power in his fortresses and locked doors, keeping others out. Herod exerted his power over others because he desired to reveal his character and presence rather than God's. The real King of the Jews offered an alternative to the lock of pride and the unrestoration of harshness. He was humble and gentle (Matthew 11:29). He was a liberator Who authoritatively freed people, healed them, gave them life, and access to a different kind of power. He searched out others, moving toward them in relationship to uncover the love of the Father in them.

Jesus searched to humbly unlock and gently restore the spiritual inner boxes of everyone: sand and stone hearts alike. In Nazareth, where He lived ninety percent of his life, Jesus and His father Joseph were most likely stonemasons. It is reasonable to surmise that they may have worked at a stone amphitheater in Sephora known as the "Ornament of Galilee," only three to four miles away from Herod's grand structures. So He knew about Herod's hard heart; He had seen the edifices that Herod had erected in his own honor. But Jesus chose a different path. In His humility, Jesus saw the power in love, exalting the humble and granting them access to His kingdom. His heart of love changed the world through the transcendent power of God.

In the end, Herod died in his palace in Jericho in 4 BC. He died *insignificant*, *discontent*, *insecure*, and *out of control*. Historians say that he passed away most likely due to a bout with syphilis. To ensure that mourning, rather than rejoicing, would take place at his death, he issued a decree that several prominent Jews be executed at his passing. His sister Salome reversed this edict.

Contrastingly, Jesus died *significant*, *content*, *secure*, and in *control*. The Gospel writers demonstrated how Jesus' desires were satisfied in the Father even in His darkest hours, evidenced in His final words on the cross—the most excruciating death devised by mankind.

Jesus died *significant*, satisfied in the Restorer's *love*: "Jesus called out with a loud voice, 'Father, into your hands I commit my spirit.' When he had said this, he breathed his last" (Luke 23:46).

Jesus died *content*, satisfied in the Restorer's *peace*, forgiving those who were crucifying him: "Jesus said, 'Father, forgive them, for they do not know what they are doing.' And they divided up his clothes by casting lots" (Luke 23:34).

Jesus died *secure*, satisfied in the Restorer's *truth*, offering that security to others including the repentant thief on the cross: "Jesus answered him, 'I tell you the truth, today you will be with me in paradise'" (Luke 23:43).

Jesus died in *control,* satisfied in the Restorer's *power.* His *control* to fulfill prophecy was evidenced in his *power:* "Later, knowing that all was now completed, and so that the Scripture would be fulfilled, Jesus said, 'I am thirsty'" (John 19:2).

While on the cross, Jesus did not breathe his last breath until he had finished his purpose, a mark of *control* discovered in the *power* of the Restorer: "When he had received the drink, Jesus said, 'It is finished.' With that, he bowed his head and gave up his spirit" (John 19:30).

The most challenging of Jesus' statements on the cross is this one: "About the ninth hour Jesus cried out in a loud voice, *'Eloi, Eloi, lama sabachthani?'* — which means, 'My God, my God, why have you forsaken me?'" (Matthew 27:46; cf. Mark 15:33). In saying this, Jesus quoted the first line of Psalm 22. Before we make a rash assessment and assume God's abandonment of Jesus on the cross, we must recognize David's purpose in writing Psalm 22 evidenced in its joyful conclusive statement, "For he has not despised or disdained the suffering of the afflicted one; he has not hidden his face from him but has listened to his cry for help" (Psalm 22:24). David's poetic prayer demonstrated that he trusted God to carry him from agony to joy when he had felt rejected by God and others.

It is possible that Matthew and Mark could have been communicating Jesus' recitation of the entire Psalm by recording only its first line. We often do the same thing with The Lord's Prayer when we refer to it as "Our Father" or assume the balance of the prayer is being recited when we hear someone say, "Our Father in heaven."

In any event, Matthew and Mark communicated that even in His agony, Jesus trusted His heavenly Father for His *significance* in being the love of God, His *contentment* in being the peace of God, His *security* in being the truth of God, and His *control* in being the power of God.

Here we see the dramatic differences in the destination of people traveling on Restoration Road. Because Jesus is alive, the humble are "in," and the proud are "out." Jesus Christ, the humility of God, lived the perfect example of being restored from the inside out so that those on the outside could come in. Christ's Master Key unlocks the gate to Restoration Road as our hearts are fully surrendered to love God, to worship him, and to serve Him only. Then we can begin to experience the limitless love, peace, truth, and power of the Father.

In His grace-filled posture toward us, the eyes of God look deep into the condition of the chambers of our heart (1 Samuel 16:7). His desire is to restore the fracture that occurs within, and He has offered His greatest gift, Jesus, to bring healing and restoration through that grace to draw us to our desired destination of a restored life.

When we begin this leg of the journey, we enter a new kingdom, run a different race, and recognize that every moment is lived by His grace and for His glory. It is a revelation of His character and presence instead of our own. Consequently, every experience becomes a divine appointment that lowers a life of pride to one of humility, pointing others to the Restorer.

Take a *poor in spirit* inventory of any prideful area in your life where you are ruling your own kingdom. It will be manifested in a relationship, a task, or a conflict that is leaving you dissatisfied. Surrender your pride to Christ, saying, "I can't. You can." Live out this humility toward Christ in your relationships where you will experience satisfaction through the surrender of your desires to Him. You will live in the kingdom of heaven, and those around you will be drawn to Christ through you.

The Importance of Gentleness

After God unlocked the spiritual box of my heart, it was time for me to experience the restoration offered through *gentleness*. I realized that I had been harsh in my relationships, and it had left me unrestored. I had been harsh in (1) my vertical relationship with God, (2) my horizontal relationships with others, and (3) the depth of others' relationships with God.

Have you ever been harsh?

Something flawed inside each of us says that we can satisfy our desires by being harsh. Whether at the airline counter or the fast-food line, in the checkout aisle or the exit lane, on the basketball sidelines or on the telephone, we believe that harshness will satisfy our desires. Yet at the same time, it leaves our relationships damaged and unrestored. Jesus gave us a different way in the third of His eight secrets to satisfaction through surrender. In the Sermon on the Mount, Jesus said, "Blessed are the meek, for they will inherit the earth" (Matthew 5:5).

In this word picture, who are satisfied? The *gentle* are satisfied. The NASB says, "Blessed are the gentle." Gentleness is power under the Spirit's control. Like a bit in a horse's mouth, the Spirit's residence in our hearts guides us when we are gentle. The Greek word for "gentle" is *praus,* taken from the word *prautes.* Aristotle defined it as the middle course of being angry, somewhere between being angry for no reason and not getting angry at all. Gentleness is getting angry at the right time with the right measure for the right reason.

Jesus told us that He was "Gentle...in heart" (Matthew 11:29). Contrary to prevailing popular opinion, the God of the universe is gentle, not harsh, in heart. Paul told us that the result of the Holy Spirit's dwelling in us is *gentleness* (Galatians 5:23). If the Spirit of God is alive in us, then we will be gentle in heart, not harsh.

Why are the gentle satisfied? Because "they will inherit the earth." This is Jewish phraseology for the blessings of God's kingdom. David said, "But the meek will inherit the land and enjoy great peace" (Psalm 37:11). We were designed to be satisfied by the kingdom of heaven, that invisible movement of God's reign, rule, and order in our lives. We find satisfaction, not through our harshness, but through our gentleness because gentleness restores relationships.

Gentleness restores (1) our relationship with God (height—the *vertical*), (2) our relationships with others (width—the *horizontal*), and (3) others' relationships with God (*depth*—the result of how effectively the vertical intersects with the horizontal). Let's take a closer look at these three aspects of a life lived in gentleness.

First, gentleness restores our relationship with God. Jesus said that His gentleness restores our souls (Matthew 11:29). James, the pastor of the New Testament church in Jerusalem, said that we should humbly, or gently, receive the word of God planted in our hearts which saves, or restores, us toward God (James 1:21).

As I began to surrender my harshness to the Restorer, I began to receive his gentleness in my vertical relationship with God. My first step was to return to the Restorer so that my tragedy, failures, and sins could be transformed into authenticity from the inside out. He was the shepherd with the lost sheep, the woman with the lost coin, and the father with the lost sons. He offered me an opportunity to cross over from worldly death into eternal life. Desperation Road had led me away from a relationship with the Restorer as I gave my resources to everything but Him; Restoration Road offered strength to lean into the Restorer, even in the midst of regret.

I was able to identify with the prodigal's regret as I pondered with deep remorse how many millions of dollars had traveled through my company's bank account, and how few of those dollars remained. As I poured my heart out to God, I was reminded that being restored was going to be an ongoing process. I was not going to flip a switch and suddenly live a perfect life. However, my trip down Restoration Road was more significant than any rare automobile I would ever auction. It was the beginning of the rest of my life. The Restorer gave me the strength to leave my regret behind.

I was lost for a long time, so my return to Restoration Road required me to face the extent of my sin as I asked the Restorer's forgiveness. I was no longer convinced that forgiveness, or restoration, depended solely on me. I thought about that shiny metal box and wondered how many times I had locked myself out of the kingdom of God, placing myself beyond the reach of His will in my life. Now I had a second chance, and I was determined to live in obedience to the Father.

I was thirsty, and just as sand and stone do not hold water, my heart was dry and needed to become clay in order to hold the Restorer's water of life. My future in the auction business dangled in the balance, but I no longer cared about controlling its outcome. Rather, I wanted to focus on the process more than the results. I had entered the restoration process with a renewed hope that the Restorer promised to transform my sand and stone heart into a heart of clay.

Are you harsh with God in any area of your life? Maybe He did not heal someone in the way or with the timing that you saw fit. Perhaps He has allowed suffering in your life that you deem unreasonable. Possibly, you don't have the career, spouse, or children that you thought He should give you. Whatever that harshness against God might be, surrender it to Him today. Say, "I can't. You can. I can't satisfy my desires through harshness toward You, but You can satisfy my desires if I surrender my harshness to You."

Second, gentleness restores our relationships with others. Jesus said that our words flow from our hearts (Luke 6:45). When we are harsh in heart, so are our words. When we are gentle in heart, our words are gentle—empowered by the Spirit's control. Solomon advised, "A gentle answer turns away wrath, but a harsh word stirs up anger" (Proverbs 15:1).

I began to surrender my harshness with others in order to receive the Restorer's gentleness in my horizontal relationships. As I've mentioned before, I had been quite harsh with my words and actions toward anyone who did not share my perspective of life, specifically in business. My harshness severely damaged my relationship with Susan, my family, my employees, my vendors, my competitors, my friends, and even my customers. My harshness in words as well as nonverbal cues flowed from a proud heart. I saw the counterfeit contents of my inner spiritual box—my desires and my time, talent, and treasure—as superior to others. The painful result of this harshness was damaged, unrestored relationships. The sand-hearted younger son experienced the same horizontal damage and subsequent unrestored relationships, especially with his older brother.

Are you harsh with your words in any of your relationships? Do you find yourself being harshest with those closest to you? Surrender your *harshness* for *gentleness* in your heart and subsequently in your words. You will find restoration in your relationships with others.

Third, gentleness restores others' relationships with God. This applies to both the surrendered and the unsurrendered heart. Paul said that when the surrendered person is caught in sin, we should restore him gently, realizing that we could be tempted as well (Galatians 6:1). Peter said that when we answer the unsurrendered person with the reason for the hope that we have in Christ, we should do so gently (1 Peter 3:15).

Prior to the night of July 1, 1992, I had not considered how my business activities might affect the depth and quality of another person's relationship with God. Did God really care how I directed my business affairs? Did He care about the spiritual effects my auction might have on others? Now, kneeling beside my bed, I was willing to consider that He might. This would make my business a ministry where the vertical would intersect with the horizontal in such a powerful way that it would permeate the depth of my impact on others. They would grasp how high, how wide, and how deep the Restorer's love was (Ephesians 3:18).

In fact, looking back, I see how this night appeared to resemble what the apostle Paul had in mind when he wrote his letter to the universal church: "For this reason I kneel before the Father, from whom his whole family in heaven and on earth derives its name. I pray that out of his glorious riches he may strengthen you with power through his Spirit in your inner being, so that Christ may dwell in your hearts through faith. And I pray that you, being rooted and established in love, may have power, together with all the saints, to grasp how wide and long and high and deep is the love of Christ, and to know this love that surpasses knowledge— that you may be filled to the measure of all the fullness of God" (Ephesians 3:14-19).

Notice that Paul saw humble surrender as the key that unlocks the restoration of our inner spiritual boxes. In order to be fully restored, we are given the Spirit of the Restorer, including His gentleness, or His power, to repair both our vertical and our horizontal relationships with God and with others. Restoration's depth reaches both the surrendered and the unsurrendered.

With whom are you harsh because of their unrestored relationship with God? It might be the self-righteous or the unrighteous. Are you harsh toward a particular person's relationship with God? It might be your spouse, a vendor, a customer, a leader in your local church, or even a friend or family member? Are you prepared to surrender that harshness to the Restorer, experiencing gentleness in heart and the inheritance of God's restorative blessings?

Full restoration has a way of bringing us face-to-face with our pretense and inner addictions. What are those things in your life that have built up walls of sand and stone around your spiritual heart? What are the addictions that have left you hopeless in your walk with the Restorer? Have you become an expert at outside in living?

The most valuable commodities in the world are locked in boxes to keep others out. Will you unlock your heart to let the gentleness of the Restorer in?

Chapter Ten

RESTORING THE FOUR CHAMBERS OF OUR HEARTS

I walked down a narrow alley, climbed the back steps and entered an unfinished storage room. Bending the knees of my body to climb those steps reminded me of the way I had been brought to my knees before God to discover the wisdom I was designed to pursue.

In these storage-room meetings, I listened to one of the most brilliant individuals I knew, my Uncle Derald. He was my earthly source for heavenly wisdom. We had been meeting together shortly before the raid as he guided me through the challenges of my business life. As you'll remember from the story of the raid, Uncle Derald was also my one telephone call courtesy of the IRS.

Many of the challenges I faced were unique to a family business. Dad was such a powerful politician-salesman that I thought I needed help to understand him from someone who knew him well—his brother. Speaking with Uncle Derald, I began to recognize that I had not connected shrewd business practices with God's heart.

This small meeting place had become my escape from the insanity that swirled around me as the IRS investigation made its way to Federal court. Surrounded by shelves filled with books, most of which Derald had read, we were meeting on a routine basis. I glanced around the room and was caught by the vertical lines and horizontal rails of the bookcases that intersected to form the shelves. It was a continual reminder of how the vertical—my relationship with God, had been designed to intersect with the horizontal—my relationships with others.

A Good Question

During one of these meetings, Derald had asked me an unexpected question: "Mitchell, have you ever thought about changing the scorecard of your life from money to wisdom?"

My response at the time had been, "No."

However, life had changed dramatically since that day. While I was convinced God had me on a new path, I was still fighting a tailspin toward a potentially career-ending, life-crushing legal nightmare. My relationships were also still a mess. I wondered, if I said "yes" to Uncle Derald's question, would that open the door to the wisdom I needed to change my life?

Derald had my undivided attention. He showed me that restoration comes about by pursuing wisdom. Money had been an idol that prevented me from recognizing my need for the Restorer. My desires needed to be transformed from *idolatry* in the form of love of money and greed, to *intimacy* with God.

God resists a heart that is proud or greedy (Proverbs 3:34). When pride is rooted in the chambers of the heart, we make a mockery out of our faith. It is only through God's generosity, flowing through a humble heart, that we find authentic restoration. With pride comes disgrace, but with humility comes wisdom through grace.

"Humility," *anavah*, in Hebrew means "to make lower than, or to bend the knee." It is the condition of the heart that fully surrenders to God and unlocks wisdom's gate (Proverbs 1:7, 9:10, 11:2, 22:4). Jesus said that He was gentle and humble in heart (Matthew 11:29). His life evidenced full surrender in its ultimate clarity as He surrendered all to the Father.

"Wisdom" is *chokma* in Hebrew. It is God's righteousness combined with street smarts. Wisdom makes our relationship with God "sticky" to our tasks and earthly relationships, the intersection of the vertical with the horizontal. It unleashes transformation from the inside out. Wisdom is not merely an idea; it is a person in whom the vertical intersects with the horizontal. Paul referred to Christ, our Restorer, as the wisdom of God (1 Corinthians 1:24), and Solomon described the pre-incarnate Christ as "wisdom" (Proverbs 8:22-36). We need the personal divine wisdom of the Restorer to unlock the four chambers of our spiritual hearts in order to travel Restoration Road.

The Four Chambers of the Heart

Whenever a vertical line intersects with a horizontal line, four quadrants appear. The same is true with the human heart (*leb* or *lebab* in Hebrew, meaning one's entire inner being). Just as the physical heart is comprised of four chambers, so the spiritual heart is comprised of four chambers remembered in the acronym, *WISE*: *Will, Intellect, Spirit,* and *Emotions.*

An easy way to think of the interrelationships of these four chambers is to imagine filling out a bracket during the NCAA's men's basketball tournament. When you look at the two teams playing each game, your *intellect* tells you which team has the better record. You think that team will win, but the opponent happens to be your alma mater, which has teetered on the brink of having a losing record. Your *emotions* are so favorable toward your school's team that you are leaning toward writing that name in the blank, even though you think the team with the better record will be victorious. So, you choose to be loyal to your school colors and pick it as the winning team with your *will*, writing its name in the blank. Finally, you pray in your *spirit* that the outcome will be in your favor.

Will

The *will* is the chamber of our *choices*. Nearly every action is preceded by a choice. In order to experience wisdom in our lives, we must surrender the will, or our choices, to God. Humbling our wills to God in order to experience wisdom is a choice (Proverbs 8:10). In essence, it is the flip of a switch. Humility says to God, "I can't. You can." When it comes to the will, humility says to God, "I won't. You will."

Jesus Christ surrendered His will to the Father. Just before His arrest and subsequent crucifixion, Jesus said, "Father if you are willing, take this cup from me; yet not my will, but yours be done" (Luke 22:42). Surrendering His will to the Father gave Jesus the wisdom to interact with Judas, the chief priests, Pilate, Herod, Peter, John, Mary, and the Roman soldiers among others in order to accomplish the will of the Father. This led to the glorification of Christ and the salvation of our souls. In other words, Jesus' surrender changed the course of the entire world. Now that's saying something about the value of submission! There is great power in humbled wills that make wise choices.

During one of our girls' varsity basketball seasons at Lakewood Park Christian High School, I stood on the sidelines with the head coach, frustrated that our post players were not taking advantage of the lane to the basket—either scoring, getting fouled, or both. With my auctioneer voice I yelled, "Would somebody, anybody, please take the ball strongly to the basket?"

Just as fate would have it, my daughter Megan got the ball, took one dribble, was fouled, and scored. I turned to the coach and added, "Do you know what that was? That was a Rosa Parks choice. Nothing else was taught. Nothing new was trained. Absolutely nothing new was introduced. All she did was flip the switch and choose to do what she was able to do." It was a perfect picture of the will engaged in the right way.

Prior to July 1, 1992, I had made proud sand choices and proud stone choices. Proud sand choices flowed from my sandy will which partially surrendered the horizontal at the expense of the vertical. I made street-smart choices void of my vertical connection. By mere definition, this would not lead to wisdom (Proverbs 1:7). I became loose and licentious in my choices, and all this left me dissatisfied.

Prior to my sand-heartedness, I had made proud choices which flowed from my stony *will*. I had partially surrendered the vertical at the expense of the horizontal. I created a neat and tidy box of right and wrong choices. Consequently, I saw blessings from God as solely dependent on my efforts, and I condemned others who could not make the same morally right choices. I became legalistic in my choices. My stone choices flowed from my stony *will* and left me dissatisfied.

It was time for me to flip the switch and choose wisdom by humbling my will to the Restorer. This meant fully surrendering the sand and stone in my will in order to choose clay.

God is saying the same thing to us. Flip the switch. Choose to change the measurement of success in your lives to wisdom. Will we humbly flip the switch of our hearts and choose wisdom? The answer begins when we choose to bend our knees to God's will.

Intellect

The *intellect* is the chamber of our thoughts. It is the content of the mind, including information, images, and ideas in both our conscious and subconscious. In order to unlock the gate to wisdom, we must humble our minds to God. The humbled intellect is a light that illuminates our hearts. King Solomon said, "The fear of the

LORD teaches a man wisdom, and humility comes before honor" (Proverbs 15:33). "The fear of the LORD" is humility toward God. When we humble our intellects to God, we learn wisdom. Solomon said that if we would accept it, store it up, listen to it, apply our hearts to it, call out for it, even cry aloud for it, look for it, and search for it, then we would understand "the fear of the LORD" because it is the Lord Who gives us wisdom (Proverbs 2:1-6). These aforementioned efforts comprise the study of wisdom that comes from a humbled mind.

Jesus is the Word, or the expression, of the mind of God (John 1:1). When walking this earth, Jesus surrendered His mind to the Father (Matthew 22:37). Paul said that we should take every thought captive and make it obedient to Christ: "We demolish arguments and every pretension that sets itself up against the knowledge of God, and we take captive every thought to make it obedient to Christ" (2 Corinthians 10:5). This restores us from pretense to authenticity. When we humble our intellects to God, we have the mind of Christ (1 Corinthians 2:16).

This proved to be significant to me.

At one point, Derald challenged me to memorize all 111 verses of the Sermon on the Mount—one per day for 111 days. I remember pushing back when he laid down the gauntlet for memorizing three chapters from Matthew. Did he not realize that my life was a 24/7 commitment to run Kruse International? How in the world would I have the time? When he wrote his challenge on the legal pad in front of him and pushed it across the table for me to sign, I felt like my leadership capabilities had been challenged. I agreed and signed the paper. What unfolded next changed my life.

I did not realize how getting into the Word would get the Word into me. I learned how the Bible could become the catalyst to my thoughts. I used to think that my thoughts were at the mercy of what was in front of my eyes. But after memorizing these chapters, I learned that I could recall Jesus' sermon, the greatest speech ever told, at any time. I found myself recalling the words while I traveled on airplanes, while driving my car, and even while awaiting a judge on a Federal court stand.

Jesus' words of wisdom began to come out in mine—not in a proud way, but in a humble one. For example, I would not tell someone, "Do you not realize Jesus said that what you are doing is wrong?" Rather I would confess my shortcoming in what I was learning, "I read the other day that the merciful find mercy. I've been working on making that evident in my life." I never had anyone push back on that approach.

As I was responding to Derald's challenge, he taught me wisdom from the book of Proverbs beginning with our joint study of its key words. I met weekly with Uncle Derald to ask him questions about my week's reading from the Scriptures. He was a Bible commentary in the flesh. He was Google before Google existed. He did not just feed me fish; rather, he taught me how to fish. He not only educated me regarding what the Bible said, he helped me understand how to study and allow the text to interpret itself.

This fueled an almost insatiable desire to fill my mind with wisdom from the Bible in order to apply it to my life. I attacked the study of the Scriptures like a college syllabus, creating four courses to apply my mind to the study of wisdom.

(1) Study Wisdom 101: I read one chapter in Proverbs each day that corresponded with the date of the month. Proverbs has 31 chapters, so I read through the book once each month during the course of the year.

(2) Study Wisdom 201: I accomplished *Study Wisdom 101,* plus I read a chapter from the New Testament each day. This allowed me to read the entire New Testament in less than a calendar year.

(3) Study Wisdom 301: I accomplished *Study Wisdom 201,* plus I read three chapters each day in the Old Testament so that I could read through the entire Bible in a year.

(4) Study Wisdom 401: I accomplished *Study Wisdom 301,* plus I memorized one verse each week that I applied to my collector car auction life, recalling it several times throughout the week.

These four disciplines have proven to be so valuable to me that I continue to pursue them each day. I encourage you to consider selecting one of the courses for your own life. **WARNING: This will radically change your life!**

I applied what I had learned from the Restorer, either from His Word, His people, or His Spirit, to my calendar. This meant that every appointment and every task would be done with the Restorer. I remember trying the five-second rule. I would take five seconds before every encounter, including telephone conversations, and ask the Restorer, "What do you want me to do?" I even tried the five-minute rule, which did not last long. I tried to arrive at every appointment five minutes early to ask God the same question, thinking through all that I thought should be wisely accomplished from the encounter.

Prior to July 1, 1992, I had thoughts of sand and thoughts of stone. Both were proud thoughts that flowed from my hardened intellect. My sand thoughts were licentious from breaking apart the horizontal from the vertical in my mind. This widely broadened my choices and feelings that often followed my thoughts, ideas, images, and information that passed through and lingered in my sandy intellect. Sand thoughts provoked sand choices, feelings, and prayers that provoked more sand thoughts. My sandy intellect left me dissatisfied.

Prior to my sand heartedness, I lived dependent on my stony intellect that broke apart the vertical from the horizontal and pretended to hold it tightly. I proudly gathered moral information and chiseled it into my stone mind. I used it to think legalistically regarding how I could manipulate God and judge others. I even saw God as one with a stone mind. My judgmental, stony intellect left me dissatisfied.

Something changed in my life as the Restorer exchanged my sand and stone intellect for a mind of clay. Softening of my thoughts illuminated the vision of my mind's eye. In my sand and stone intellect, I used to see nearly every encounter as an interruption. Whenever employees, prospects, customers, competitors, vendors, or even family members who took the initiative to walk into my office, call me, or write me took my time, I saw it as a negative theft of my precious seconds. But, as the Restorer transformed my thoughts with wisdom, I began to see every encounter as a divine appointment. This one shift in perspective has probably made the biggest impact on my life and still exists today.

Spirit

The *spirit* is the chamber of our *prayers*. The Bible refers to the spirit as the *lamp* of God (Proverbs 20:27). He uses it to search our innermost being. *Prayer* is the connection of our hearts with God's. In essence, it is being online with the Creator. Paul said that he prayed with his mind and with his spirit, indicating that prayer is not limited to just one quadrant of the heart (1 Corinthians 14:15). However, the spirit is the lead chamber of prayer. In order to humbly surrender our spirits to the Father, we must pray for wisdom.

James is believed to have had calloused knees from the amount of time he spent humbling his body as well as his heart in prayer. He penned, "If any of you lacks wisdom, he should ask God, who gives generously to all without finding fault, and it will be given to him" (James 1:5). Solomon said, "The LORD is far from the wicked but he hears the prayers of the righteous" (Proverbs 15:29).

When we humble all four chambers of our hearts, including our spirits, to the Restorer we receive His righteousness. This gives us a clear connection to the heart of God, and God has a strict policy against dropping calls.

Jesus surrendered His spirit to the Father. Each of the Gospel writers recorded Jesus praying alone daily with the Father and living online 24/7 with Him. Luke captured Jesus' last words complete with the inflection that only eyewitnesses would have known, "Jesus called out with a loud voice, 'Father, into your hands I commit my spirit'" (Luke 23:46).

Prior to July 1, 1992, my spirit had been hardened in sand and stone. This led to prayers that were similarly hardened. My sand-hearted prayers flowed loosely from partially surrendering the horizontal at the expense of the vertical. I neglected God until I needed Him. Consequently, my sand-hearted prayers were random and crisis-oriented. After hitting the pause button on God while I led my own life, I attempted to use prayer as a magic wand to manipulate God into fixing my crisis. Needless to say, my sand-hearted prayer life left me dissatisfied.

Prior to my sand-heartedness, I had prayers of stone. My partial surrender of the vertical at the expense of the horizontal led to prayers that were like stone rubbing on stone. I asked God to help me be good and do right so that I could be an example of righteousness which in the end was no more than self-righteousness. I saw God's movement in my life as solely dependent on my petitions. If I forgot to tell Him my requests, then He would not do what I needed Him to do. This created an enormous amount of pressure on me as I attempted to control everything that happened in my universe. Actually, I attempted to control only my ego-centric universe because I rarely prayed for others. My stone-hearted spirit with its legalistic prayers left me dissatisfied.

After the raid, I began surrendering my spirit to wisdom, praying for the Restorer to grant me the intersection of God's heart with street smarts. I was bookending my days with reading the Bible and praying for God to help me make sense of the wisdom in order to apply it to my auction world. I remember one time coming to a difficult verse to understand in Galatians. I was troubled that Paul would write something so difficult for a first-century person to understand. I decided to pray. I put down my Bible and asked God to help me understand the verse. After this I said, "Amen," and I picked up the Bible and read the verse again, studying the context around it. I finally understood it!

I created another acronym to assimilate into my life "The Lord's Prayer," where Jesus taught each of His disciples how to be a person who *PRAYS* (Matthew 6:9-15). This five-fold pattern transformed my prayer life. Jesus said, "This, then, is how you should pray" (Matthew 6:9).

(1) Praise. Jesus prayed, "Our Father in heaven, hallowed be your name" (Matt. 6:9). "Heaven" has three meanings: (1) where we go when we die, (2) the stars in the sky, and (3) the air in and around us. "Hallowed" means "holy." When I pray, I praise our heavenly Father for who He is (holy) and for being as close as the air is in and around me.

(2) Renew. Jesus prayed, "Your kingdom come, your will be done on earth as it is in heaven" (Matthew 6:10). It was understood that after God's kingdom came, His will would be done on earth as in heaven. Jesus ushered in God's kingdom. As a result, this part of Jesus' prayer calls for a renewing of our minds in order to experience God's kingdom and will in our lives (Romans 12:1-3). This is a 180-degree turn from our world's standards. Jesus prayed for His Father's will (Matthew 26:39). When I pray, He renews my mind to be about His kingdom.

(3) Ask. Jesus prayed, "Give us today our daily bread" (Matthew 6:11). This referenced God's provision of Manna in the desert for the Israelites. It is an illustration of total dependence on God for our needs to advance His kingdom. When I pray, I ask God for what I need to advance His kingdom.

(4) Yield. Jesus prayed, "Forgive us our debts, as we also have forgiven our debtors" (Matthew 6:12). C. S. Lewis said that "as" was the most sobering two-letter word in all Scripture because the prayer is for God to forgive us in the same exact manner in which we have forgiven others. For some of us, this is a scary prayer. We have to yield all unsettled accounts to

God, radically issuing to others the forgiveness that we have received from Him. If we do not, then we really have not received God's forgiveness (Matthew 6:14-15). When I pray, I yield all unsettled relational accounts to God.

(5) Surrender to be Spirit-led. Jesus prayed, "And lead us not into temptation, but deliver us from the evil one" (Matthew 6:13). The Aramaic sentence structure might indicate "Let us not sin when tempted," rather than "Let us not be tempted." This is supported by the fact that Scripture tells us that God does not tempt anyone (James 1:13). When I pray, I surrender my heart to be Spirit-led in order to become a rapid Holy Spirit responder.

Humble your spirit, and pray for wisdom. Ask God to lead you to the intersection of His heart with street smarts. Pray this request to God before, during, and after your Scripture reading as well as when you are making a significant decision, or encountering another person during a divine appointment. Become a rapid Holy Spirit responder as a person who *PRAYS*.

Emotions

Our *emotions* represent the chamber of our *feelings*. These are the multiple reflectors, or mirrors, of the light in us. Although the exhaustive list of emotions is a difficult one to complete, a simple way that Derald categorized them was: *mad*, *sad*, *glad* or *afraid*. In order to fully surrender our hearts to the Father, we must feel like it. We must want to bend our knees to His will. This is a desire that includes an emotive reflection.

Solomon not only challenged young leaders to choose wisdom (Proverbs 8:10), but he also went on to say that they should desire it above all else, "For wisdom is more precious than rubies, and nothing you desire can compare with her" (Proverbs 8:11). Many of us need to make a shift in what we desire. Too often, we enter a conflict emotionally seeking victory that is measured in time, talent, or treasure, wishing for falsely promised significance, contentment, control, or security. Consequently, we become mad, sad, glad, or afraid over whether or not we will win when we pursue our satisfaction apart from God. The irony is that we find ourselves dissatisfied because only He can truly satisfy our desires (Psalm 145:16, 19). He does this through wisdom—the sweet spot where the vertical intersects with the horizontal.

Jesus surrendered His emotions to the Father. While being crucified with criminals as Roman soldiers divided up His clothes by casting lots, Jesus said, "Father, forgive them, for they do not know what they are doing" (Luke 23:34). Peter, who witnessed this said, "When they hurled their insults at him, he did not retaliate; when he suffered, he made no threats. Instead, he entrusted himself to him who judges justly" (1 Peter 2:23).

Recently, I was trying to teach my daughter Kelsey about emotions and how they reflect our hearts to others.

"Kelsey, I want you to vacuum the cars, all three of them."

Kelsey is our perfectionist who almost always attempts to do what is right, but out of character she gave me push back. I was amazed at how I had to return to her over the course of an hour in order to entice her to do it.

Finally, she vacuumed the cars. I checked in as she made her way through the floors of the vehicles. She was a little sad and a little mad—totally out of character for Kelsey. I checked in one last time, only to be amazed by the sight of the vacuum hose and attachments lying on the garage floor, where she knew they should never be. So I walked upstairs for an overdue appointment with Kelsey in her room.

In my sweatpants' pocket were three denominations of dollar bills: a five, a twenty, and a hundred. I walked into Kelsey's room and placed the pictures of Abe, Andrew, and Benny on her bed.

"Kelsey, when I asked you the first time to vacuum the cars, I knew these were in my pocket. I thought I'd give you the twenty.

Kelsey, there was even something inside of me that said, 'She's been supporting a girl through Compassion International; she needs money to buy Christmas presents; maybe I'll just go for it and give her a hundred.'" Kelsey's big blue eyes got even bigger as she stared down Benjamin Franklin, noting how his hairstyle resembled her dad's.

I asked, "Kelsey, look at these three denominations and tell me what kind of job you did."

"Maybe the five," she replied.

"That's right, and that's what I'm giving you," I proclaimed.

"I just want you to know that your emotions cost you something. What do you think they cost you?"

"Probably dinged my relationship with God," Kelsey said spiritually.

"What else?" I asked.

Kelsey's eyes scanned all three bills as her mind seemed to race. She responded, "Somewhere between fifteen and ninety-five dollars."

I explained, "Kelsey, your emotions cost something today. They dinged your relationship with God and me because you didn't reflect His heart during the process." Then it was time for the altar call. I continued, "You know what? That's the same thing that's happening all over our world today. Ministries and businesses are getting killed because their leaders and employees are reflecting negative emotions to those they encounter, and it is dinging the advancement of the kingdom of God!" I began to sweat as I preached, driving this message home. I walked away and decided to return to my perfectionist daughter a few minutes later to give her the twenty and a lesson on grace. I just could not bring myself to give her the $100!

I could relate to Kelsey's emotions because I had lived in the unrestored state of sand and stone emotions. My sand feelings ebbed and flowed from partially surrendering the horizontal while foregoing the vertical. At different times I was mad, sad, glad, afraid, or frustrated over my sand-hearted beliefs that flowed from my sandy intellect. Life had been all about me as I attempted to gratify my desires in selfish horizontal fulfillment. My feelings about others loosened as I developed more of an affinity for the licentious. People who were not religious elitists seemed more accepting of others. Consequently, I lowered my formerly perfectionistic expectations in order to feel better when they were unmet.

When I spoke to Derald about my dilemma between licentiously low sand-hearted expectations and legalistically high stone-hearted ones, Derald offered me clay-hearted advice: *remove the expectations*. He suggested that I stop trying to figure out every encounter before it happened. I needed to remove my prideful expectations in order to live wisely in the present. This one minor change provided major renewal in my emotional health. As a result, I desired wisdom more than ever.

When I affirmatively answered Derald's challenge to me regarding wisdom as the scorecard of my life, I felt differently. I began to engage every transaction in search of wisdom. I wanted it more than money. I believe that this emotive transformation enticed others to do business with me. This occurred because my search was authentic from the inside out. It began with desiring wisdom from God in order to live it with others.

Humble your emotions and desire wisdom. Shift the target of your life from your measurement of choice to wisdom—God's heart intersecting with street smarts. In every encounter, desire wisdom. Feel it. Want it. Joyfully embrace it. Just as changing your diet will create a desire for different tastes, so desiring wisdom will lead to a different appetite for life.

When we humble all four chambers of our hearts to God, we receive Christ, the wisdom of God, dwelling in us (1 Corinthians 1:24). Jesus Christ is the intersection of the vertical with the horizontal. He walked the earth as fully God and fully man. He is

God's heart combined with street smarts. He has reconciled man with God and man with man. Paul referred to Christ in us as "the hope of glory" (Colossians 1:27). Hope is confident assurance, not wishful thinking as we tend to use it in our English language. Glory is the revelation of the character and presence. When we humbly surrender all four chambers of our hearts to God, we can be confident and assured that God's wisdom in Christ will manifest itself in us.

Learning to Yield

As a recovering perfectionist, I realized that I had attempted to control every outcome in my life. After losing almost everything and subsequently studying the Bible, I learned that I could only control my input into situations. Consequently, I needed to yield the outcomes to the Restorer. This was one of the most freeing concepts I ever applied to my journey. It meant letting go, literally leaving the *go*, or the ripple effect, to the Restorer. Shifting my target of success from money to wisdom freed me to surrender the outcomes of my efforts to God.

I learned that I needed to yield my heart fully to God. This meant fully surrendering all four chambers of my heart to him including my: *will*, *intellect*, *spirit*, and *emotions*. Paul communicated it clearly, "Yield yourselves unto God." However, there is a prerequisite to full surrender.

Joshua, after conquering the Promised Land, noted full surrender's prerequisite to the people of Israel, "Throw away the foreign gods that are among you and yield your hearts to the Lord" (Joshua 24:23). Yielding our hearts to God means throwing away any foreign gods that are desired by sand and stone hearts. In my life, they included the gods of money and perfectionism. In Israel's journey, they included a potpourri of gods from other cultures and generations. In three and a half millennia, little has changed.

Joshua challenged the people of Israel regarding their allegiance to these foreign gods that they must have been white knuckling,

"Choose this day whom you will serve, whether the gods your forefathers served beyond the river or the gods of the Amorites, in whose land you are living. But as for me and my household, we will serve the Lord" (Joshua 24:15). It is interesting that we were created to serve, to fully surrender to someone or something. Consequently, the telling question is not whether we will fully surrender, but, "To whom will we bend the knee?" As a humble and wise leader, Joshua initiated full surrender of all four chambers of his heart to God.

The people of Israel replied again to Joshua's challenge in self-restorative pride, "Far be it from us to forsake the Lord to serve other gods!" (Joshua 24:16).

Joshua answered their reply with the fact that left to themselves they would never be set free from the prison of pride. They could not yield, or fully surrender, their hearts to God while locked in self-restoration, "You are not able to serve the Lord. He is a holy God; he is a jealous God," (Joshua 24:19). Neither are we able to fully surrender our hearts to God when we continue to hold onto the gods of our past cultural and generational experiences. For example, I could not continue to white-knuckle money and fully surrender my heart to God. The net effect would be only partial surrender.

Again the people of Israel replied, "No! We will serve the Lord" (Joshua 24:21). Joshua knew what they had to do in order to yield their hearts fully to God. Joshua commanded them to rid themselves of what they had been holding back, "Now then... throw away the foreign gods that are among you and yield your hearts to the Lord, the God of Israel" (Joshua 24:23).

Due to being pulled over multiple times for driving at high speeds, I have taken the Indiana State Driver's Test on more than one occasion. One of the questions on my most recent written test asked what was the name of a triangular highway sign, the *yield* sign. It directs people *to let go*. When approaching the yield sign, we let any oncoming traffic go first. When we yield our hearts

1908 Auburn Model G Touring original design

In the fall of 1907, the Vehslage family of Seymour, Indiana purchased three new Auburns in an attempt to become Auburn dealers to get a discount from the factory. They sold two Auburns and retained one for themselves, thus ending their careers as Auburn dealers. They purchased a Model G Touring, one of 356 cars built by Auburn for the 1908 model run. The family maintained the Auburn in running condition until 1971 when a tornado hit the barn in which the Auburn was stored. Part of the barn collapsed, and the upper floor fell in on the car. The remains were dug out of the barn and were stored until 1984 when the vehicle was donated to the Auburn Cord Duesenberg Museum. The vehicle was placed on exhibit until 1993 when it was put into storage. In 1997, restoration began and the car was brought back to life. The restoration was finished in the spring of 2002.

1908 Auburn Model G Touring remains after a tornado demolished the barn where it was stored

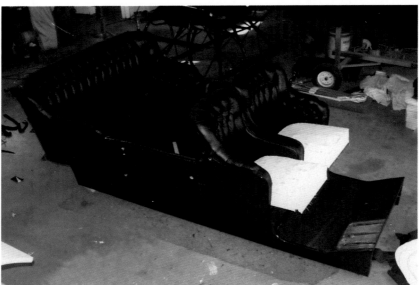

*1908 Auburn Model G Touring being restored piece by piece
(chassis and body)*

1908 Auburn Model G Touring restored to its original design

1922 Duesenberg Model A Roadster, owner Tom Mix behind the wheel

*1924 Duesenberg Special Indianapolis 500 winner, Driver L. L. Corum
(Fred Duesenberg standing)*

*1925 Duesenberg Special Indianapolis 500 winner, Driver Pete DePaolo
(Fred Duesenberg standing)*

1927 Duesenberg Special Indianapolis 500 winner, Driver George Souders

1929 Cord L-29 four door sedan with the Graf Zeppelin that touched down in California, September 10, 1929

1929 Cord L-29 convertible sedan with the four Marx Brothers, one of four Cord automobiles owned by the famous radio, film, and stage family

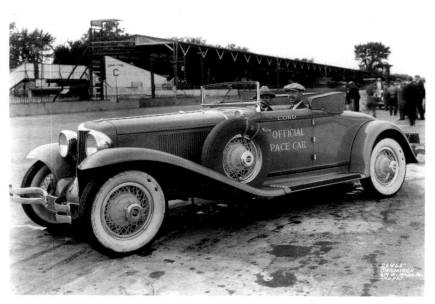

1930 Cord L-29 Indianapolis 500 Pace Car

1930 Duesenberg J-431 Derham Tourster photographed with owner, Gary Cooper

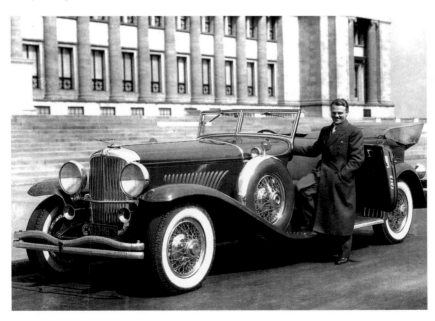

1932 Duesenberg J Dietrich four door convertible with James Cagney posing in front of Chicago's Museum of Science and Industry

1933 Duesenberg J-481 Fernandez and Darrin Convertible Victoria designed for actress Greta Garbo. The car was reportedly fashioned for her recluse personality. Her chauffer would be exposed; she would be hidden. The car also featured secret compartments for Garbo to safely stow her jewels.

1934 Auburn V-12 Cabriolet with its owner James Cagney sitting behind the wheel on the Warner Brothers Studios lot during the filming of their silver screen hit, The Mayor of Hell

1935 Duesenberg SJ Mormon Meteor piloted by Ab Jenkins to a World Land Endurance Speed Record both for one hour and 24 hours (154 mph average) at Utah's Bonneville Salt Flats in 1935

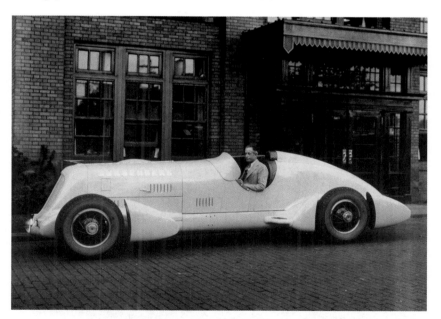

Ab Jenkins with his Duesenberg Special known as the Mormon Meteor, June 4, 1935

1935 Auburn 851 Supercharged Boattail Speedster with Ab Jenkins and friends in the summer of 1935 after breaking the Flying Mile World Speed Record (one of 70 American Stock Car Speed Records set by Jenkins in an Auburn automobile). Each supercharged Auburn was sold with a dash plate engraved with the words, "Driven by Ab Jenkins at 101.1 miles per hour." Recovered dash plates indicate a variation of speeds up to 101.8 miles per hour. Grandpa Russell remembered as a teenager hearing the supercharged Auburns roar down the dirt road during their test-drives, the same dirt road where I grew up.

1935 Auburn 851 Supercharged Boattail Speedsters with big screen stars Mary Astor (seated behind the wheel) and George Murphy (standing)

1935 Duesenberg J-560 Rollston convertible coupe pictured with owner, Clark Gable

1936 Cord 810 Phaeton with Sonya Henie, the only three-time female Gold Medalist Olympic Figure Skater (1928, 1932, and 1936). Photo was taken around the time of the release of her first movie, One in a Million.

1936 Cord 810 Phaeton on movie set

1937 Cord 810 Phaeton with owner, Tom Mix, who was later killed in this vehicle after swerving to miss a road construction barrier on an Arizona highway in the dark of night. His car struck a cactus head-on. The impact caused his luggage that was stored in the back of the vehicle to thrust forward, breaking his neck.

1930 Duesenberg J-249 Murphy Torpedo Roadster factory photo; side view and rear view

The restored Duesenberg legendary grille fronted by Trippe lights that articulate with the steering wheel in order to illuminate the road ahead

J-249 is equipped with external side exhaust pipes signifying its supercharger that increased its engine output from 265 to 320 horsepower

The prestigious Duesenberg hood ornament is a status symbol of E. L. Cord's dream for Fred and August Duesenberg to build the largest, fastest, most expensive, and simply the best automobile in the world

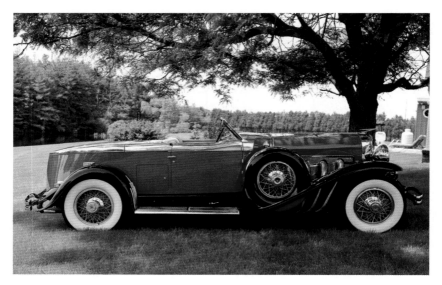

This 1930 Duesenberg J-249 Murphy Torpedo Roadster is one of the most beautifully restored classic automobiles ever reassembled. The thousands of hours invested in both the research of its history and design, as well as the meticulous reconstruction of the body, make it a priceless contribution to the preservation of the automobile and specifically to the heritage of the Auburn Automobile Company. As I traveled across the globe seeking rare and desirable collectible vehicles for auction, I toured many of the world's finest public and private car collections. Consequently, I believe that Richard Losee's donation of this Duesenberg to the Kruse Automotive and Carriage Museum is one of the most significant gifts made to any nonprofit entity dedicated to communicating the riveting story of rolling sculptures.

to God, we need to first let go of what we are holding back from Him in the form of other gods and let His priorities go first in our lives. This yielding takes place in the four chambers of our hearts. We *choose* to let go; we *think* to let go; we *pray* to let go; and we *want* to let go.

In order to yield ourselves to God, we need to eliminate any desire for life apart from God, any sin that separates us from a heart of clay and manifests itself in a foreign god. In order to yield ourselves unto God, we need to ask ourselves, *"What god am I white knuckling?"* It might be money, an illicit relationship, improper use of the internet, a career, or anything we see or hold in our hands that is not God. It might even be a position in the church where we desire to find significance, contentment, control, and security in ministry, but not in God.

Joshua learned a great deal from his apprenticeship with Moses. I love what Moses shared from the heart of God before the Israelites battled to conquer the Promised Land. He clearly stated the people's close proximity to the key that could unlock all four chambers of their hearts to God. It resided inside them: "Now what I am commanding you today is not too difficult for you or beyond your reach. It is not up in heaven so that you have to ask, 'Who will ascend into heaven to get it and proclaim it to us so we may obey it?' Nor is it beyond the sea so that you have to ask, 'Who will cross the sea to get it and proclaim it to us so we may obey it?' No, the word is very near you. It is in your mouth and in your heart so that you may obey it" (Deuteronomy 30:11-14). The power to yield ourselves to God lies in our hearts (cf. James 1:21). It lies in the spark of the Restorer placed in each one of us. It lies in the Master Key of full surrender to the Restorer. It occurs when we utter these simple words to the Restorer: "I can't. You can."

Moses continued regarding this life-giving power of a humble choice, "This day I call heaven and earth as witnesses against you that I have set before you life and death, blessings and curses.

Now choose life so that you and your children may live and that you may love the Lord Your God, listen to His voice, and hold fast to Him. For the Lord is your life" (Deuteronomy 30:19-20a).

To yield ourselves fully to God, we need to: *yield* all four chambers of our hearts to Him, *love* Him, *listen* to His voice, and *hold fast* to Him, for He is our *life*. No other god can provide restorative breath, only death resulting from the imprisonment of our pride.

When we yield all four chambers of our hearts to God, we begin to live abundantly and eternally. We become free to yield our desires, as well as our time, talent, and treasure to God. This yielding provides us the wisdom to control only the things we can and yield those we cannot.

I learned that I had lived a fantasy of pretending that I could control the *outcomes* of my life; whereas, all the while I could only control the *input*. One of my favorite Bible verses first became familiar to me during my high school basketball career. My teammates with whom I had practiced daily for almost six years would often remind me to read it before a game. It said, *"I can do everything through him who gives me strength"* (Philippians 4:13). I had interpreted that verse from basketball to business as "I can do everything." In other words, "I can control the outcomes in my life." I tried to live this by breaking apart the vertical from the horizontal, just as I had done with the words in the verse. I used God (the vertical) as a magic wand to provide all of my desired outcomes (the horizontal). The result was the imprisonment of pride followed by my self-restoration attempt to free myself.

As I began to study the wisdom of the Bible, I saw an important nuance that I had missed. It lied in what was possibly the most telling word in the verse, *"through."* God did not promise that I could do all things—that is, control the outcomes in my life. Rather, God promised that I could do all things *through* the One who would renew my strength. I could do all of my inputs *through* a relationship with the Restorer, *through* the sweet spot where the vertical intersected with the horizontal. I could choose to, think to, pray to, and want to yield all four chambers of my heart to the Restorer. In doing so, I would be free to yield the outcomes to Him as well. After years of attempting to control the outcomes in my life, I finally surrendered to the Master Key.

God searches all our hearts to find the Master Key of full surrender (2 Chronicles 16:9). He designed us to fully surrender all four chambers of our hearts vertically to Him so that, through our horizontal humility, He would reach the hearts of others. He desires that we seek *life* in Him with all of our hearts (Deuteronomy 4:29; Jeremiah 29:13). He wants us to cast His vision to *light* the world with all of our hearts (John 8:12; Colossians 3:23). He designed us to *listen* with all of our hearts (Psalm 119:34, 69, 145). He created us to *lean* into Him with all of our hearts (Proverbs 3:5). He invites us to *learn* with all of our hearts (Proverbs 4:4). He wants to lead us in order to *lead* others with all of our hearts (Ephesians 6:7; 1 Corinthians 11:1). He shaped us to *love* with all of our hearts (Deuteronomy 6:5; Matthew 22:37-40). He restores us to *let go,* or to forgive, with all of our hearts (Matthew 18:35).

The Master Key of full surrender unlocks the gate of our hearts to walk Restoration Road in authenticity, reflecting the design of the Designer.

To help you do the same, I developed a pattern for a simple *Restore Your Heart Chart.* Too often, our thoughts, feelings, choices, and prayers flow from sand- and stone-hearted perspectives that see ourselves in pretense. This is due to our own self-restoration programs that attempt to unlock ourselves from the prison of pride from the outside in. This is a tool for us to see ourselves not with the clouded perspectives of others, nor from our own clouded perspectives, but from God's authentic perspective of 20/20 vision.

Take out a sheet of paper and make five columns. Entitle the first column, *Time.* Underneath this heading, record the time when you have a destructive thought.

Entitle the second column, *Thoughts*. Write down the destructive thought. Search for any thought that compares, labels, or focuses on the outside at the expense of the inside.

Entitle the third column, *Feelings*. Write down the feelings that stem from the destructive thought: mad, sad, glad, afraid, or frustrated. Now you have a listing of emotions that correspond with the often-elusive thoughts that act as a catalyst.

Entitle the fourth column, *Choices*. Write down the choice you made regarding the specific thought and its corresponding emotion. For example, it could include speaking certain words, walking in a different direction, eating, drinking, smoking, exercising, buying, selling, or sleeping.

Entitle the fifth column, *Prayers*. After each destructive thought, feeling, and choice, take that thought captive and make it obedient to the Restorer who will transform pretense into authenticity over the course of time (2 Corinthians 10:5). Pray these words, *"I can't. You can. I can't deliver myself from this destructive thought. You can. Please take it away and restore me to seeing myself as You see me."*

In those storage room meetings with Derald, I discovered that everything in my life changed when I surrendered all four chambers of my spiritual heart to the Restorer. I chose, studied, prayed for, and wanted wisdom. That intersection of the vertical with the horizontal restored my heart, my desires, and my three resources of life. It all began by answering one question, a question I will ask you, "Have you ever thought about changing your scorecard of life from money and all that it promises to wisdom found in a heart of clay?"

The Restorer's Water

Partial surrender hardens an individual chamber of the heart. It results in compartmentalizing our lives. This, I have observed, becomes evident when we make New Year's resolutions. I have noticed that we typically make them in five areas of life: (1)

physical (body, to lose weight, work out more), (2) *financial* (the amount of money we choose to earn and invest, the purchases we plan to make, the expenses we decide to cut, or any other marketplace choices), (3) *mental* (books we plan to read or degrees we desire to achieve), (4) *spiritual* (a church we plan to attend, a ministry we desire to help, or a prayer life we desire to renew), and (5) *social* (relationships and the tasks we plan to accomplish with them).

Every New Year's Day, I used to set goals in each compartment of my life. A funny thing would happen. When I set these goals with a sand or stone heart, I created boundaries that did not previously exist. As a result, I compartmentalized God. However, as I grew in my vertical relationship, I began to realize that what I had written down on paper was designed to be much more a matter of the heart to release the Holy Spirit, or the Spirit of Christ, within me. Consequently, I desired a heart of clay that would be malleable in the hands of the Restorer, one that would align my vertical relationship with all of my horizontal life because *clay holds water.*

Water is a symbol for the Spirit of God used in the Old and New Testaments. When I compartmentalized my world, I hardened my heart in those respective chambers, damming up the flow of the Holy Spirit in my life. I became god, with a little *g*, in each area: whether it was physical, financial, mental, spiritual, or social. These represent the four chambers of the heart enveloped in our physical bodies: financial emphasizes the chamber of the *will;* mental represents the chamber of the *intellect*; spiritual is the chamber of the *spirit*; and social comprises the chamber of the *emotions.*

Because of the first sin, we have compartmentalized God and dammed the flow of the Holy Spirit in each chamber of our hearts. We have created boundaries that did not previously exist in God's design. We have chosen to become god in each chamber of our hardened hearts of sand and stone. However, God did not intend for it to be this way. Through the prophet Jeremiah, God said,

"My people have committed two sins: They have forsaken me, the spring of living water, and have dug their own cisterns, broken cisterns that cannot hold water" (Jeremiah 2:13).

Imagine the five compartments of life as five cisterns. A cistern is a receptacle for holding liquids. Cisterns are usually built to catch and store rainwater. Two thousand years ago in Palestine, early engineers would create cisterns at the bases of mountainous terrain. They would cover a basin of stone with plaster in order to fashion a cistern to hold water. After years of use, the plaster would crack, causing the stone cisterns to leak.

When we surrender all four chambers of our hearts along with our physical bodies via a heart of clay, we begin the flow of *water* in our lives. Whereas sand and stone hearts represent cisterns that separate the vertical from the horizontal, clay allows for flow at the sweet spot where the vertical intersects with the horizontal. Sand, stone, and clay are made from the same substances, but clay is finer. Clay allows our hearts to hold water that flows from our inlet to our outlet.

A *physical* cistern dams the flow of the Holy Spirit into our bodies. This is a big idea that we need to grasp. In the course of Scripture, God moved by dwelling in a tent, or a tabernacle, in the wilderness with the Israelites who had fled Egyptian slavery. Then God dwelled in a temple originally built by Solomon. The writers of Scripture indicate that God could never be confined to only the tabernacle or the temple; rather, these were holy places that depicted the vertical intersecting with the horizontal. The temple in Jerusalem was even referred to as "heaven and earth," the intersection of the vertical with the horizontal. Finally, Paul said that each of us who fully surrenders all four chambers of his heart to the Restorer becomes the walking temple of the Holy Spirit (1 Corinthians 6:19).

A heart of clay asks how the Holy Spirit can be released in our physical lives. If our pride prevents us from living with a heart of clay, we find our physical cistern begins to crack and is unable to hold the Living Water of life. We dam the flow of the Holy Spirit in our lives.

As I pondered the ramifications of releasing the Holy Spirit in my physical life, I considered how I could become more intentional in caring for the temple that God had given me. I began to do something that radically transformed my physical life: (1) *Word*, (2) *worship*, and (3) *workout*. I started to read the *Word* in the mornings. I almost always worked out in the mornings, but I had never worked out with aggressive *worship* music playing loudly. So I began each day with reading the *Word* and listening to *worship* music as I performed my *workout*. Often times, I would do all three at the same time on an elliptical machine. This produced a unique flow of *norepinephrine* and *endorphins* in me that gave me a *relaxed energy* for the day. I inhaled God so that I could exhale Him throughout the next twenty-four hours. Focusing on my inlet empowered me to bring the flow of water to my outlet.

A *financial* cistern represents the damming of the *will*, especially for a business owner. This hardening of the will stops the flow of the Holy Spirit in our financial world. An example of choosing to compartmentalize God from our finances occurs when we decide to arbitrarily give him ten percent of our gross income. This places God and our finances in a neat and tidy box. However, willfully surrendering our finances is not that simple. Someone's five percent might be more than most people's ten percent. God has intended something totally different than neat and tidy boxes that dam the flow of the Holy Spirit in our financial lives. Instead, He calls clay hearts to give one hundred percent of our time, talent, and treasure to release the Holy Spirit in our lives.

In essence, we give it *all* to God. Read carefully what God said to His people through Moses: "Be careful that you do not forget the Lord your God, failing to observe his commands, his laws and his decrees that I am giving you this day. Otherwise, when you eat and are satisfied, when you build fine houses and settle down, and when your herds and flocks grow large and your silver and gold increase and all you have is multiplied, then your heart will become proud and you will forget the Lord your God, who brought you out of Egypt, out of the land of slavery. He led you through the vast and dreadful desert, that thirsty and waterless land, with its venomous snakes and scorpions. He brought you water out of hard rock. He gave you manna to eat in the desert, something your fathers had never known, to humble and to test you so that in the end it might go well with you. You may say to yourself, 'My power and the strength of my hands have produced this wealth for me.' But remember the Lord your God, for it is he who gives you the ability to produce wealth, and so confirms his covenant, which he swore to your forefathers, as it is today" (Deuteronomy 8:11-18).

The Restorer was the spiritual rock providing the spiritual water to the Israelites (1 Corinthians 10:4). As I read about the cisterns in the Bible, and as my will softened, I was beginning to see Him as my inlet as well. When I applied this passage to my life, I realized that while I had made a lot of money, I had willfully built a cistern. I measured success and failure all in terms of money: my accomplishments and my shortfalls as well as my profits and my losses. Consequently, I had dammed the flow of water in my life. On my dirt road toward restoration, I began to see that a heart of clay called me to release my financial resources for God to use how He desired. My role was to surrender my heart to Him, including the chamber of my *will* which housed my financial decisions.

About the time that our business had made some improvement in our financial dilemma, I was invited to view our local homeless shelter's new facility. The first person who greeted me was a four year-old girl playing on the floor. She was the same age as my daughter. For the first time in my life, I realized that a child in DeKalb County could be homeless. After my tour, I went back to my office and wrote a check to the shelter that really stretched my sacrificial cardiac muscles. I learned that when my clay heart recognized God as the inlet for my financial resources, the result was an increased desire to help those in need through my outlet.

When we look at our *mental* cisterns, we see how often we seek knowledge for knowledge's sake apart from God. We grow from the newly retained information, and then we go on auto pilot making decisions predicated on the knowledge that we collected apart from God. Thoughts become a very safe place for a Christian to sin, to lust for someone who is not our spouse, or to desire a life we do not have. These will eventually come out of our mouths as well as in the way we steward our bodies. Consequently, we must release the Holy Spirit in our thoughts. Paul offered a solution to mental cisterns, "We demolish arguments and every pretension that sets itself up against the knowledge of God, and we take captive every thought to make it obedient to Christ" (2 Corinthians 10:5).

A heart of clay shows us that we will not succeed until we first release the Holy Spirit in our *intellects* and learn more about the Bible. If we continue to rely on our own knowledge, we will watch as another cistern begins to crack and the Living Water escapes. "Taking captive every thought" means that we identify any destructive idea or image in our minds that flows from a sand and stone cistern of pride. "Making it obedient to Christ" means that we surrender it to Him, experiencing His perspective, His mind, His wisdom. Identifying and surrendering destructive thoughts to the Restorer will transform our emotions that tend to follow our beliefs.

In order to release the water of the Holy Spirit in the clay chamber of my intellect, I committed to not only read a different translation of the Bible each year, but also to allow the Word to permeate my thoughts. I discovered that on my road toward authenticity I needed to have the Word of God in my mind. This empowered me to not think about merely what was in front of me; rather, I could indeed take captive every thought and make it obedient to the Restorer as His Living Water transformed my mind. I continue to identify destructive thoughts in my intellect and surrender them to the Restorer.

A *spiritual* cistern also compartmentalizes God. You might ask, *"How do we do that?"* Actually, this is one of the easiest to explain. We limit God to a particular worship style, in a specific building, during one hour, on a certain day of the week, or even a quiet time, a Bible study, or a small group. Then we take control of the other 167 hours of the week. Mankind has been doing this with sand and stone hearts since the first sin. However, God created a different design for His people, one that allowed the Holy Spirit to saturate all of our hearts all 168 hours a week.

"Hear, O Israel: The Lord our God, the Lord is one. Love the Lord your God with all your heart and with all your soul and with all your strength. These commandments that I give you today are to be upon your hearts. Impress them on your children. Talk about them when you sit at home and when you walk along the road, when you lie down and when you get up. Tie them as symbols on your hands and bind them on your foreheads. Write them on the doorframes of your houses and on your gates" (Deuteronomy 6:4-9).

I memorized these verses and recited them twice a day because I learned that was the pattern of its original audience, a pattern that was maintained for millennia. I took my spiritual cistern and surrendered it to God who released the Holy Spirit in my spiritual life. In turn, I gave God every moment that encapsulated every act as a spiritual one. With a heart of clay, I discovered that God was not meant to be compartmentalized. The spiritual was not fashioned for religion, but for relationships. When I fully surrendered my spirit to the Restorer, something unique happened. He restored my heart to authenticity, the way God designed it to be.

When we look at the *social* cistern we find friends, business associates, spouses, and children with whom we leverage relationships for our benefit only. We leverage these relationships for our benefit only. John offered a different way, one that would allow the flow of the Holy Spirit, "We love because he first loved us. If anyone says, 'I love God,' yet hates his brother, he is a liar. For anyone who does not love his brother, whom he has seen, cannot love God, whom he has not seen. And he has given us this command: Whoever loves God must also love his brother" (1 John 4:19-21). God calls us to self-sacrificial love. Solomon weighed in with his wisdom regarding relationships, "A man of many companions may come to ruin, but there is a friend who sticks closer than a brother" (Proverbs 18:24).

In Hebrew the phrase "many companions" and the word "ruin" come from the same root word. It is a picture of hardening our hearts and creating a cracked cistern that will not hold water. If we leave this cistern in its current state, it will break into pieces when it becomes brittle. Jesus' half-brother James warned, "You adulterous people, don't you know that friendship with the world is hatred toward God? Anyone who chooses to be a friend of the world becomes an enemy of God" (James 4:4). Does this mean we should not be friends with sinners like Jesus was? No; rather James revealed how having a heart of clay means being a friend to the lost of the world. A broken social cistern makes every re-lationship for our selfish benefit, but what would happen if we would release those relationships for God's glory, an increased thirst for God, a heart to release the Holy Spirit in them?

Releasing the Holy Spirit's water in my relationships meant demolishing my social cistern. This translated into reclaiming all of my relationships for advancing the heart of God in them. I ex-amined my friendships for ways in which I could help my friends experience the Spirit of God. I quit being stone-hearted with stone hearts and sand-hearted with sand hearts. Instead, I sought to have a clay heart in all of my friendships. This led to studying the Bible with several of my friends.

I focused on my business associates in order to discover how I could make sense of my relationship with God in my marketplace encounters. In my conversations with my customers, employ-ees, competitors, and vendors, I began to be transparent about my journey on Restoration Road. When I started having these conversations, I found out that many people were on the same journey that I was traveling.

The water of the Holy Spirit realigned my relationship with Susan and our girls by revealing the heart of the Restorer. I began to prioritize the most sacred relationships that I had neglected, searching for ways that I could travel less or bring my family to auctions with me. Living Water refreshed my relationships to resemble what the Designer had intended.

Jesus said that anyone who fully surrendered his heart to Him would experience the Living Water of the Holy Spirit flowing from his heart: "On the last day, that great day of the feast, Jesus stood and cried out, saying, 'If anyone thirsts, let him come to Me and drink. He who believes in Me, as the Scripture has said, out of his heart will flow rivers of Living Water.' But this He spoke concerning the Spirit, whom those believing in Him would receive; for the Holy Spirit was not yet given, because Jesus was not yet glorified" (John 7:37-39 NKJV).

Jesus' words were spoken in a loud voice during the last feast of the year, in the temple, where a crowd of hundreds of thousands had gathered. At the Feast of Tabernacles, the priests would lead the people out each day to their source of water, a process they repeated for seven days. They would come through the water gate that surrounded Jerusalem with a gold pitcher of water, and pour it on the altar to commemorate God leading them and providing physical water through the Exodus. Then they would pray for the autumn rains for their crops.

God's answer to those prayers far exceeds physical rain. He pours out Living Water that refreshes thirsty hearts by restoring their foolish desires to wisdom. The Restorer's ripple effect flows to you and me.

"At one time we too were foolish, disobedient, deceived and enslaved by all kinds of passions and pleasures. We lived in malice and envy, being hated and hating one another. But when the kindness and love of God our Savior appeared, he saved us, not because of righteous things we had done, but because of his mercy. He saved us through the washing of rebirth and renewal by the Holy Spirit, whom he poured out on us generously through Jesus Christ our Savior, so that, having been justified by his grace, we might become heirs having the hope of eternal life" (Titus 3:3-7).

Jesus Christ lived, died, was buried, resurrected, ascended into heaven, and provided His Spirit to live through those who fully surrender their hearts and lives to Him. God never intended for us to make cisterns. Rather, He designed all of life as an opportunity to release the Holy Spirit, or the Spirit of Christ, in us as we drink from the Spring of Living Water. *Flow* has always been the design of the Designer.

Here's an interesting experiment to do with your children in describing how God's influence needs to permeate every area of our lives. Fill five glasses with water as a symbol of the ways we compartmentalize God. Add a drop of red food coloring to one of the glasses, and observe that the color doesn't flow from one glass to any of the others. Next, pour the contents of each glass into a crystal pitcher. Then add a couple of more drops of red food coloring (indicative of the blood of Christ). Watch as the drops permeate the water, transforming the color from clear to red. This imagery represents how the flow of the Holy Spirit changes our lives to living color.

God said, "My people have committed two sins: They have forsaken me, the spring of living water, and have dug their own cisterns, broken cisterns that cannot hold water," (Jeremiah 2:13). The Restorer's blood paid the price for those sins. When we fully surrender our hearts to Him, He transforms our lives of black and white to living color by releasing the Holy Spirit in us. The Restorer flows through us and changes a culture thirsting for authenticity, the design of the Designer. The flow of the water of the

Holy Spirit transforms each person who fully surrenders his heart, desires, and life to Him.

I have learned that the Holy Spirit is enough to satisfy my heart's desires. I traveled across the globe struggling to build my own kingdom as I searched for something, anything, to quench the thirst in my heart. I tried compartmentalizing my life with cisterns: the *physical* pursuit, the *willful* drive for *financial* security, the *mental* exercise for more *intellectual* knowledge, the *spiritual* treadmill of good works, the *socio-emotional* experiment for more surface relationships. The flow of the Spirit of Christ was the only answer. He satisfied me when I fully surrendered my heart, desires, and life to Him. Today, the flow of His water of life continually satisfies my thirsty heart, allowing the Spirit of the Restorer in me to bring satisfaction to other thirsty hearts who desire to be restored to authenticity.

Chapter Eleven

RESTORING OUR FOUR DESIRES

A few years ago I flew in a private jet with hopes to auction an elderly couple's estate. This couple had never had children. I was asked by the executor to view their remaining assets (real estate, antiques, and collectible vehicles) to develop an appraisal and auction marketing plan. When I arrived, I discovered a farmhouse on one side and a barn on the other, nestled in a beautiful New England setting. When I was led inside to view the collectible items that would be auctioned, I was shocked at the condition of the interior of the farmhouse. It was literally filled with junk stuffed in boxes that were spread apart widely enough to form a maze through the various rooms. This is how the couple had lived, evidently for years. The boxes were filled with uncollectible items that the miserly couple could not bear to throw away. I also noticed I could see through the wood floor to the foundation underneath.

The man walking with me told me that this place was generating publicity all over New England. At first, I speculated that interest had been due to the old unrestored antique and classic cars parked in the couple's barn. Even in their dilapidated state, they were worth millions of dollars. However, that was not the reason why this estate was garnering the attention of the media. The estate's executors had discovered something unfathomable to add to this story. One million dollars worth of gold bars was hidden in the house's foundation.

The wealthy couple had lived like misers since the Great Depression, allowing their car collection to rust as they remained apathetic toward the potential impact of the resources lying at their fingertips. When I flew home, I thought about how their house had been a picture of my old unrestored life.

Like that old house, I had gold hidden away, nestled in the foundation of my life. I had desired to be a billionaire by the time I turned 40; I wanted to prove to the world that a Christian could do it. Building on that foundation resulted in a life that tilted with crooked priorities as its framework. With money rather than wisdom as my foundation, I failed to recognize the warning offered in Scripture: "But each one should be careful how he builds. For no one can lay any foundation other than the one already laid, which is Jesus Christ. If any man builds on this foundation using gold, silver, costly stones, wood, hay or straw, his work will be shown for what it is, because the Day will bring it to light. It will be revealed with fire, and the fire will test the quality of each man's work" (1 Corinthians 3:10-13).

In order to fuel my addiction, I desired more and more of a fix to feel the rush. I desired money like an addict desires his next hit. All four chambers of my spiritual heart proudly said, "I choose it. I think about it. I need it. I want it." Like an addict, the more I desired money, the less I had and the more I needed. My pursuit of the satisfaction of my desires apart from the Restorer left me dissatisfied.

The Designer created a blueprint for life that has wisdom as its foundation. Wisdom teaches that our desires are not for our gratification. They are intended to point us toward desiring God and lead us to transformation. These are desires that can only be satisfied in full surrender to the Restorer.

Along Desperation Road, the Restorer drew me to Himself in order to free me from my addiction. His desire that I pursue a heart filled with wisdom offered me that freedom. Solomon described its source, "Then you will understand the fear of the Lord and find the knowledge of God. For the Lord gives wisdom, and from his mouth come knowledge and understanding" (Proverbs 2:5-6). Through the Master Key of full surrender to the Restorer, He allowed me to discover wisdom that could only be found on Restoration Road.

Four Desires

Four primary God-given desires reside in each one of us to represent the heartbeat that connects our hearts with our three resources of life. Every choice, every thought, every prayer, every feeling is connected with every investment of time, talent, and treasure by the heartbeat to satisfy these desires. We see them in the very first book of the Bible. That's how foundational they are to our lives: "So God created man in his own image, in the image of God he created him; male and female he created them. God blessed them and said to them, 'Be fruitful and increase in number; fill the earth and subdue it. Rule over the fish of the sea and the birds of the air and over every living creature that moves on the ground.' Then God said, 'I give you every seed-bearing plant on the face of the whole earth and every tree that has fruit with seed in it. They will be yours for food. And to all the beasts of the earth and all the birds of the air and all the creatures that move on the ground—everything that has breath of life in it—I give every green plant for food.' And it was so" (Genesis 1:27-30).

The first primary God-given desire is *significance,* which comes from being created in God's image (Genesis 1:27). The second desire is *contentment* from being blessed by God to be fruitful, multiply, and subdue (to bring contentment to) the earth (Genesis 1:28). The third desire is *control* from being empowered by God to rule over the earth (Genesis 1:28). The fourth desire is *security* from being provided with every seed-bearing plant and fruit-bearing tree (Genesis 1:29-30).

Notice that each desire is from our *being*, or our identity in the Designer, who is also our Restorer. These desires flow vertically from the heart of God into each one of our spiritual hearts, and they flow horizontally into our relationships with others (Genesis 2:18).

Our pursuit of the satisfaction of each desire leads with a particular chamber of the heart. One who attempts to satisfy his desire for *significance* leads with *emotions*. One who attempts to satisfy his desire for *contentment* leads with the *spirit*. One who attempts to satisfy his desire for *control* leads with the *will*. One who attempts to satisfy his desire for *security* leads with the *intellect*. Even though one leads with a heart chamber when pursuing a particular desire, all four chambers of the heart flow toward each pursuit.

God has given us these desires for a purpose: to be satisfied in Him and to bring a saving knowledge of that satisfaction to others.

David fully surrendered his heart and his desires to God. He described the process of knowing God's heart in a psalm, "Delight yourself in the LORD and he will give you the desires of your heart" (Psalm 37:4). "Delight," *anag* in Hebrew, means "to make one's heart pliable." In essence, it is a surrendered heart that is humble toward God like clay in the Potter's hands. "Give" is translated from *nathan* in Hebrew, meaning "to orchestrate." As previously stated, desires represent the heartbeat that connects our hearts with our three resources of life. Thus, when our hearts become malleable in God's hands, He makes our desires to be like His. This is how we experience God's will in our lives.

God created Adam and Eve with humble hearts. The focal point of their satisfaction was God. In their pride, they desired *significance*, *contentment*, *control* and *security* apart from God. With a little encouragement from the serpent, they convinced themselves they were making the right decision. The result was pride, the first sin recorded in Scripture.

In the Sermon on the Mount, Jesus offered an authentic alternative to the satisfaction of our desires: *wisdom*. When we examine them individually, we learn that attempting to satisfy our desires by gaining wealth measured by money will never be enough to satisfy us. It will always leave us dissatisfied. Additionally, we discover that wisdom not only satisfies our four primary desires, but it also leads to their restoration.

Significance

Would a little extra money satisfy any of your desires? Do you want to decrease your liabilities? Perhaps you desire to reduce your mortgage, pay off your car, or eliminate credit-card debt. Do you want to increase your assets? Maybe you want to buy a new car, a new boat, a new house, a new set of golf clubs, a new technological device, or a new piece of jewelry. Money, in and of itself, is not evil. Owning stuff is not from the devil, as some of us were told growing up in the church. Our problem occurs when the stuff owns us. Ironically, it is not money that we desire, rather it is something deeper.

Money is pride's measurement of our giftedness (time, talent, and treasures). Wisdom is humility's measurement of our godliness (Christ in us). Jesus is "gentle and humble in heart" (Matthew 11:29), and He is the "wisdom of God" (1 Corinthians 1:24). Humility toward Christ is the beginning of His wisdom in our lives. Solomon noted, "When pride comes, then comes disgrace, but with humility comes wisdom" (Proverbs 11:2).

In the Sermon on the Mount, we see Jesus, the Restorer, warn His disciples about attempting to satisfy their desires with money. He offered wisdom as an alternative. The first desire He addressed was *significance* (Matthew 6:19-21).

Pride seeks significance from money. Jesus said, "Do not store up for yourselves treasures on earth" (Matthew 6:19). Why do we store up treasures on earth? We do it to find significance. Significance is "expressed meaning, purpose, importance, or value." Significance can be encapsulated in attention, acceptance, affection, and approval. Notice that the first four letters of significance comprise the word "sign" which says, "Look at me." People might say, "Look at him. He is successful." Others say, "Look at her. She's got it all." We often say to ourselves, "Storing up this stuff really satisfies. I feel significant."

The result is insignificance. Jesus continued, "…where moth and rust destroy and thieves break in and steal" (Matthew 6:19). In the end, the stuff is just that: stuff. The more we pursue it as the satisfaction of our desires, the more we thirst for more. The result is a never-ending cycle of dissatisfaction.

But humility stores up relationships. Jesus said, "Store up for yourselves treasures in heaven, where moth and rust do not destroy, and thieves do not break in and steal" (Matthew 5:20). Relationships are the only treasure that we can store up in heaven because they are eternal. These relationships flow vertically in communion with God and horizontally in community with others.

The truth is that our treasures reveal the object of our desires. Jesus said, "For where your treasure is, there your heart will be also" (Matthew 5:21). Valuing people over profit, or relationships over remuneration, is what God designed for our lives. A proud heart searches for significance from money. A humble heart discovers significance in a relationship with the Restorer and shares that relationship with others.

The result is the love of God in Christ (John 3:16).

Christ is the love of God, a love that is so undeserved, a favor that is so unmerited, that it is called "grace." John recorded the ultimate picture of this undeserved love in one of Scripture's most popular verses, "For God so loved the world that he gave his one and only Son, that whoever believes in him shall not perish but have eternal life" (John 3:16). When we believe this we are free to bring His satisfying Spirit to our relationships with a love that sacrificially serves others.

Paul defined the sacrifice of the Restorer's grace, "For you know the grace of our Lord Jesus Christ, that though he was rich, yet for your sakes he became poor, so that you through his poverty might become rich" (2 Corinthians 8:9). Christ is our image of God.

Christ, the father in the parable, is the answer to every single person's desire. We were created to be satisfied in Him. Christ is the answer to transforming our desires. Christ actually created us, sustains us, and restores us (Colossians 1:15-23). Our answer for *significance* is found in His love. There is no greater love than that which the father shows in the parable, the same love that Jesus Christ offered every single person when He walked the earth: "The Word became flesh and made his dwelling among us. We have seen his glory, the glory of the One and Only, who came from the Father, full of grace and truth" (John 1:14).

I had decided to forego my dream of earning an MBA from Harvard to learn from billionaires how they had amassed such great wealth. One of the most successful real estate holders in America was a mentor of mine when I graduated from Indiana University. I stayed at his home, a 22,000 square-foot stone chateau that had been imported piece by piece from France. Many celebrities had stayed in his guest house.

Interestingly, when I asked him why he sold a particular car that he had sought for so long for $1,500,000 profit, he responded that he liked counting the extra 1,500 one thousand dollar bills better than having the car, which was a symbol of status and significance.

This man had it all. He had money, coveted income-producing assets, and hundreds of the greatest classic and sports cars on the planet. Yet, something I said on the telephone one day seemed to be significant to him.

We were discussing the cars he was going to consign to our Labor Day Weekend Auction. At the close of our discussion, in appreciation for all he had done for me, I said, "I love you, man." Each of us placed the receiver back on the telephone. Thirty seconds later, I received an all-page as I walked through our office. I picked up the telephone. The voice on the other end was my same mentor.

"Do you really mean that?" He asked.

"Mean what?" I inquired.

"What you said."

"When I was hanging up the phone?"

"Yes."

"Of course," I said.

"God will get you if you don't mean it," he replied with a hint of humor.

"I do," I said reassuringly, and we said, "Good bye."

I learned that day that our desire for significance is only satisfied in love, a love that is manifested in storing up relationships, both vertically with the Restorer through His unmerited favor, or undeserved love, and horizontally in relationships where we seek the best for all involved.

I took this learning into my everyday life. For example, I thought for a while about the reasons why I called my customers, and I realized that the answer to that question was that I called solely to help them buy or sell something. So I began to call once in a while just to ask about their lives, to learn about their needs, to understand their desires, and to build relationships rather than focus on remuneration. I learned the tremendous value of community. It was something that money could never buy.

When you discover the satisfaction of your desire for significance in the love of Christ, you take that love to others. You initiate conversations with your customers, prospects, friends and family. You get to know them, ask questions and listen, rather than attempt to work those relationships for your benefit. You do it just for the sake of relationships—storing up treasures in heaven rather than storing up stuff on earth. When your spouse, family, friends, associates and those in need connect relationally through the way you serve them, then you'll find satisfaction. You will be significant. You will be loved. You will no longer be an addict with a sand or stone heart, like the two sons, but a lover of a clay heart, like the father in Jesus' trilogy.

Seek God's wisdom, allowing money to be a byproduct of relationships. Seek intimacy with your customers, vendors, employees, employers, family, or friends as you seek intimacy with God. Read a chapter in Proverbs each day corresponding to the date of the month, applying this wisdom to your tasks and relationships, including your finances.

When life is centered in Christ as we become clay in His hands, we discover that His *love* is greater than our desire for *significance*.

Contentment

Who is more content, the person with a million dollars or the person with ten children? You probably guessed the person with ten children, and you are correct. He is more content because he does not want any more. That is the definition of contentment: being in a state or a situation where you're not wanting anything more or anything different. It literally means "held together."

The desire for *contentment* comes from being blessed by God to be fruitful, multiply, and subdue (bring contentment to) the earth (Genesis 1:28). This desire flows vertically from the heart of God into each one of our hearts. It also flows horizontally in our relationships with one another (Genesis 2:18).

Pride seeks contentment from money. Jesus taught, "But if your eyes are bad, your whole body will be full of darkness" (Matthew 6:23). Two thousand years ago, a "bad eye" was a greedy one. It desired something more or different than the time, talent, and treasure given by God. We read earlier how Paul equated greed with idolatry (Colossians 3:5) because the eyes of the heart are focused on something other than God for contentment.

Today, when we want something more or something different we believe money will get it. With more money, we can acquire a different car, a different spouse, a different house, a different job, or even a different church.

The result is discontentment. Jesus continued, "If then the light within you is darkness, how great is that darkness" (Matthew 6:23). Darkness is discontentment. Solomon said, "Whoever loves money never has money enough; whoever loves wealth is never satisfied with his income. This too is meaningless" (Ecclesiastes 5:10). Jesus and Solomon both said that seeking contentment apart from God leads to discontentment. Regardless of how much money we have, we will never be satisfied.

Humility seeks generosity. "The eye is the lamp of the body. If your eyes are good, your whole body will be full of light" (Matthew 6:22). The figurative meaning here is clear: what you choose to take in with your eyes, that's what your heart focuses on. Two thousand years ago, saying that a person had a good eye meant that he had a generous, content, loyal, and focused eye.

Today, we use the term "good eye" when a batter lets a bad pitch go by. The batter is content enough to let the foolish opportunity pass. When we are content, we do not need something more or something different. We are wise enough to allow life's bad pitches to go by as we become generous with our time, talent, and treasure. Rather than focus on our giftedness, we focus on our godliness and live in contentment.

The result is the peace of God in Christ (Ephesians 2:14).

Light is a metaphor in Scripture used for the spiritual vitality of life. Christ is that light. John recorded, "When Jesus spoke again to the people, he said, 'I am the light of the world. Whoever follows me will never walk in darkness, but will have the light of life" (John 8:12). When we fully surrender our hearts and desires to Christ, we embody and reflect His light. A body full of light is a body full of peace, and Christ is the peace of God who holds us together. Paul said, "For he himself is our peace, who has made the two one and has destroyed the barrier, the dividing wall of hostility" (Ephesians 2:14). Christ brings that divine peace into our lives in communion with Him so that we will share it in community with others. Jesus proclaimed to his disciples, "Peace I leave with you; my peace I give you. I do not give to you as the world gives. Do not let your hearts be troubled and do not be afraid" (John 14:27). He summarized, "I have told you these things, so that in me you may have peace. In this world you will have trouble. But take heart! I have overcome the world" (John 16:33). Christ is our blessing of peace.

Paul taught that focusing on our godliness over our giftedness brings contentment, but he offered a warning against the pursuit of money for contentment, saying, "Godliness with contentment is great gain. For we brought nothing into the world, and we can take nothing out of it. But if we have food and clothing, we will be content with that. People who want to get rich fall into temptation and a trap and into many foolish and harmful desires that plunge men into ruin and destruction. For the love of money is a root of all kinds of evil. Some people, eager for money, have wandered from the faith and pierced themselves with many griefs" (1 Timothy 6:6-10).

In Paul's letter to the church at Philippi, he communicated that the peace that passes all understanding comes from a content, or thankful, heart surrendered to Christ in prayer (Philippians 4:6-7). He went on to say that the secret of contentment was that he could do all things through Christ who gave him restorative strength. "I know what it is to be in need, and I know what it is to have plenty. I have learned the secret of being content in any and every situation, whether well fed or hungry, whether living in plenty or want. I can do everything through him who gives me strength" (Philippians 4:12-13).

Paul discovered contentment in the Giver, not the gifts.

Although I had read Paul's words many times, I thought that contentment came from money. I deduced that if I had enough, I would be free to help others. I had a dream of building my family a symbol of my supposed contentment: a large Georgian classic house. I had kept a "new home" file that was almost 6 inches thick. It included exterior and interior photos of attractive designs torn from magazines that I had combed for ideas to incorporate into our dream home, *someday*. After July 1, 1992, I realized that I might never build that place, or palace, I should say, and strangely enough, that was okay. For the first time in a long time, I was content.

Just before the restoration of Kruse International, I had been struggling in my sand-hearted condition. During a trip through Germany where I had been meeting with prospective buyers and sellers of premier classic and sports cars, I had discovered a proverbial hidden treasure. It was a Horch twelve-cylinder special roadster built in the 1930's, now stored in a small garage across from the owner's flat in a gorgeous German village. As the owner and I were looking at the restored twelve cylinder power plant under the hood, he shared his philosophy about contentment and money. He was most likely describing why he valued this multi-million dollar car, yet lived in a modest home. In his German-accented English, he reflected.

"You know Mitchell, there are two ways to live life. One is to make a lot of money in hopes that you will *someday* be able to enjoy it. The other is to enjoy it as you go. I've chosen the latter."

His wisdom foreshadowed my restored clay heart perspective in the pursuit of contentment.

Several years later, after multiple seasons of huge losses and seemingly infinite accounts payable at Kruse International, we finally experienced the first twelve months of breaking even on the bottom line. I sat behind the wheel of my car overcome with a new perspective on money. I realized how content I was—not from money, but from realizing that I could trust the Restorer for contentment. I was not spending time worrying about our income tax burden, nor was I stressing over being unable to pay vendors. Breaking even was a symbol of contentment. For a moment, I did not want anymore.

I remember calling Derald from my car to tell him of my newly discovered thankfulness that had been revealed to me at the intersection of 15th and Grandstaff Streets in Auburn. I realized that contentment is satisfied in the peace of the Restorer. By trusting in my godliness rather than my giftedness, I was freed from micromanaging profitable outcomes. The Apostle Paul summed it up when he spoke against those who used godliness as a means to financial gain, "But godliness with contentment is great gain" (1 Timothy. 6:6).

What would happen if you were generous with your time, talent, and treasure? Would you be content enough in Christ to give to someone in need? Would you spend extra time with your spouse or children, allowing them to set the agenda? Would you invest your talent into a coworker? Would you give some of your treasure to a neighbor who's struggling? Imagine if you let life's bad pitches go by and lived content in the peace of God in Christ, the focal point of the eyes of your heart. This is yet another step you can take as you travel Restoration Road to live restored to authenticity.

When life is centered in Christ as we become clay in His hands, we discover that His *peace* is greater than our desire for *contentment*.

Control

Do you desire money for the control that it brings?

"Control" literally means "to roll against." It is the extension of our will over another person or object. We attempt to control others, our own lives, or even God. The desire for control comes from people being empowered by God to rule over the earth and to use that control to humbly serve Him (Genesis 1:28).

One aspect of pride for many people involves serving money instead of God. But Jesus taught, "No one can serve two masters"

(Matthew 6:24). Jesus knew that our desire for control would be abused in a dualistic lifestyle where we would attempt to selfishly control others for our own purposes to try to bring some order into our own lives. When we serve multiple masters, we have to find different ways to manage those relationships. Our lives, as a result, can become out of control. Jesus continued, "Either he will hate the one and love the other, or he will be devoted to the one and despise the other" (Matthew 6:24). The attempt to serve two masters really boils down to just serving one—our own selfish desires. At some point the two interests collide, leaving us with a choice of which master we will serve. The attempt to serve two masters really boils down to just serving one—our own selfish desires. The question is "Who or what has ultimate control of our lives, God or money?" It depends on whether we are controlled by the Spirit of the Restorer or our own sinful, dinged up nature.

Paul elaborated, "Those who live according to the sinful nature have their minds set on what that nature desires; but those who live in accordance with the Spirit have their minds set on what the Spirit desires. The mind of sinful man is death, but the mind controlled by the Spirit is life and peace; the sinful mind is hostile to God. It does not submit to God's law, nor can it do so. Those controlled by the sinful nature cannot please God" (Romans 8:5-8).

Humility seeks to serve God. Jesus concluded, "You cannot serve both God and money" (Matthew 6:24). As previously mentioned, God's design for control was for us to serve Him. We flesh this out by humbly serving others rather than controlling them. In doing so, our unselfish desires are satisfied as well as the desires of God and the person served (Philippians 2:3-5).

The result is the power of God in Christ being made known in our relationships (1 Corinthians 1:24).

Paul taught that he had discovered power in humility: "But he said to me, 'My grace is sufficient for you, for my power is made perfect in weakness.' Therefore I will boast all the more gladly about my weaknesses, so that Christ's power may rest on me.

That is why, for Christ's sake, I delight in weaknesses, in insults, in hardships, in persecutions, in difficulties. For when I am weak, then I am strong" (2 Corinthians 12:9-10). This power is the Spirit of the Restorer dwelling in us.

Great power resides in humbly serving others because it frees us from pride's bondage and draws others to Christ in us while we grow in our intimacy with both. The more we give up control, the more we find it resides in us. Christ is the power of God (1 Corinthians 1:24) and His complete power is unlocked in our lives through the key of humility. The sooner we realize that ultimate control rests in the hands of the Restorer, the sooner we're able to live our lives in greater freedom.

Paul communicated to those who desired to be restored to authenticity that they were to be controlled by the Spirit of the Restorer, "You, however, are controlled not by the sinful nature but by the Spirit, if the Spirit of God lives in you. And if anyone does not have the Spirit of Christ, he does not belong to Christ. But if Christ is in you, your body is dead because of sin, yet your spirit is alive because of righteousness. And if the Spirit of him who raised Jesus from the dead is living in you, he who raised Christ from the dead will also give life to your mortal bodies through his Spirit, who lives in you" (Romans 8:9-11).

In an effort to fully surrender my business to the Restorer, I developed a mission statement for Kruse International, "Serve God and others." I placed it on our brochures discreetly under the postal indicia. Sometimes, I would include a verse from Proverbs merely to spark the thought of wisdom's relevance to anyone who would read it. One day I received a call from Australia from a collector who wanted to sell a rare and desirable vehicle in one of our mainland events. After walking through how we would market the vehicle upon its arrival, he agreed to sell it through us. This was his first time to auction a collector car.

I met the collector from down under for the first time at our corporate offices in Auburn. We were standing in a foyer beside a display of brochures for our upcoming events when he selected one from the rack and turned to the back cover containing our mission statement and the verse from Proverbs. When he picked up the brochure, I thought that maybe he wanted to purchase another vehicle pictured on the cover with the proceeds from the sale of his car. But instead he touched the brochure just below the mission statement and Bible verse.

Now the recovering perfectionist's voice sounded off inside my head, *"Oh no. I blew it with that idea. I'm sure I turned him off. Here it comes."*

"You know, before I called you, I noticed this line on your brochures," he said as he referenced this statement and the verse. "I just want you to know that I noticed it. I realize someone can talk these things and walk a totally different path; however, I felt like it was worth taking a chance to cross the pond for someone who was willing to stand up and be counted."

I learned that day that our desire for control is satisfied in the power discovered in the Restorer, who calls us to serve Him and others. Paul offered the secret to the satisfaction of our desires as well as the desires of those around us, "Do nothing out of selfish ambition or vain conceit, but in humility consider others better than yourselves. Each of you should look not only to your own interests, but also the interests of others. Your attitude should be the same as that of Christ Jesus" (Philippians 2:3-5). When we humble ourselves vertically to God and horizontally to others, we discover the sweet spot where our unselfish desires intersect with God's interest and the interests of others. This became a benchmark for me to discover wisdom in every business deal.

I began an enduring and profitable relationship with my friend from the Outback who had many more significant cars to auction. In serving him and building an authentic friendship, I found the proverbial sweet spot where my unselfish interests intersected with his as well as the interests of the Restorer.

When presented with the choice of serving God or money, choose God because serving two masters is serving one. Flesh this out by humbly serving every person that you encounter with your time, talent, and treasure. You can serve the other person's interests while at the same time serving your unselfish interests and God's — the sweet spot where the vertical intersects with the horizontal. It will not merely be you who is serving, but Christ in you.

When life is centered in Christ, as we become clay in His hands, we discover that His *power* is greater than our desire for *control*.

Security

Would you like to achieve financial security? How much money would it take for you to have it? Having security means that one does not have to worry; there is an assured supply of resources available to fill our needs. We can trust in one resource to be true all the time. This desire for security comes from God providing man every seed-bearing plant and every fruit-bearing tree (Genesis 1:29). In so doing, he provided everything Adam and Eve needed in the garden. That was true security!

But pride seeks security from money. Jesus taught, "Therefore I tell you, do not worry about your life, what you will eat or drink; or about your body, what you will wear" (Matthew 6:25a). When our hearts are hard, we focus on our own selfish desires; we see money as the ticket to the doorway of security. We desire to be financially secure so that our needs will always be met. This leads us to a life of worry, because the pursuit of money always leaves us fearful that we will not have enough. Deep inside our hearts, we are not merely trusting in money for security, we are trusting in ourselves — our ability to earn, keep, and grow a stockpile of cash.

The result is insecurity. "Is not life more important than food, and the body more important than clothes? Look at the birds of the air; they do not sow or reap or store away in barns, and yet your heavenly Father feeds them. Are you not much more valuable than they? Who of you by worrying can add a single hour to his life? And why do you worry about clothes? See how the lilies of the field grow. They do not labor or spin. Yet I tell you that not even Solomon in all his splendor was dressed like one of these. If that is how God clothes the grass of the field, which is here today and tomorrow is thrown into the fire, will he not much more clothe you, O you of little faith? So do not worry, saying, 'What shall we eat?' or 'What shall we drink?' of 'What shall we wear?' For the pagans run after all these things, and your heavenly Father knows that you need them" (Matthew 6:25b-32). The more we pursue the satisfaction of our desire for security apart from God, the more insecure we become. Insecurity is worrying that our resource of supply will not remain true. Worry is literally a divided mind, or heart. We trust in God a little and in ourselves a lot. We think that by doing so we will add security to our lives.

A multi-billionaire gave a billion dollars (a million thousand dollar bills) to one of his favorite causes. He was interviewed by a national network's morning news anchor who insightfully asked him about financial security. He replied, "I wake up every morning afraid that I'm going to lose it all." Imagine a billionaire worrying about that! Yet, remember the older couple that we talked about at the start of this chapter. Again we are reminded that financial security is not discovered in money.

We were created by God to function by trust in Him; however, sometimes we have trust in the wrong object—that which is temporary, rather than that which is eternal. Jesus summed it up as having *"little faith"* (Matthew 6:30). Paul called it walking by sight—having faith in what we see around us rather than believing in Who is in us (2 Corinthians 4:18; 5:7). When we worry, we trust in the gifts rather than the Giver, in our giftedness rather than our godliness.

Our insecurity perpetuates the need to test and prove that our resources are true. So we find ourselves leveraging our time, talent, and treasure toward those ends. This occurs most frequently where our self-trust is highest: in tasks where we are skilled or in relationships where we are most familiar. The outcome is a never-ending cycle of trusting in our giftedness to prove our security, and the outcome is further insecurity.

Jesus commanded us to stop the cycle of insecurity, saying, "Do not worry" (Matthew 6:31). Worrying is for the proud who do not trust God; the humble trust that God knows their needs (Matthew 6:32).

Humility seeks first God's kingdom and His righteousness. Jesus began to bottom-line the pursuit of our desires, "But seek first his kingdom and his righteousness, and all these things will be given to you as well" (Matthew 6:33a). Remember, God's kingdom is His divine reign, rule, and order in the hearts and lives of people on this earth now and in the future. It is the effective reach of His will. God's righteousness is what is right in His sight. The two intersect to form wisdom: God's righteousness combined with street smarts (the shrewd reach of God's will into our tasks and relationships).

Wisdom is not a principle; it is a person. Christ the wisdom of God came as the Righteous One (1 John 2:1) to inaugurate the renewal of God's kingdom (Mark 1:15). When we humble our hearts to Him, we experience the security of God's kingdom and righteousness in our lives. Solomon, the pinnacle of wisdom, said that the fear of the Lord (humility) was the ticket to the door-way of security (Proverbs 14:26). This humility seeks to prioritize God's will in our tasks and our relationships.

The result is the truth of God in Christ (John 14:6). Jesus con-cluded, "And all these things will be given to you as well. There-fore do not worry about tomorrow, for tomorrow will worry about itself. Each day has enough trouble of its own" (Matthew 6:33b-34). These things represent our needs. Paul reiterated, "And my God will meet all your needs according to his glorious riches in Christ Jesus" (Philippians 4:19). God satisfies our desire for security with the truth of God in Christ. John recorded Jesus' response to Thomas' question inquiring the way to God, "Jesus answered, 'I am the way and the truth and the life. No one comes to the Father except through me'" (John 14:6). Christ is the truth of God. He is the well of wisdom that will never run dry.

When I was growing up, I was privileged to get to know one of my dad's best friends, Fred Hunter. Fred owned thousands of apartment units and knew each tenant by name. He was a brilliant, deep voiced, tall, charismatic Scotsman. One time when being pulled over by a police officer for speeding, Fred rolled down the window of his car and spoke solely in Scottish. The officer let him go.

Fred talked to me about how all the anxiety of his business interests caused him to spend so much time worrying. One day he decided to make an appointment to set aside twenty minutes to worry about money. The appointment began at one o'clock.

I remember Fred describing it this way. "Mitchell, I sat in my desk chair and started to worry about money. I was about five minutes into my worry time when I realized something. How stupid was this? What a waste of time! Mitchell, how many more times do you think I made an appointment to worry? None!"

Fred was indirectly quoting the Restorer when He asked, "Who of you by worrying can add a single hour to his life?" (Matthew 6:27). I learned that day that security is satisfied in the truth of the Restorer even though many still worry about their financial security. A renowned financial advisor told me, "I know many billionaires. None of them would say he is financially secure." He was saying that financial security merely based on money does not exist.

Solomon said, "Wisdom is a shelter as money is a shelter, but the advantage of knowledge is this: that wisdom preserves the life of its possessor" (Ecclesiastes 7:12). That extra hour of life that we are seeking by worrying is infinitely found in wisdom. The psalmist added that the person who humbly trusts God will have no fear, and his heart will be secure (Psalm 112:7-8).

Try this little experiment. First, sit down for twenty minutes and write down everything that worries you. After you experience the insanity of this simple exercise, commit to not worry again about the things on the page in front of you. Give them back to God, the only One Who can heal your concerns. Second, pray. Humbly trust God with all of your concerns by seeking first His will in your life. Make your muscles move with your prayers by working wisely.

When life is centered in Christ as we become clay in His hands, we discover His truth is greater than our desire for security.

Solomon philosophized, "Of what use is money in the hand of a fool, since he has no desire to get wisdom?" (Proverbs 17:16).

Changing my target of success from money to wisdom unlocked the door to restoration and brought me closer to my authentic condition. I had been a fool for desiring money at the expense of wisdom. I was amazed to discover how the book of Proverbs positioned wisdom as our target to the satisfaction of our four primary desires. If you do not believe it, read what King Solomon said.

Wisdom as our target satisfies our desire for *significance* in *love*. Wisdom personified proclaimed, "I love those who love me, and those who seek me find me" (Proverbs 8:17). Solomon reflected on what satisfies our hearts, "What a man desires is unfailing love" (Proverbs 19:22).

Wisdom as our target satisfies our desire for *contentment* in *peace*. Solomon advised young leaders about this, "Her ways are pleasant ways, and all her paths are peace" (Proverbs 3:17). He went on to say that humility toward the Restorer renews contentment, "The fear of the Lord leads to life: Then one rests content, untouched by trouble" (Proverbs 19:23).

Wisdom as our target satisfies our desire for *control* in *power*. Solomon noted, "A wise man has great power, and a man of knowledge increases strength" (Proverbs 24:5). It is interesting how wisdom and control are so practically intertwined, "A fool gives full vent to his anger, but a wise man keeps himself under control" (Proverbs 29:11). Wisdom helps us control ourselves.

Wisdom as our target satisfies our desire for *security* in *truth*. In The Thirty Sayings of the Wise, Solomon recorded, "Buy the truth and do not sell it; get wisdom, discipline and understanding" (Proverbs 23:23). Again, wisdom personified calls out, "My mouth speaks what is true" (Proverbs 3:7). Solomon elaborated on how humility toward the Restorer was the key that unlocked the door to an enduring transferable satisfaction of the desire for security, "He who fears the Lord has a secure fortress, and for his children it will be a refuge" (Proverbs 14:26). Contrastingly, Solomon communicated that the pursuit of money at the expense of wisdom does not satisfy one's desire for lasting security, "For riches do not endure forever, and a crown is not secure for all generations" (Proverbs 27:24).

The Pure in Heart

What do you add to your devotion to God to satisfy your desires?

The equation usually looks like this: God + blank = satisfaction. What do you place in your blank? It might be money, sex outside of God's design, pornography, risk, a rush, a smoke, a toke, a drink or a line. It might seem as innocent as attention, affection, acceptance, approval, influence, an attractive spouse, well-behaved children, or even religion. The result is a mixed devotion of the heart because of those desires. The Bible alludes to these mixed devotions as impurities, or idols, because they compete with our full devotion to God. The apostle John said that anyone who does evil has not seen God. (3 John 11). Jesus offered us a different way. He said, "Blessed are the pure in heart, for they will see God" (Matthew 5:8).

Who are satisfied?

The pure in heart.

The Bible uses the word "pure" most frequently to reference precious metal—usually gold. Precious metals must be refined to become pure. This process involves generating intense heat that brings impurities to the top of the crucible (silver) or the furnace (gold) so that the refiner, our Restorer, can remove them. The deepest impurities rise last, after an intense time of being tested by fire. Just like the crucible is used for silver, and the furnace for gold, so God tests our hearts to discover whether they are pure—wholly devoted, or fully surrendered, to Him (Proverbs 17:3). Paul warned us to not be led away from our pure and sincere devotion to Christ, the Restorer (2 Corinthians 11:3).

Our ultimate example of a pure heart is the heart of the Restorer. The Bible tells us that Christ is pure in heart (1 John 3:3; Hebrews 7:26). He demonstrated a fully surrendered heart that was fully devoted to the Father, a heart with unmixed devotion to God.

Why are they satisfied?

Because they will see God.

The God of the universe will demonstrate His kingdom in their hearts and lives. They will see the Restorer in themselves. This is illustrated in the molding of silver or gold. The metal refining process continues until we see the reflection of the Restorer's pure heart in us (Romans 8:29). When God sees the Restorer in us, we see God. David said that our desires will be satisfied when we see Him. "And I—in righteousness I will see your face; when I awake, I will be satisfied with seeing your likeness" (Psalm 17:15). David said that God shows Himself pure to the pure in heart, but He judges those with mixed devotions (2 Samuel 22:27; cf. Psalms 18:26). Addressing those with impurities, God promised to reveal Himself to anyone who would seek Him with all of his heart (Jeremiah 29:13).

How are they satisfied?

They surrender their impurities, their mixed devotions, and relying on their giftedness rather than their godliness.

Surrender says to God, "I can't. You can. I can't satisfy my desires with mixed devotions. You can when I am fully devoted to You." In order to do this, we need to do what David did.

First, we ask God to search our heart for any mixed devotions: "Search me, O God, and know my heart; test me and know my anxious thoughts. See if there is any offensive way in me, and lead me in the way everlasting" (Psalm 139:23-24).

Second, we ask God to create in us a pure heart. "Create in me a pure heart, O God, and renew a steadfast spirit within me" (Psalm 51:10).

A life restored to authenticity moves us to search our hearts for any mixed devotion, any selfish desires, to renew in us a pure heart—one that is fully devoted to restoration in the Father.

What I learned from both sons in Jesus' trilogy, as well as my own journey, was that sin is a desire for *any* life apart from God. It attempts to find *significance*, *contentment*, *control*, and *security* in everything else but Him. The irony is that the more I tried to find significance in my giftedness and not my godliness, the more insignificant I became. The more I tried to find contentment in my giftedness and not my godliness, the more discontent I became. The more I pursued control in my giftedness and not my godliness, the more out of control my life became. The more I tried to find security in my giftedness and not my godliness, the more insecure I became.

Paul described a pure heart condition, the object of our search, and the resulting satisfaction of full surrender to the Restorer when he said, "Flee the evil desires of youth, and pursue righteousness, faith, love and peace, along with those who call on the LORD out of a pure heart" (2 Timothy 2:22). When we flee our evil desires of proudly searching for satisfaction apart from Christ, we humbly turn with a pure heart to the Restorer where we find satisfaction of our desires. Righteousness is what is right in God's sight, which is truth that satisfies our desire for security. Faith is trusting in God rather than ourselves for control, and that brings power. Love is self-sacrificial serving where we discover our ultimate significance. Peace is absence of strife in our relationships, satisfying our desire for contentment.

Imagine life being like a wheel. Two roads travel to the outside of the wheel: stone and sand. One road leads to the center: clay. In our hurriedness, business ambition, worry or anxiety, we attempt to live at the outside of a wheel that seems to move faster and cover more ground as we trust in our giftedness rather than our godliness. However, Christ is at the hub of the wheel, drawing each of us to true life in Him. He is the answer to our search.

Christ is the *grace* of God (John 3:16; 2 Corinthians 8:9). Christ is the *peace* of God (Ephesians 2:14). Christ is the *power* of God (1 Corinthians 1:24). Christ is the *truth* of God (John 14:6). When we fully surrender our hearts, desires, and three resources of life to Him, we receive His Holy Spirit. The Holy Spirit is the Spirit of *love* and *grace* (Romans 15:30; John 14:23; Hebrews 10:29). The Holy Spirit is the Spirit of *peace* (John 14:26-27). The Holy Spirit is the Spirit of *power* (Acts 10:38; Romans 15:19). The Holy Spirit is the Spirit of *truth* (John 14:17; 16:13). The fellowship of the Father and Son brings these four characteristics of the Spirit to our lives (Galatians 5:22). This is the result of *love*, *peace*, *power*, and *truth* flowing from the heart of the Father. The Father is *love* (1 John 4:8). The Father is *peace* (1 Corinthians 14:33). The Father is *power* (Psalm 68:34; 2 Corinthians 4:7). The Father is *truth* (Psalm 25:5; Isaiah 45:19). The ultimate clarity of the satisfaction of our desires is embodied in the Restorer, Jesus Christ.

When we fully surrender our desires to the Restorer, we translate His satisfying restoration horizontally to others. This is a secret that I will only share with you. The apostle Paul used four nouns to describe the gospel of God's restoration which we share with others: *grace*, *peace*, *power*, and *truth*—the satisfaction of our four primary desires. We were designed to relate restoration to others in this pattern.

We translate restoration to others through the gospel of *grace*. "However, I consider my life worth nothing to me, if only I may finish the race and complete the task the Lord Jesus has given me— the task of testifying the gospel of God's grace" (Acts 20:24).

We translate restoration to others through the gospel of *peace*. "And with your feet fitted with the readiness that comes from the gospel of peace" (Ephesians 6:15).

We translate restoration to others through the gospel of *power*. "I am not ashamed of the gospel, because it is the power of God for the salvation of everyone who believes: first for the Jew, then for the Gentile (Romans 1:16).

We translate restoration to others through the gospel of *truth*. "And you also were included in Christ when you heard the word of truth, the gospel of your salvation. Having believed, you were marked in him with a seal, the promised Holy Spirit" (Ephesians 1:13).

God's design is that we vertically receive the Restorer's *grace*, *peace*, *power*, and *truth* in order to transfer them horizontally to others.

Let's go back to the story of the two lost sons to illustrate these ideas. In Jesus' trilogy, the father satisfied the desires of his sand-hearted younger son as well as the desires of his stone-hearted elder son through the gift of restoration.

When the younger son returned home, *sandals* were placed on his feet, which transformed him from a slave back into a son. This illustrated the father satisfying the younger son's desire for *significance* translated in the *love*, or *grace*, of the patriarch.

A *calf*, rather than a goat, implied that everyone in the community was invited, not just the family. This noted the father satisfying the younger son's desire for *contentment* translated in the *peace* of the father's reconciliation of the son with the community.

The father instructed the servants to place the *ring* on his son's finger to restore his ability to make business deals, an act that committed the father's resources. This demonstrated the father satisfying the younger son's desire for *control* translated in the *power* that he had transferred.

The servants scattered to find the father's *robe*, since it was the best. This symbolized the father satisfying the younger son's desire for *security* translated in the *truth* that everything he owned had belonged to the son.

These were acts by the father that restored his younger son to authenticity, the original design of the Designer.

The father offered the same satisfaction of the elder son's desires that he had provided in the four images restoring his younger son. *"My son"* demonstrates *significance* translated in the *love* of the father for his son pictured in *sandals* covering his elder son's feet.

The father's plea, "But we had to celebrate and be glad, because this brother of yours was dead and is alive again; he was lost and is found" points to *contentment* translated in the father's *peace* symbolized by the *calf* reconciling two lost sons with the community totally at the father's expense.

"You are always with me" reveals *control* translated in the *power* of the father noted in the *ring* that would always be on his elder son's finger.

"Everything I have is yours" illustrates *security* translated in the *truth* of the father providing all that his son had needed, evidenced in the father's *robe* draping over his elder heir.

The father offered restoration of his elder son's stone heart through the transformation of his desires.

What would happen if you surrendered your desires vertically to the Restorer and became significant in the grace of God, content in the peace of God, under control in the power of God, and secure in the truth of God? If you trusted in your godliness rather than your giftedness, would you transfer the satisfaction of your desires in the Restorer horizontally to others?

How you answer these questions can bring you one step closer to living with a malleable heart of clay—one that the father can use to expand his kingdom. Like the father in the trilogy who reached out to his two sons, the Restorer offers us *grace*, *peace*, *power*, and *truth,* enabling us to live restored to our authentic condition in an effort to bring authentic restoration to others through the power of Christ in us.

Chapter Twelve

RESTORING OUR TIME, TALENT, AND TREASURE

I was in a conference center at the Ritz Carlton in Naples, Florida, surrounded by eight hundred onlookers who listened intently as Tim Keller taught about the father who had two sons. I was on the edge of my seat as his words brought clarity to what I was still defining about sand, stone, and clay.

Keller preached, "Our goodness is just as much of a barrier as our badness to God because we trust in it. The younger brother's relativistic grid says that the liberal and licentious are in, and the narrow are out. The older brother's traditional values grid says that the moral are in, and the immoral are out." He had just blown away the resulting perspectives of my sand- and stone-hearted past when he rocked my world with his third option. "The gospel grid says that the humble are in, and the proud are out because only the humble receive grace." This represented the heart of the father.

He continued with a story to explain the heart of the older brother, who I would later refer to as a stone heart. His story was inspiration for the following modern-day parable.

An entrepreneur owned a start-up social-networking business. He strategically placed his office in the center of his one hundred employees so that they could observe his work ethic through the glass panes that surrounded his office area—command central.

One day, an intern whose family made wine in their spare time brought him one of her family's best bottles. She wanted to thank this man for taking a risk to hire her during her last semester of college.

"You're heading up new client management, aren't you?" the entrepreneur inquired.

"Yes sir," the intern answered tentatively.

"How does a promotion sound?" the entrepreneur asked. Assuming the affirmative reply, he continued with issuing his decree, "As of today, you are vice president of marketing. Your salary will triple, you will drive a corporate sport utility vehicle, enjoy an expense account, and receive full health benefits. Your first assignment is to recruit a team of fifty sales associates."

His generosity garnered the attention of a sales manager who overheard this conversation and thought to himself, "Wow, if a cheap bottle of wine gets a six-figure salary and benefits, I wonder what I would get if I gave the boss a week's vacation to the Atlantis?"

After a quick online purchase during his lunch break, the sales manager skipped in to the entrepreneur's suite with his $10,000 gift certificate in hand. His eyes beamed as he placed the envelope on his leader's desk, waiting for him to open it.

"Wow, thank you so much!" said the grateful business mogul as he pulled the certificate from the envelope and looked it over. After a matter of seconds he tossed the gift on his desk and began to walk out of his office to his next appointment. He had barely passed through the threshold of his doorway when the enraged sales manager shouted loudly enough for all to hear.

"Wait a minute!" he screamed. "I saw the intern give you a cheap bottle of homemade merlot, and you made her vice president of marketing with a six-figure salary and full benefits. I gave you a $10,000 gift certificate to travel to one of the world's finest resorts, and you give me nothing in return?"

The entrepreneur looked at his sales manager and spoke with heart-piercing words: "The intern gave the gift to *me*," the chairman replied. "You gave the gift to *yourself*."

The Search for Authenticity

We all do it.

A non-profit corporation CEO offers a favor to a potential donor. Later, he plans to ask that person for a charitable contribution that will advance his agenda for the organization. He gave the gift to himself.

A busy husband reluctantly agrees to his wife's request to pick up the kids from school, knowing that he's going to ask for a reward that night in return. He gave the gift to himself.

A car salesman buys lunch for a prospective new car purchaser. He gave the gift to himself.

A politician serves the homeless for five minutes by filling their plates with food at a local soup kitchen while the television cameras capture the footage. The airing will garner him votes. He gave the gift to himself.

Jesus' disciple Peter addressed this pattern by offering a picture of God's design in this regard: "Each one should use whatever gift he has received to serve others, faithfully administering God's grace in its various forms" (1 Peter 4:10). We were designed to be generous with our gifts of time, talent, and treasure. God desires that we use them to serve, faithfully administering divine grace—his undeserved love—in its various forms. We were designed to use our gifts received vertically to serve those horizontally, so that they connect vertically with the grace of the Generous One.

The words "generous" and "generate" come from the same Latin word, *genus*, meaning "race or kind." "Generous" means "giving." "Generate" means "multiply." Consequently, generosity multiplies giving in the human race. God's desire is to multiply our gifts through us to generate generosity in others. Yet many of us still believe that our grasp at significance, contentment, control, and security apart from the Restorer will ultimately satisfy our desires. Attempting to satisfy our desires apart from God creates the gap of pretense in each one of us. This gap misaligns our hearts, desires, and three resources of life.

In our postmodern culture we deconstruct, or peel back, the layers of a person beginning with the outside working inward, in search of one of the most valuable words in today's society—authenticity. Authenticity involves the alignment of our spiritual hearts with our desires, and placing our three resources of life in the hands of the Restorer. If we delve deeper into the aligned life, desires, and heart of a fully surrendered person, we see that authenticity grows in power. We are surprised to find that this person is someone who is the same in all places at all times. In today's culture we find it increasingly difficult to find a person without pretense. When we do, we say, "He's the real deal."

For example, we watch the news and see how politicians answer questions with the words we want to hear, yet we find that they vary their responses to tickle the ears of the audiences they are addressing. We watch celebrities support personal convictions that place them in high esteem, yet embrace lifestyles behind closed doors that are in direct opposition to those ideals. We listen to preachers stand before congregations on Sunday mornings pointing out all the wrongs in the world, while they neglect to confess the sins they have hidden in their shiny metal boxes.

Pretense surfaces in us when we build ourselves up from the outside in, trying to convince others in our community that we are authentic, restored, and the real deal. The irony is that the very act of pretending to be the real deal is inauthentic, unrestored, and counterfeit. We must keep in mind that we will always come up short if we are searching for someone who is authentic *all* of the time and in *all* circumstances, unless we are looking toward the Restorer.

The Restorer is completely authentic. His heart, His desires, and His three resources of life are perfectly aligned from the inside out. He generously uses His gifts to serve others, faithfully administering God's grace in its various forms. Consequently, we find the most power in our lives when we pursue a life centered around the Restorer. When we seek to be like Jesus, His attitudes and actions permeate our hearts, desires, and our time, talent and treasure.

The true test of our authenticity comes when we use our time, talent, and treasure in *generosity* that flows in the cracks where only God sees our obedience and disobedience, namely our *greed*. It is revealed when the voting is over, when the cameras are gone, and when the lights in the church are turned off. Those are the moments where living restored to authenticity really matters.

Is there any room in your heart, desires, and life for the generosity of the Restorer?

A generous heart is open and recognizes God as the Provider, while a greedy heart remains closed. When we are restored to authenticity, we are renewed with God's heart in order to reflect Him. He aligns our hearts, desires, and three resources of life with His. On Restoration Road, we find that God is a generous God Who redeems us. He generously paid for us to be restored to authenticity. Consequently a deeply rooted need resides in each one of us to respond to Him.

What I experienced the night of the raid was not unlike what countless others have experienced in their search for authenticity. Some reject God's gift. They hear about it and witness it in action, yet they remain prideful in heart—legalistic in stone or licentious in sand—and have a hard time accepting it. Others humbly bend their knees in full surrender to the Restorer, the response of an authentic clay heart.

As our culture searches for the real deal in politicians, political activists, celebrities, talk-show hosts or other rich and famous people, it neglects to embrace the truth that there is only One who exemplified this authenticity perfectly: Jesus, who was nailed to a cross and forever demonstrated His true heart's condition with a relentless act of radical generosity. He gave His life to intersect the vertical, our relationship with the Father, and the horizontal, our relationships with others. His heart of clay fully surrendered His life to God, the generous Giver of time, talent and treasure, and horizontally offered them to others in need. He did it perfectly. He showed us how generosity flowed from God toward others. He taught the duplicity of someone who claimed to have received God's generosity without passing it on to someone else. A vertical generosity that is void of a horizontal generosity is not authentic.

A stone heart partially surrenders the three resources of life vertically at the expense of the horizontal. A sand heart partially surrenders these same resources horizontally at the expense of the vertical. When it comes to time, a stone heart focuses on the eternal at the expense of the abundant. A sand heart focuses on the abundant at the expense of the eternal. In terms of talent, a stone heart fixes his priorities on ministry at the expense of the marketplace. A sand heart fixes his priorities on the marketplace at the expense of ministry. With treasure, a stone heart says, "How little can I give?" A sand heart says, "How much can I keep?" Both stone and sand hearts act from a hard heart of greed. Both give the gift of life to themselves.

The Restorer gave His life to connect us with restoration and authenticity. Only He can turn a politician, a celebrity, a preacher, a teacher, an entrepreneur, a stay-at-home mom, a student, or someone who is seeking spiritual truth into the "real deal." Rich or poor, the Restorer challenges us to be generous with the resources the Father has given us because it becomes an outpouring of who we truly are from the inside out. If we hold anything back from the Restorer, then we are relying on our giftedness—what we will gain, instead of our godliness—what we will give for God to receive the glory. As with the sales manager in the story above, we give the gift to ourselves.

Evidently, this was an issue in the early church. James, the leader of the Jerusalem church and the half-brother of Jesus, observed: "Suppose a man comes into your meeting wearing a gold ring and fine clothes, and a poor man in shabby clothes also comes in. If you show special attention to the man wearing fine clothes and say, 'Here's a good seat for you,' but say to the poor man, 'You stand there' or 'sit on the floor by my feet,' have you not discriminated among yourselves and become Judges with evil thoughts? Listen, my dear brothers: Has not God chosen those who are poor in the eyes of the world to be rich in faith and to inherit the kingdom he promised those who love him? But you have insulted the poor. Is it not the rich who are exploiting you? Are they not the ones who are dragging you into court? Are they not the ones who are slandering the noble name of him to whom you belong? If you really keep the royal law found in Scripture, 'Love your neighbor as yourself,' you are doing right. But if you show favoritism, you sin and are convicted by the law as lawbreakers. For whoever keeps the whole law and yet stumbles at just one point is guilty of breaking all of it. For he who said, 'Do not commit adultery,' also said, 'Do not murder.' If you do not commit adultery but do commit murder, you have become a lawbreaker. Speak and act as those who are going to be judged by the law that gives freedom" (James 2:1-12).

As we see in James, favoritism is giving the gift to ourselves. We misuse our gifts to use others in order to serve ourselves. Favoritism flows from a greedy, partially surrendered heart of sand or stone. However, our generous God desires full surrender from a heart of clay so that His generosity has an opportunity to flow through us and to others so that He can be made known and his kingdom expanded.

In our fallenness, when we offer only partial surrender of our time, talent or treasure, we are actually surrendering nothing. Surrendering half of the four chambers of the heart (for example: choosing to, thinking to, but not praying to, or wanting to) is surrendering none. Surrendering some of our desires is surrendering none. Surrendering some of our time, talent, and treasure is, in effect, surrendering none. Partial surrender is non-surrender because it uses others to serve ourselves. God knows our motivations and sees what lies behind our actions.

James said that we cannot obey the commandments halfway. We cannot offer help to the rich while we neglect the poor. We cannot be half-heartedly generous without actually being greedy. We cannot receive God's generous gifts and white-knuckle them, refusing to give back to Him and those in need without greed, or hardness, in our hearts. Greed that flows from a proud heart breaks apart the vertical from the horizontal and forms a four-walled prison, pride's incarceration of greed.

Conversely, we must beware of discriminating against the rich in order to help the poor (Exodus 23:3). This is another kind of greed. *Posturing greed* is pretense: helping the poor with a disguised internal jealousy against the rich. We attempt to satisfy our four primary desires as we pursue social justice apart from the loving heart of God. Too often, our hearts for social justice become hardened toward the economically rich, the very ones that we depend on for helping the poor. This dichotomy frequently arises both inside and outside churches where we pursue selfish *significance*, *contentment*, *control*, and *security* in helping the poor as we hatefully bash the rich. Posturing greed can still take place whenever we seek to help the poor merely to draw attention to our self-serving agendas. In either case, we give the gift to ourselves.

Based on the Bible and the clarity of Jesus' teachings, I came to the personal conclusion that both the rich and the poor needed to find Restoration Road. I realized that not all economically rich people were spiritually bankrupt, nor were the impoverished all saints. Whether rich or poor, God focuses on the heart (1 Samuel 16:7)—

and He focuses on our hearts as well, as we give to those in need or interrelate with those who are not in financial need.

The Restorer warned against greed, "Watch out! Be on your guard against all kinds of greed; a man's life does not consist in the abundance of his possessions" (Luke 12:15).

Are you locked inside the thought that life consists in the abundance of your possessions? Do you respond to God's generosity and the needs of others with *greed*? Has your attempt at self-restoration been about what you can gain, or has it been about protecting what you are afraid to lose? Have you tried to be restored, but your self-ambition has pulled you away from living generously? Perhaps you placed your trust in a uniquely gifted leader, but were disappointed by the lack of authenticity in his life, and that experience has caused you to be cautious to release the resources of your life. Has it made you apprehensive to trust in the Restorer?

If your answer to any of these questions is "yes," then consider whether your heart has been hardened toward becoming the kind of generous person that God desires you to be. Think about this— is your generosity reserved only for giving to those who will offer something in return? If so, then you give the gift to yourself. Perhaps you think, "Why not? I earned it."

God gave insight to pride's problem of seeing only ourselves as providers:

"When you have eaten and are satisfied, praise the Lord your God for the good land he has given you. Be careful that you do not forget the Lord your God, failing to observe his commands, his laws and his decrees that I am giving you this day. Otherwise, when you eat and are satisfied, when you build fine houses and settle down, and when your herds and flocks grow large and your silver and gold increase and all you have is multiplied, then your heart will become proud and you will forget the Lord your God, who brought you out of Egypt, out of the land of slavery. He led you through the vast and dreadful desert, that thirsty and waterless land, with its venomous snakes and scorpions. He brought you water out of hard rock. He gave you manna to eat in the desert, something your fathers had never known, to humble and to test you so that in the end it might go well with you. You may say to yourself, 'My power and the strength of my hands have produced this wealth for me.' But remember the Lord your God, for it is he who gives you the ability to produce wealth, and so confirms his covenant, which he swore to your forefathers, as it is today.

If you ever forget the Lord your God and follow other gods and worship and bow down to them, I testify against you today that you will surely be destroyed. Like the nations the Lord destroyed before you, so you will be destroyed for not obeying the Lord your God" (Deuteronomy 8:10-20).

I am convinced this is how I lived during my sand-hearted marketplace days. After each deal, I kept thinking that it was *my* power and the strength of *my* hands, or *my* abilities, that produced *my* wealth. I was generous to those who offered me something in return. I neglected the God who gave me the ability to produce wealth. I forgot Him. After losing everything with my loose sand heart, I even had the gall to try to earn it back with a legalistic heart of stone, all the while still neglecting God. My attempts to protect myself brought me to an overdue appointment with the Restorer.

Do you respond to God's generosity and to the needs of others with generosity in kind? What have you done with the three resources of your life when no one was looking that changed the circumstances of someone else? When have you helped someone who offered nothing in return? Take a moment and write down a few of those things and determine, to the best of your ability, if you did them out of greed or generosity. Was it the real deal or was it your attempt at a self-restoration program?

Greed flows from a hard heart to a tight fist, but generosity flows from a soft heart to an open hand. God's design aligns the heart with our three resources of life. Rather than being *hardhearted* and *tightfisted* with our resources, God's desire is that we be *softhearted* and *openhanded*.

"If there is a poor man among your brothers in any of the towns of the land that the Lord your God is giving you, do not be hardhearted or tightfisted toward your poor brother. Rather be openhanded and freely lend him whatever he needs. Be careful not to harbor this wicket thought: 'The seventh year, the year for canceling debts, is near,' so that you do not show ill will toward your needy brother and give him nothing. He may then appeal to the Lord against you, and you will be found guilty of sin. Give generously to him and do so without a grudging heart; then because of this the Lord your God will bless you in all your work and in everything you put your hand to. There will always be poor people in the land. Therefore I command you to be openhanded toward your brothers and toward the poor and needy in your land" (Deuteronomy 15:7-11).

Fairness in Our Relationships

We can determine if our hearts are full of greed or generosity by examining how we offer to others the three resources of life: our time, talent and treasure. When we are generous with these resources, we pursue authentic relationships, which includes acting in fairness toward others.

Through studying wisdom, I learned that what is fair includes straight paths. Uncle Derald's foundational approach to life was: "Trust in the Lord with all your heart and lean not on your own understanding; in all your ways acknowledge him, and he will make your paths straight" (Proverbs 3:5-6). Solomon passed along his father's advice, saying, "I guide you in the way of wisdom and lead you along straight paths" (Proverbs 4:11). "Straight" is translated from the same root as "equity," pointing toward what is fair. That root can be interpreted as "smooth," or "evenly applied," a reference to the fashioning of metal. Typically, in the course of interpersonal conflict in our lives, we do not evenly apply risk and return between ourselves and the other person involved. Risk is the potential for loss. Return is the profit, gain, or reward. When relational tension arises, we tend to pile up risk on the other party while we attempt to retain all of the return for ourselves. Consequently, our paths become crooked, uneven, or full of greed.

Wisdom's tool for evening our paths is "equity" which begins by placing the possibility for risk into God's hands. When we risk all four chambers of our hearts: (1) choices, (2) thoughts, (3) prayers, and (4) feelings, we desire to risk all of our ways on Restoration Road where the vertical intersects with the horizontal. Our desires represent the heartbeat that connects our hearts with our ways. God responds by making our paths, or all three resources of life, straight or fair. The antithesis of equity is trusting in our own fallen understanding which minimizes our relational risk, or vulnerability, in a false attempt to maximize our egocentric return.

When we fully surrender our hearts and desires on Restoration Road, we fully surrender our time, talent, and treasure to God, Who restores our paths with *generosity*, resulting in a total reallocation of our resources toward the destination of a restored life.

Time

In order to be restored to authenticity, we need to surrender our *time*.

Paul referenced this as, "Redeeming the time" (Ephesians 5:16 KJV). The NIV translates this phrase, "making the most of every opportunity" (Ephesians 5:16 NIV). Paul had at least two word choices for this word: *chronos* or *kairos*. *Chronos* is where we get our English word "chronology," meaning "the clock." *Kairos* means "the right time, or just in time." That is why the NIV translates "redeeming the time" as "making the most of every opportunity." Both translations imply that in order to surrender our time to the Restorer, we must transition from *chronos* to *kairos*, from following our own selfish agendas on the clock to making the most of every opportunity to meet the needs of others at the right time. As we do so, we move from trusting in the gift to trusting in the Giver.

Some of us are managing our lives backwards from the design God has in store for us. We focus on the past or the future and lock out the present. Consequently, we are so busy accomplishing our selfish tasks that we rarely have time to listen to His small still voice, His whisper (1 Kings 19:12). All we hear is the static of our fallen culture that tells us how to hurry through life on this side. But the key that unlocks His restoration is full surrender of our time to the Restorer.

After the raid and my early meetings with Derald, I began to re-prioritize my time. I was fascinated to find that the commodity in my life that appeared to be most scarce seemed to be more abundant after I surrendered it to the Restorer. I responded to the Spirit's promptings to meet with different groups each week.

Monday began our daily stand-up management meetings where we reviewed and prayed for our desired goals. Tuesday featured our early morning Bible study at the office led by my brother Stuart. Wednesday included a meeting with my friend who became my walking partner, lunch with Derald, and an evening meeting at our home with a small group of couples from our church. (I had helped champion this initiative at County Line after unwillingly engaging in a small group program at a conference that Susan and I attended. I remember in a period of twenty minutes changing my perspective from thinking, "There is no way that I'm going to share the shambles of my life with a bunch of strangers," to feeling a strong connection with people who were experiencing the same challenges in life that I was.) Thursday and Friday were reserved for travel.

I also began reading through the Bible and praying every morning and every evening to bookend my days with the Restorer's perspective. Uncle Derald said, "Time is the only true democracy." While surrendering my time to the Restorer did not add any minutes to my day or days to my calendar, it redeemed my time to make it more abundant and eternal. Rather than an interruption, I began to see every encounter with a human being as a divine appointment to discover the Restorer at work. This made my encounters and my days more productive. I chose more wisely, thought more clearly, prayed more frequently, and felt more nobly. As I turned my time over to God, I found that I needed less time to deal with the consequences of my foolish decisions. Time became more about developing relationships than it was about giving gifts to myself. As a result, I became more generous with my time.

Take a moment and pull out your calendar. What appointments have you set for the next week? Is it all about busyness or relationships? Are you trusting in the gift of time for your own selfish benefit or are you trusting in the Giver?

Talent

In order to be restored to authenticity, we need to surrender our *talent*.

Talent is our unique identity. From that identity flows our passions. We need to discover and develop the unique expression of the Restorer in us to advance His message of restoration in the lives of each person we encounter. CPA's need to discover how to account with the Restorer. Realtors must uncover how to broker real estate with the Restorer. Attorneys...never mind. (Seriously, attorneys need to learn how to practice law with the Restorer.) The key that unlocks this restoration is full surrender of our talent to the Restorer. He will help us reinvest that talent to bring restoration to others (1 Peter 4:10).

A snapshot of our talent, God's unique design expressed in each one of us, can be found on our business cards or in the title we use at the end of an e-mail to define who we are and what we do. If it says, "CPA," "MBA," "AVP," "CEO," "CFO," "DIR," "MOM," or "DAD," the telling question is, "Are we using our talent for our selfish advantage or for the glory of God and the benefit of others?"

A generous clay heart reveals the heart of the Restorer through every relational encounter. To keep us grounded and focused, we ask ourselves, *"Are we being selfish or unselfish with our God-given talent?"*

Years ago I began the journey of examining and surrendering my talent to the Restorer. I reflected on what tools God had given me and how I had misappropriated them. I had always been a leader, but sand and stone in my heart made me resemble a manipulator. I asked myself one of the most telling questions I had ever pondered, "How have I misused for greed what God intended for generosity?" All along, sand and stone caused me to give the gift to myself.

I read countless books, listened to hours of sermons, and sought a plethora of information from Derald to discover the answer to my foundational question. I needed to know if God cared about a collector car auction. The answer I uncovered rocked my world. It was a resounding, "Yes!" In fact, the Hebrew word, *abad*, can be translated either as "work" or "worship." I learned that I had been designed to worship God 24/7, including in my work. The result would be that I worshiped God the most where others expected it the least.

Unfortunately, prior to the night of July 1, 1992, I never thought that my work world had anything to do with my worship. I had proudly trusted in the gifts rather than the Giver. This newly discovered reality meant that I needed to surrender my talent to the Restorer. My business would somehow become a ministry to serve God and others along Restoration Road.

One example of the Restorer renewing my talent occurred at our Labor Day Weekend kickoff press conference luncheon held at the Auburn Cord Duesenberg Museum. Each year in that historic setting, we offered a preview of the premier vehicles that would cross the auction block. Just prior to walking on stage to take the microphone, I was made aware of a situation that moved my heart. My best friend from elementary school and his wife, who had also been one of our high school classmates, recently gave birth to their daughter who was in need of a heart transplant. She would become the youngest person in the United States to receive a new heart.

Responding to what I believed was a Holy Spirit prompting, I stepped up to the podium and made the crowd aware of the need. As I finished describing her dilemma, I saw a raised hand in my peripheral vision. It was racing legend and heart transplant recipient Carroll Shelby seated next to me offering the first $25,000 toward the infant's operation. Jerry J. Moore matched it, and her funded operation was a success. When I look back at the surrender of my talent to the Restorer, I realize how trusting in the Giver rather than my gifts led to two new hearts that day: mine and the baby girl's.

Are you trusting in the gift of your talent or in the Giver? Look at your business card, and ask yourself this question, "How have I misused for greed what God intended for generosity?"

After you examine the use of your talent, surrender it to the Restorer. You don't have to engage in full-time church or ministry work to worship God with your work. Ask Him to make your career a ministry. Underneath the title of your card, write, "Surrendered," and carry it with you as a reminder of your desire for restoration of your talent. Next, keep a journal of Spirit-prompted objectives that will restore your talent to generously serve others, faithfully administering God's grace in its various forms. Ask a wise and trusted friend to help you implement strategies to achieve your Spirit-prompted objectives.

Treasure

In order to be restored to authenticity, we need to surrender our *treasure*.

We can get one rather obvious indication of how we're managing our treasure by looking at our checking accounts. Our checking accounts reveal the costs of our needs: mortgage or rent payments, school tuition, groceries, utilities, gas for our cars, and the balance of expenses for survival. Our checking accounts also reveal the costs of our wants: new car payments, new boat payments, lake cottage payments, vacations, electronics, and other luxuries that we often prioritize. Consequently, treasure is oftentimes the most difficult of our three resources to give away.

Most of us keep the status of our checking accounts private for fear that someone will take advantage of us. Sometimes we include the church in that fear. When we walk through its front doors, we protect our treasure at all costs, carefully hoarding our often over-extended resources. This is the natural bent of hard hearts — they result in clenched fists.

If you were raised in the church, you probably encountered the ongoing debate over tithes and offerings. You may ask yourself, "Do I tithe off the gross or the net? Do I have to give my money to a church, or can I give it to another non-profit? Is it acceptable to spend my treasure on myself, or is that sin?"

In our hard-heartedness, we become diligent about nailing down the specifics of exactly how generous we must be to stay in line with the rules. In our attempt to follow the rules, we remove the heart of God. Jesus offered the following admonishment to stone hearts: "Woe to you, teachers of the law and Pharisees, you hypocrites! You give a tenth of your spices — mint, dill and cumin. But you have neglected the more important matters of the law — justice, mercy and faithfulness. You should have practiced the latter, without neglecting the former" (Matthew 23:23). A greedy heart follows the letter of the law and misses the spirit of the law. A generous heart follows the spirit of the law and receives the heart of the Restorer.

Having a greedy perspective toward my treasure led to me having less treasure. Like the younger son in Jesus' trilogy, money slipped like sand through my fingers. Millions of dollars had traveled through my accounts, and only deficits remained. The minus signs were a result of my foolish sand-hearted decisions. Ironically, now that I had less than nothing, I was ready to surrender my treasure to the Restorer. I was even ready to consider giving to the advancement of God's heart in others.

In order to surrender all of my treasure to the Restorer, I developed a financial plan to get out of debt. I created a conservative pro forma of revenue and expenses, including repayment of past due accounts payables to our vendors. As I was finalizing the plan, I considered tithing in our business as an act of surrendering our treasure. Consequently, the natural question arose, "Should we tithe off the gross or the net?" My perspective of our past-due payables caused me to think that tithing, whether off the gross or the net, would be giving away other people's money—the money I owed to my vendors. As a result, I thought about first paying off our vendors in the spirit of tithing before we gave a dime to charitable causes. After our vendors were paid in full, we could continue with our pattern, but instead give to entities that advanced authentic restoration.

When I finalized my plan, I realized that two years would pass before our vendors would be paid in full. This meant that I would have to undertake many humbling face-to-face meetings and telephone conversations. Through this process I learned a valuable lesson, one that I would not take a million dollars for, nor give ten cents to repeat: never again did I want to be foolish with my treasure. I saw the ripple effect it had on others, and I was ashamed of how poorly it had reflected on the cause of the Restorer in my personal and business life.

At the same time, I found great comfort in seeing the light at the end of the tunnel, though it lingered two years down Restoration Road. Now that I had the plan, I was free to trust in the Giver rather than the gifts. This was a radical shift in my life that flowed from a heart of clay. I began to see God as my Provider, a belief that restored my treasure to authenticity. By the way, we made it to the end of the tunnel. We paid every vendor at the rate of 10 percent of our gross income. Through my meetings with vendors, I learned that on the other side of every expense, whether a need or a want, is a person. Wisely valuing those relationships allowed me to experience generosity as God restored my treasure.

As I moved toward the heart of the father in Jesus' trilogy, God shaped my business into a ministry that put people ahead of profit, relationship before remuneration, and ministry above my old greedy marketplace philosophy. I realized that I needed to give all of my three resources of life to God, which would loosen my grip on money and achievement. When I opened my tight-fisted heart, God blessed my life and made it possible for me to send those blessings out to help others. My clay heart enabled me to see business as a way to generously give back resources to God's kingdom, multiplying His generous heart in others.

Have you ever considered the relationships on the other side of your expenses? If not, take a moment to reflect on the names and faces on the other side of your needs and wants. Have you generously used your treasures to serve them, faithfully administering God's grace in its various forms, or have you used others to serve yourself? Do you see any names and faces of those in need with whom you might have neglected to share your gifts? Would you say that you have been *greedy* or *generous* with your treasure?

Create a treasure restoration plan. Assemble a conservative estimate of your next two years' revenue and expenses. Ask God and a wise friend what percentage you should attempt to give, whether calculated from the gross or net. At the same time, pursue wise counsel as to where you should direct those dollars for the highest and best use. Never lose sight of giving generously, with godly wisdom, in both your personal and business dealings. Let every relationship—including customers, vendors, employees, competitors, family, friends, or those you may not know who are in need—reflect the heart of the Giver.

Fully surrendering my *time*, *talent*, and *treasure* to the Restorer, I began to use the gifts I had received vertically to serve others horizontally, so that others would connect vertically with the grace of the Generous One.

When we consider the three resources of life, we need to constantly evaluate our use of this generous inheritance. Perhaps you will want to align your *time*, *talent*, and *treasure* with one or two charities. Maybe you will create a foundation to serve others. The Restorer reminds us that He gave everything for us so that we can live life authentically, working as His agent in the world to the furtherance of his kingdom. If the Restorer is truly dwelling in us, then our three resources of life will reflect His generosity on Restoration Road.

Chapter Thirteen

RESTORING LIVING HOPE

I s there anything in your heart, your desires, or your three resources of life that you would like to make new? Often, we
hold on to our old relational patterns that hinder growth in our
relationships with God and with others. When we experience trials, these sin patterns are the first patterns we follow. For example, when we're stressed we snap when asked to volunteer for
something that will take more of our time; our fuse is short, our
temper quick. When we're stressed, many of us indulge ourselves
in things that are not beneficial to us, be it food, alcohol, or whatever. When we do, the smooth operating machinery that makes up
our walk with God gets gunked up with sin. Would you like those
junky parts of your inner being to be restored to a living hope that
makes what's old and corroded in your heart new?

No one understood the concept of restoration like Peter. He
had been humbled, softened, and sanctified when he wrote his
first letter to those who walked Restoration Road near the end of
his lifetime. His audience was Christians who were experiencing
social pressures to renounce their faith and go back to their old
lives that had been controlled by sin. His message was of a *living
hope* that made the old new.

Living hope means "the confident assurance of eternal and abundant life with God in Christ." It comes to us as a gift of God's great mercy through the resurrection of Jesus Christ from the dead. We receive this gift by fully surrendering: (1) our old lives, (2) our sins (piece by piece), and (3) our new lives to Christ, the Restorer. After surrendering our old lives to Christ, His Spirit convicts us of our sins. Just as a gold refiner's fire brings the impurities to the top, so also faith's trials bring to light our old sin patterns. We surrender these by confessing them to God and to a close confidant or a trusted friend in Christ. When we confess, God forgives us and restores us from the impurities in our lives. Then God molds and shapes us to be useful in helping others surrender their sins as they draw nearer to Him. The result is a fully surrendered life restored to living hope.

The Auburn Cord Duesenberg museum has a vintage 1908 Auburn touring car that for years had rested peacefully in an old barn. For decades, this rare automobile remained untouched, until one day, a tornado ripped away the barn's roof, leaving the car buried under a pile of rubble. The pieces of the Auburn miraculously survived, but now the car needed to be restored. The value of this Auburn would be at its greatest when it was restored to its authentic condition. Consequently, the Auburn's owner surrendered his basket case of a car to the Auburn Cord Duesenberg Museum, saying, "I can't restore it. You can. When you do, keep it and use it as a sign for all to see the authentic design of its designer."

The same holds true for us. In order to be restored to authenticity, each of us must surrender his old basket case of a life to the Restorer, saying, "I can't restore it. You can. When you do, keep it and use it as a sign for all to see the authentic design of the Designer." When we compare the condition of the 1908 Auburn with our unrestored condition of God's design, we see hearts and lives that are rusted, corroded, worn, and dinged by life's storms, leaving us damaged seemingly beyond repair. When we confess to the Restorer that we have held tightly to a heart of sand or stone, we surrender to *living hope*. Let's examine the different aspects of this living hope.

Surrendering Our Old Lives

First, *living hope surrenders our old lives*. We surrender our old pattern of desiring life apart from God into the hands of the Restorer for an inheritance of abundant life now and eternal life in the future. We see this in Peter's first letter to those on Restoration Road: "Praise be to the God and Father of our Lord Jesus Christ! In his great mercy he has given us new birth into a living hope through the resurrection of Jesus Christ from the dead, and into an inheritance that can never perish, spoil or fade—kept in heaven for you, who through faith are shielded by God's power until the coming of the salvation that is ready to be revealed in the last time" (1 Peter 1:3-5).

"Resurrection," "inheritance," and "future salvation" are all terms that the Jews used to refer to the last days, or the end times. But Peter told them that the Messiah had already come. Jesus was God in the flesh. He lived a perfect life and died on a cross, bearing the penalty of the old unrestored life for all who believe. He gave restoration: new life and new hope for all of the sand- and stone-hearted.

In Peter's time, pagan religions preached a much different version of a restored life. Their message for new hope and new life depended upon self-restoration. How true this is for us today. Often, we rely on the words of self-help evangelists and wonder how much has really changed over the last two thousand years. Peter tells us that living hope is not based on our works or the works of others, but solely on the hope that we have in the Restorer.

We deserve justice. However, God unleashes mercy so that we do not get what we deserve because of our sins. He offers us the opportunity to surrender our old life into the hands of the Restorer and receive what we do not deserve: grace.

When we look at both sand and stone hearts who fight alone, outside the Restorer's grace, we uncover unrestored sinners. In the end, we discover that our attempts at self-restoration will always fail. The gate to Restoration Road is unlocked when we fully surrender our old lives, confessing to the Restorer, "I can't. You can. I can't restore my old life. Jesus Christ, You can. I can't pay the penalty of my sin. Jesus Christ, You can. I can't be lord of my own life, free from the power of sin. Jesus Christ, You can."

A stone heart basically says, "I can restore my life; Christ can't." A sand heart might say, "I can't restore my life; Christ can't either." These are two devastating ideas that come with the misguided belief that God either expects us to self-restore or never be restored. If either is true, then we will remain unrestored in our old vices. Our only hope to be restored to authenticity is God's mercy and grace — that which conquers the penalty and power of sin in our hearts. We are restored through Christ, the Restorer. He already sees the evil within us, even if we have kept it hidden in a shiny metal box.

The apostle Paul said that in order to be restored, we must surrender our old life including our old desires, "You were taught, with regard to your former way of life, to put off your old self, which is being corrupted by its deceitful desires; to be made new in the attitude of your minds; and to put on the new self, created to be like God in true righteousness and holiness" (Ephesians 4:24).

Juxtaposing the self-restoration of stone hearts who offer half-hearted sacrifice with a clay heart who surrenders the old life, Jesus said, "But go and learn what this means: 'I desire mercy, not sacrifice. For I have not come to call the righteous, but sinners" (Matthew 9:13). Jesus communicated that humility was the key that unlocked the gate to new life on Restoration Road (Matthew 18:3-4).

Surrendering Our Sins, Piece by Piece

Second, *living hope fully surrenders our sins, piece by piece*. If we are going to live restored to authenticity, we must confess our sins to God, one at a time. Peter continued, "In this you greatly rejoice, though now for a little while you may have had to suffer grief in all kinds of trials. These have come so your faith—of greater worth than gold, which perishes even though refined by fire—may be proved genuine and may result in praise, glory and honor when Jesus Christ is revealed" (1 Peter 1:6-7).

The first thing an automobile restorer does is disassemble the vehicle in order to restore it piece by piece. In a similar way, if we desire to walk Restoration Road, the Restorer will dismantle our old lives piece by piece. We can no longer hold on to old vices when they surface amidst our trials. We must surrender our individual sins as the Restorer reveals them. "Surrender" means that we confess our sins, piece by piece, first of all vertically to God and then horizontally to others.

Peter spoke to the early Christians because many of them were losing their physical inheritance when they chose to leave their old lives behind. They had refused to go to the guild meetings at the temple and were seen as unprofessional in business. They were criticized for not being family-oriented because they refused to go to the family events that were held at pagan temples. They were even criticized for being unpatriotic because they would not bow down to Caesar, who called himself divine.

Fast-forward to our postmodern culture, and we see how many Christians try to live out their relationship with God with boundaries in the marketplace, fight for the sanctity of marriage, raise families with Christian values, and speak out for things such as prayer in school or a rating system for movies and video games. How often are these efforts snubbed by secular society? The similarities to the background of Peter's words two thousand years ago makes this text applicable to us today.

Living hope surrenders our *old life* and our *sins, piece by piece,* so that our faith will be proved genuine to all. Peter illustrates this with the imagery of a refiner of metal. Refinement brings heat to the metal. The hotter the fire, the more the metal's impurities rise to the top. This is the case when trials of our faith come our way, and our impurities rise to the surface. In the refinement process, the biggest, baddest impurities ooze out near the end when the fire is at its hottest. In the heat of our trials, the Refiner removes our impurities. He continues the process until He sees His reflection in the metal.

Jesus, the Restorer, is refining us amidst our trials and temptations, ready to remove the impurities that rise to the surface so that we will be proved genuine and authentic. Being restored to authenticity means that we will be proven to have His heart and subsequently reflect Him. In essence, we reflect the design of the Designer, our Restorer.

Restoration is impossible without confessing our sins to God, who makes living hope available by His grace and mercy. God already knows our sins anyway. We have not fooled Him by hiding our sins behind a secret wall, inside a shiny metal box, or disguising them in the scorecards of life. If we hold on to our sins, then we will always struggle with sand and stone hearts at the expense of a deeper relationship with Christ.

You might be reading this right now and have flashes of areas in your life that have remained unconfessed to the Restorer. You believe you can make it right on your own, but the struggle has evolved into years of battling sin patterns that never go away. Your heart of sand and stone has prevented you from living with a heart of clay where Jesus has the opportunity to mold you into His image.

You know that I have been there. The heat of my trials brought the impurities of my heart, desires, and life to the surface. For a season, I had found a safe place to hide, but after the IRS walked through our company's doors—those that had been locked to wisdom—I decided to have my late-night conversation with God. The impurities that had remained unconfessed threatened to destroy any thread of faith left to be restored to authenticity.

In those secret places of confession, we bend the knee and have a face-to-face encounter with the Restorer. We communicate with brutal honesty our unadulterated rage, hurt, fear, and shame. These are the moments where our impurities can either bring us closer to God through confession, or further away through sandy license or stony legalism. Rarely is the net effect of the refining fire neutral. In our sand and stone hearts, the Restorer makes us aware of our sins in the heat of our trials. When we receive clay hearts that confess in authenticity, we are liberated to walk Restoration Road free from white knuckling our impurities in pride and pretense.

If we avoid the truth and hide our sins, life may appear outwardly stable, but our hearts will always remain inwardly unrestored. Our stone hearts harden and our sand hearts loosen to the point where there is no remaining spiritual heartbeat. When we harbor our sins apart from God, we create prisons where we spend time in the solitary confinement of our guilt, locking us away from being restored to authenticity.

Often, we refuse to confess sins to God because we know that if we do, He will take them away. We would rather find short-term pleasure in holding on to a sin, mulling over the fantasy of it in our hearts. One of the most difficult decisions that we will make on Restoration Road is to let go of our old life and the resulting sins that have imprisoned us.

The apostle John described vertical confession and its benefit, "If we confess our sins, he is faithful and just and will forgive us our sins and purify us from all unrighteousness" (1 John 1:9). When we confess our sins vertically to the Restorer, He first forgives us and then restores us.

This is why we must confess *all* of our sins to Him. The word "confession" means *"to agree with God,"* from His perspective, that our sins are real. We admit that our impurities have risen to the top, and our only restorative option is to let the Refiner remove them. Anything less than raw confession leaves our heart conditions fractured and unrestored in sand and stone.

I once sat in a hearse with a Monsignor who told me that few of his parishioners used confession. They had chosen to live with their unrestored hearts when confession would have freed them to be restored. Authentic confession restores the heart.

Anything less is pretense, "If we claim that we're free of sin, we're only fooling ourselves. A claim like that is errant nonsense. On the other hand, if we admit our sins, make a clean breast of them, He won't let us down; He'll be true to himself. He'll forgive our sins and purge us of all wrongdoing. If we claim that we've never sinned, we out-and-out contradict God—making a liar out of Him. A claim like that only shows off our ignorance of God" (1 John 1:8-10 The Message). We must vertically surrender our unconfessed sins, piece by piece, as they surface from the Refiner's fire.

Not only must we confess our sins vertically to God, we must confess our sins horizontally to someone we trust to walk us through the restoration process. James taught: "Therefore confess your sins to each other and pray for each other so that you may be healed. The prayer of a righteous man is powerful and effective" (James 5:16).

In my meetings with Uncle Derald, I began to confess my deepest sins horizontally with another person. I was surprised to find understanding embedded in grace and truth. Derald was the most righteous person I knew, yet he was also the most understanding, forgiving, and wisdom-offering. Those characteristics flowed from a heart that knew its own sin. From Derald, I learned a different kind of righteousness than the type that I had contrived in my sand and stone heart. I learned that a clay heart depended on the righteousness of another, the righteousness of the Restorer.

Vertical confession leads to *communion*: intimacy with God. Horizontal confession leads to *community*: intimacy with others in Christ. Each represents relationship. Confession helps us live in the sweet spot where our vertical relationship with God intersects with our horizontal relationships with others. The result is communion intersecting with community.

The Restorer lives in the sweet spot where communion intersects with community. He refuses to play religious games. He is unconcerned with which church has the largest attendance. He understands that the messages we preach, the songs we sing, and the recovery groups we attend are virtually in vain unless we are honestly being restored to an authentic relationship with Him. I believe that the Restorer cares most about transforming our hearts, desires, and three resources of life so that others can see our lives and also find restoration.

Living hope made relationships paramount in my life. First to be restored was my relationship with God. As I mentioned previously, for months after my late-night conversation with God, I immersed myself in Scripture. I knew that I was forgiven, but I also knew that I was starting a new journey on Restoration Road. I refused to read the Bible simply as an exercise or a task performed from guilt. Instead, it became a habit, one that I still engage in today as I read through the Bible cover to cover every year. This is my connecting point with God, part of my ongoing refinement and restoration process. I quickly learned how relationship was God's idea, while religion was a human idea. Relationships released the Spirit of Christ in my life in order to live restored to authenticity. My heart now defines restoration with God in authentic communion that is lived from the inside out.

Living hope restored me to live in community horizontally with others. Authentic community moves us to hearts that are open to relationships that help us live satisfied lives. We go deeper than a church program, a Sunday message, or singing a worship song. All of these simply point us toward the core of who God created us to be as a community.

I began a mutual walk with a friend of mine with whom I began to share everything in our weekly meetings. We read the Bible, prayed, confessed, and ran. That relationship taught me the power of the Word of God, the Spirit of God, and the people of God. The Word of God provided me the benchmark of wisdom to apply to my life 24/7. The Spirit of God guided me on the fly in every step of my life's path, making my connection with God relational, rather than religious. However, I learned even more about horizontal confession with the people of God.

I experienced the freedom offered through confession. Over time, I learned that confessing a sin usually led to the death of that sin. Confessing a temptation led to deliverance from desiring that object outside God's design. I also learned that sharing a Holy Spirit prompting to act on a vision led to experiencing God's provision.

I was surprised when, not long after the raid, Derald had asked me to begin teaching chapels at Lakewood Park Christian School. In an attempt to make the gatherings relevant to the students, the school's leadership had entitled the learning opportunity, *Life-lab*. On all fronts, I was still in the early stages of restoration and never imagined being put into a ministry position so quickly. Derald believed people could minister even in the midst of their sin or fallenness, as long as they were held accountable and humbly pursued restoration with the Father. My Wednesday chapels began that desire in me to use my gifts of communication to teach the wisdom that I was learning—to live by God's grace as I was restored to authenticity.

The Restoration Begins

For years, that 1908 Auburn sat untouched until a group of volunteers showed up on a mission to restore this work of art to its original authentic state. The first step of the restoring community was to disassemble the vehicle and restore the parts, piece by piece. After months of hard work, they reassembled the work of art, and the process was finished. Paint was shiny. Brass was buffed.

Leather was stitched perfectly. Tires were new. When the engine fired, the room filled with applause. It was a beautiful sight.

This is exactly how the restoration of living hope works with us. First, we surrender our basket cases of the old life to the Restorer. Second, we surrender our sins, piece by piece, through vertical and horizontal confession. We agree with God regarding our sins as He disassembles our old lives in order to forgive us and restore us, piece by piece. The result is deeper communion with God. And when we confess our sins horizontally to others in a safe place, the result is community. Finally, living hope surrenders the rest of our stories.

Paul described this restoration process, "For it is by grace you have been saved, through faith—and this not from yourselves, it is the gift of God—not by works, so that no one can boast. For we are God's workmanship, created in Christ Jesus to do good works, which God prepared in advance for us to do" (Ephesians 2:8-10). After surrendering the old as well as our sins, piece by piece, we surrender the upcoming good works that we were designed to do.

Surrendering our New Lives

Third, living hope surrenders our new lives. Peter concluded, "Though you have not seen him, you love him; and even though you do not see him now, you believe in him and are filled with an inexpressible and glorious joy, for you are receiving the goal of your faith, the salvation of your souls" (1 Peter 1:8-9).

The goal of our faith is the restoration of our hearts. When the Restorer connects with us, His invisible presence in our lives becomes visible through deeds of love that happen in our lives. These deeds are done because of the inexpressible and glorious joy we have within us that becomes contagious to those around us. Living hope surrenders this new life—both its tragedies and its triumphs.

Living hope surrenders our new tragedies. Will the 1908 Auburn ever get a paint chip? Will the metal rust? Will the interior get torn? Will the rubber on the tires ever wear out? Will the engine need more fluids? The answer to all of these questions is, "Yes."

Our desire to live restored to authenticity is much the same. We will face times when we are dinged, torn, worn, and rusty. Our hearts will wear down when our focus turns to the scorecard of life and our selfish desires. In those times, we must hold tightly to what we have learned along our restoration journey—the Restorer never perishes, never fades, and never spoils. We were not created to travel Restoration Road alone. The Restorer instills a living hope in us that transforms us into the unique expression of His image, His original design for us. We learn to be men and women who receive His righteousness as He bridges the gap between authentic communion with the Father and authentic community with others. He reminds us that without the promise of God restoring us, the scorecard of life will always remain a fight between sand and stone.

Living hope surrenders our new triumphs. When we are restored to authenticity, we reflect a new heart, the heart of the Restorer. The Bible writers refer to this as a mystery that was hidden, but is now revealed, much like the 1908 Auburn that was hidden in a barn in its dilapidated state and restored in community to be revealed to others. When we are restored, we can affect others' restoration as well. We begin to do the good works that the Restorer designed in advance for us to do. When we surrender our triumph, or the good works, then others see the Restorer in us. This mystery is that the invisible becomes visible.

The Apostle Paul wrote that the true mystery of God is Christ, in whom are hidden all the treasures of wisdom and knowledge (Colossians 2:2-3). Christ restores a pretending pulpit-thumping stone- and sand-hearted deal maker into an authentic clay-hearted restoring agent of the Father. A clay heart's Master Key of full surrender unlocks the gate to Restoration Road where the Restorer continues to shape our clay hearts to reflect His unique design for our lives.

When we come to the Restorer in humility, the invisible becomes visible. The apostle Paul described a paradigm shift in perspective from temporary to eternal, "We fix our eyes not on what is seen, for what is seen is temporary, and what is unseen is eternal" (2 Corinthians 4:18).

David's famous Psalm 23 demonstrates that God's restoration is a continual process. When one has a heart of clay that is newly surrendered to God's purposes, "He restores my soul. He guides me in paths of righteousness for his name's sake" (Psalm 23:3).

Jesus is the Restorer, our living hope, our confident assurance. He is the Master Key to abundant life now and eternal life on the other side. He holds the key to humility through His grace and mercy. Jesus said, "I have made and am making all things new on this side" (Revelation 21:5 [my paraphrase]). However, restoration is only available when we fully surrender our old lives; our sins, piece by piece, and our new lives.

Paul wrote, "If anyone is in Christ, he has fully surrendered his life to the Restorer, he is a new creation, the old has passed and the new has come" (2 Corinthians 5:17 [my paraphrase]). The Restorer offers us a new heart, a new Lord, and a new journey. He is our living hope (1 Timothy 1:1).

Peter said that the Restorer is making the old new, and Peter knew what having a newly restored heart was all about. Peter experienced this by walking the earth with the Restorer, who gave him a glimpse of his future just before his temporary denial of Christ. Jesus prophesied to Peter, "Simon, Simon, Satan has asked to sift you as wheat. But I have prayed for you, Simon, that your faith may not fail. And when you have turned back, strengthen your brothers" (Luke 22:31-32). And this is just what Peter did. The fisherman-turned-evangelist surrendered to the Restorer his old life, his sins, piece by piece, and his new life: both tragedies and triumphs.

Jesus has prayed the same prayer for you and me (John 17:20-21). Consequently, we must ask ourselves, "Will I surrender my old basket-case of a life; my sins, piece by piece; and my new life: both tragedies and triumphs?"

What would happen if you surrendered your old life to Him: secrets, struggles, pains, addictions, religion, or pursuit of earthly treasures? What if you asked the Restorer to come into those dark places and clean house? Maybe you gossip about one of your close friends. Maybe you abuse the internet. Maybe your old vice manifests itself in infidelity. Maybe you see it in greed or pride.

Would you like to put a stake in the ground, draw a line in the sand, and fully surrender your life to Christ the Restorer as Savior and Lord?

Restoration Road is filled with sand and stone speed bumps, so we need to continually surrender our new tragedies and triumphs to the Restorer as we live in wisdom.

For those of you already walking Restoration Road, are you committed to live in this restoration process through both tragedies and triumphs? Will you surrender your sins, piece by piece, through the refinement process and confess them both vertically and horizontally?

What has hindered you from living in authentic communion with God or authentic community with others? For me, it was outside in living. However, when I immersed myself in Scripture, I was reminded of how Christ literally died inside out so that those on the outside could come into His kingdom. He was crucified outside the city gates, which is the same place where the father chased down his younger son in Jesus' trilogy. "So he got up and went to his father. But while he was still a long way off, his father saw him and was filled with compassion for him; he ran to his son, threw his arms around him and kissed him.

The son said to him, 'Father, I have sinned against heaven and against you. I am no longer worthy to be called your son" (Luke 15:20-21). Filled with compassion, Christ our Living Hope runs to us in order to unlock the gates of our hearts with His Master Key of full surrender.

When we fully surrender our hearts to the Restorer, saying, "I can't. You can," we know that we deserve to be judged for the sins in our life, so we plan to ask for mercy, less than we deserve. However, like the father in the parable, the Restorer responds with radical grace, more than we deserve, because He is the only one who can reconcile us with our heavenly Father.

Remember that "I can't" is *repentance*; "You can" is *faith*. These are two inseparable sides of the same coin. Kenneth Bailey defines the prodigal's humble heart of repentance as "accepting to be found," receiving the gracious love the father offers.

Repentance says, "I can't restore my way to God"; yet faith says to God, "You can."

The Lost Child

I understand the pursuit of a lost child by a reconciling father. When my oldest daughter, Megan, was three years old she traveled with Susan and me to a collector car auction in Missouri. One morning we walked together about a half-mile from our hotel to a restaurant for breakfast. Due to a combination of death threats that had been made toward Dad and anonymous kidnapping threats made toward me when I was a child, we lived with a subconscious fear that Megan could be a target because of our high profile. So, I gripped her hand tightly as we talked during our morning stroll.

When we arrived at the restaurant, I let go of her hand only for a few seconds to read a menu mounted on a display. When I turned around, I noticed she was gone. Panic shot through my body when I realized she wasn't close by. I screamed out her name and I *ran*. I sprinted up and down the restaurant's large foyer. I burst through the exterior doors and attempted to memorize license plate numbers, makes, and models of cars that passed through the parking lot.

In that moment, I didn't care how much money I had or how much money I owed. Not one concern regarding self-dignity entered my mind. I just wanted my daughter back safe. A few minutes later, I found Megan in the women's restroom with an older girl who had taken her to the bathroom. Even though this was the first place that I had looked, somehow I had missed the fact that she was inside a stall. When I found her, I held her in my arms and told her how much I loved her. I felt her breath on my face when I whispered, "Don't ever tell your mother about this."

This is exactly how God feels about any of His lost, or unrestored, children. He looks for lost sheep, lost coins, and lost sons. He moves mountains, parts seas, and sends manna from heaven to pull us from circumstances that are far greater than anything we can ever handle on our own, but we must first humble ourselves to be found.

We have to *choose*, *think*, *pray*, and *want* to leave those things behind that stop us from running into the arms of the Father. If we do not, we will always remain lost with a sand or stone heart filled with pride and its subsequent pain. We need to *fully surrender* all four chambers of our hearts, our desires, and our three resources of life.

My late night conversation with God after the IRS raid had convinced me of one thing: the Restorer had seen me coming for a long time, yet He waited patiently. Like the father in the parable, He saw me when I was a long way off in my sin. When I finally returned, He did not hesitate to run with open arms to embrace me with His tireless compassion.

Would you fully surrender your heart, desires, and three resources of life to the Restorer for a million dollars? Jesus' disciple Peter, who knew quite a bit about the need, the process, and the benefits of restoration said that our faith is of greater worth than gold, more valuable than any Bugatti ever created. Interestingly the apostle Paul said that we were bought for a world-record price (1 Corinthians 6:20). A more expensive purchase will never occur than what God paid for you and me to be restored to authenticity. God fully surrendered all He had in Jesus Christ because we are priceless in the eyes of our heavenly Father.

I know this is true because I have witnessed it in my own life as well as those I have traveled with along Restoration Road. We don't have to restore ourselves to come to Christ, rather in our repentance and faith we come to Christ to be restored.

God wants to restore you to authenticity in order to use you to restore others. In the words of Russell, "If I can get you convinced, I can get them convinced." We can walk together on the dirt road toward restoring others to authenticity. It all begins when you say to Christ the Restorer, "I can't. You can."

Chapter Fourteen

RESTORING NEW LIFE: 2 MINUTES TO EBAY

On May 17, 1996, I sat at my desk busy beyond belief because of our Auburn Spring Auction, preparing for the memorabilia sale planned for that afternoon. My high-school buddy, Tom Hoffer, who had worked in our marketing department since graduating from college, buzzed me on the intercom with news that Scott Brayton was involved in an accident during practice at the Indianapolis 500.

Scott was one of the best qualifiers in Indianapolis 500 history and one of my best friends. His best performance was sixth place where he finished twice: 1989, just six seconds behind the winner, and 1993. Scott and I talked almost every single day. He lived forty-five minutes north of Auburn in Coldwater, Michigan. We were so excited that he had just won his second consecutive pole position at the Brickyard, a feat achieved by only eight other legendary drivers: Ralph DePalma (1920-21), Rex Mays (1935-36), Eddie Sachs (1960-61), Parnelli Jones (1962-63), Mario Andretti

(1966-67), A.J. Foyt (1974-75), Tom Sneva (1977-78), and Rick Mears (1988-89).

"It's probably no big deal," Hoff added regarding Scott's accident.

I left voicemail messages for Scott on his cell and at his Indy garage, his Indy apartment, and his Coldwater home and office. No answer.

I talked with Dad about the accident and the fact that I had not heard from Scott; so, he went home to watch the television for Indy updates. Dad called me about an hour later to tell me that ESPN was running a special on drivers who had previously died at the track. My heart sank, but I replied, "That's just coincidence. I'll hear from him soon."

A few minutes later, Dad called again with the news that Scott would not be calling. I remember getting this news, and the pit that formed in my stomach as Dad told me what had happened. Scott had been driving a teammate's car for about twenty-five laps when a faulty tire on his race car disintegrated. He had just entered turn two and was driving at more than 230 miles per hour. When the tire exploded, the metal rim hit the hot, oily surface of the track and his car slid like it was on ice. His vehicle spun and hit the outside retaining wall at a G-force beyond what the human body could endure.

At the age of thirty-seven, Scott Brayton died.

I went out to the auction, told Susan what happened, then drove home where I climbed in bed and watched the crash over and over again on network television.

Regardless of how tightly Scott held onto the steering wheel of his race car, because one of his four tires was bad, he was destined for death. When his car hit the wall, the steering column was broken from the front axle. For me, this represented a picture of the vertical being torn from the horizontal. The same is true for us.

Regardless of how tightly we hold on to the steering wheel of our lives, if we hold back just one of the four chambers of our hearts, then we will break apart the vertical from the horizontal. If we do not choose, do not think, do not pray, do not want full surrender, then we will not live in the sweet spot where our vertical relationship with God intersects with our horizontal relationships with others. Consequently, we will never experience restorative change to authenticity. Instead, we will encounter relational wreckage and death.

Scott's death is still one of my greatest losses. We had so much planned. While on his way to spend the month of May at Indy, Scott stopped in Auburn to donate his Cisitalia roadster to the Auburn Cord Duesenberg Museum. But with the donation, he reserved the right for us to take it from the collection to transport the vintage sports car to Europe to compete in the Mille Miglia, the famed race through the streets of Italy. We would speed around the boot with the same vigor that Scott's two year-old daughter Carly and our two-year-old daughter Kelsey displayed as they raced through the Museum during our press conference when we announced his gift.

Scott, his wife Becky, Carly, Susan, the two girls and I enjoyed lunch after the press conference in Auburn as we discussed plans for an upcoming vacation together. During our meal, Scott talked me out of being in his pits when he competed for his second consecutive pole position at the Brickyard. He did not want me to miss my daughter Megan's birthday party, scheduled for the same day.

I struggled with the decision, but I wisely decided to attend Megan's sixth birthday celebration at our local bowling alley. However, I missed the most dramatic capturing of the pole position in Indy 500 history when Scott waved off his second row position to go for the pole. His was an unprecedented decision due to its timing. He sprinted to his car to beat the 6:00 PM qualification deadline and went on to win the pole, establishing a new track record in the process. I screamed and cheered as I listened to the live radio broadcast in my car parked outside the Auburn Bowl.

The Aftermath

While the Restorer walked with me on Restoration Road, life was drastically different as we rebuilt Kruse International. In my study of the Bible, I learned that after the Jewish captivity, Nehemiah rebuilt the Jerusalem wall, Zerubbabel rebuilt the temple, and Ezra rebuilt the people. God had shaped my clay heart to be like Ezra's. I had a passion to rebuild people.

After the IRS raid and my encounter with the Restorer, I attempted to place relationships ahead of everything else, including business. The result was deepened community with our customers, vendors, employees, and even our competitors. Years later, I was able to charter a private jet to travel to and from our fifty-two annual auctions in order to gain thirty additional days each year to invest in my family while I visited prospective sellers along the way. From my perspective, all of this resulted from fully surrendering my heart, desires, and three resources of life to the Restorer.

I learned that when the Restorer unlocked my gate to Restoration Road with the Master Key of full surrender, my destination of life-giving restoration included some unexpected stops along the way.

Not long after Scott's death, the criminal portion of the IRS case was settled. However, we later received news that the IRS was going to pursue a civil case seeking penalties totaling millions of dollars. While that struggle in my life continued, it no longer defined me. I surrendered the challenge to Him and sought wisdom to walk through this valley. It lasted a decade until it was resolved. When I chose to risk my heart, desires, and three resources of life with God, He made my path straight down Restoration Road.

In 1996, we conducted our most successful annual Labor Day Weekend event in our history at Kruse Auction Park in Auburn. It was renowned as the third largest crowd-drawing event in Indiana. We auctioned two thousand cars and featured nearly another three thousand for private sale in the car corral. Sales topped $37 million, including several premier cars from private collections that sold to the highest bidder. Our live, ninety-minute television broadcast on ESPN2 received the highest ratings of any Labor Day show aired on the network. I believe that this success was merely a byproduct of changing my target of success from money to wisdom. I shared that revelation with anyone who inquired about our business.

In December of 1998, we were concluding our best year in business history. I was also attending a continuing education seminar on our grounds so that I could renew my real estate broker's license. I had traveled about forty-five weekends that year, so this was one of the only Friday nights that I would be home. Susan and I had planned to go out that evening. Consequently, I was in a hurry to finish the class. I tapped the table in front of me and waited as the instructor began to pass out our certificates of completion. This precious piece of paper was mandatory to verify that I had completed the course; I needed it to have the State renew my license. Since I had provided the facility for the instructor to hold the seminar, I believed that I would receive my certificate first (before the rest of my employees and other attendees).

The instructor began to pass out the certificates in alphabetical order. I glanced down at my watch and attempted to harness my frustration from not receiving mine first. When he reached the *K's* without saying my name, I realized that my certificate might not be in the stack. As he handed out the certificates to attendees whose last names began from *L* to *Z*, each passing letter dramatically increased the temperature inside my heart. Finally, after he had handed the certificate of completion to the guy whose last name started with *Z*, he came to mine. I decided that he had misplaced it at the bottom of the stack rather than the top. Reflecting on my new journey of the heart with all its valuable lessons, I realized that it was time to learn another.

Immediately, I left the facility and began an internal audit. As a recovering perfectionist, I began an exercise that had been beneficial to me: I attempted to *quantify* the *qualitative*. I deduced that if I could quantify the amount of time that had passed while I had been waiting for my certificate, then I could let go of the frustration (the qualitative) that had ripped through my heart and body. I looked at my watch and determined how long it had taken for me to get upset due to the delay in my schedule. The answer was: *two minutes*. That was all it took for me to feel the sense of frustration begin to rise — a flash of a sand and stone heart.

Behind the wheel of my sport utility vehicle, I exited Kruse Auction Park to take my normal southbound route home. I made it about a mile and a half to a bridge when I encountered four people looking over its edge. Subconsciously, I pulled over and rolled down my window.

"Do you need a cell phone?" I asked.

"No, there's somebody down there," one responded.

"Okay."

"No. No. No," one of the others stepped forward. "A northbound truck just crossed the center line and drove over the bridge. We just called EMS, and they are on their way."

I tried to take in what they had just said. Meanwhile a friend, who was an officer, arrived and began to look inside the truck that was upside down.

"How long ago did the truck cross the line?" I asked.

"Oh, about two minutes ago."

It is difficult to describe the feeling that resonated inside me at that moment. I realized that had I not been delayed, this truck could have hit me, possibly ending my life. Once I recognized that everything was under control, I pulled away and headed toward my house.

When I turned onto County Road 68, I sensed God speaking to me, not in an audible voice, but from within my heart. What I believed He communicated to me was that He was going to open the flood gates for me. Now was the time. I knew little about floodgates, but that was the impression I discerned. This was confirmation for me that I was to take my changed heart, transformed desires, and renewed three resources of my life to become a direct carrier of the message of authentic restoration. Yet I wondered how I could ever escape being the owner and leader of Kruse International to be free to do so.

One month later, Dad and I stood offstage minutes prior to the start of our annual Ft. Lauderdale collector car auction. He was pushing me for something out of the norm for our upcoming Scottsdale event. I responded by telling him my two-minute story. Like a politician, he saw an opening and attempted to convince me of his perspective in our discussion. He encouraged me to pursue my "Holy Spirit prompting" to connect the culture with the Restorer by communicating the Bible through writing, teaching, and preaching. He suggested that I take off the following week's Scottsdale auction, our second or third largest event of the year, to discover God's will for my life. I believed that Dad's motivation was for me to move on from the company. His reaction that day took me one step closer to finding an exit strategy from Kruse International.

Two years earlier, Dad had decided to divorce mom. She was a class act throughout the process. I will never forget the letter that we received from an attorney involved in the process commenting on her graciousness. She was a picture of the vertical intersecting with the horizontal. Humility and wisdom flowed from her heart, beat through her desires, and poured out through her three resources of life into others. I have used her posture throughout the challenge of divorce as an example with others who were going through a similar experience. She taught me a great lesson with her actions regarding the power of humility and wisdom. I realized that her heart had been clay all along.

During that time, the Restorer in Mom must have been working overtime in me because I had to craft the settlement documents since Dad and I had jointly owned the business. This was a scenario we had not foreseen, but Dad returned Mom's graciousness at the level that he was able, and a complicated situation was simplified.

However, back stage in Ft. Lauderdale, I remembered that since July 1, 1992, I had ceased blindly following Dad. I had discovered that as an adult, when we obey a parent, we assimilate not only his assets, but also his liabilities. Perhaps that is why the Bible calls us to "honor" our parents when we become adults, not to simply just continue to obey them.

The book of Proverbs gave me a filter to discern, or sift, the wisdom of my heavenly Father from the street smarts of my earthly father. One proved to reveal divine wisdom, while the other demonstrated political savvy. Traveling down Restoration Road, my pursuit of the Restorer forever shifted my relationship with Dad. While I had placed him on a pedestal as a child, as an adult I learned that he was human just like me. Consequently, I could let go of satisfying my desires of *significance*, *contentment*, *control*, and *security* through his approval.

When I came to this realization, it was as if a dam inside me opened wide and released a flow of water that swept me up and took me deeper in my journey with the Restorer. Instead of seeking Dad's approval, I learned to seek God's wisdom, relying on the Restorer to transform our relationship. Restorative change carried wisdom into my relationship with Dad because I had fully surrendered all four chambers of my heart where the vertical intersected with the horizontal on Restoration Road.

Restorative Encouragement

Encouragement from others was a catalyst for me to journey forward on Restoration Road. *Cor* is Latin for "heart." Therefore, "encouragement" means "to restore another's heart." Encouragement restores the heart, and it is only authentic when the vertical intersects with the horizontal.

Chris Schenkel, the Hall of Fame ABC sportscaster, was one of the greatest encouragers in my life. Whereas millions recognized him as an ABC sportscaster, I knew him as an "ABC encourager." His heart beat with three characteristics that restored my heart. He was: (1) Aware, (2) a Builder, and (3) a Comforter.

Chris was *aware* of people's hearts, desires, and lives. Chris remembered people's names and details about their lives at a level that I had never seen. He called me weekly to check up on me. He was aware of all that was taking place in my life. During the season of life when I was living with a sand heart, he showed up in Scottsdale, Arizona, to surprise me the day before one of our auctions. He was on his way to be inducted into the Sports Broadcaster's Hall of Fame and had received international publicity that week for his well-deserved achievement. He knew that I had been struggling. In the back seat of a limousine, he encouraged me in an unthreatening way—a way that only he could—because he was close enough relationally to be *aware* of my need.

I learned that if I was going to encourage others, I needed to assimilate the communication skills that made Chris aware of people's hearts, desires, and lives. First, Chris locked eyes with every person he met. Second, he asked questions that communicated genuine interest and revealed the heart, desires, and life of the person. Third, Chris listened intently, often repeating what he had heard. These three traits helped me receive restoration as well as bring it to others.

Scripture records that Jesus was also acutely aware of the people He encountered. He locked eyes with them, asked questions that revealed their hearts, and he listened intently. As a result, His encouragement restored them. There is something about encouragement that restores the heart.

What about you? Are you an encourager? Are you aware of the hearts, desires, and lives of those around you?

Chris was a *builder*. I remember many times when he built me up. However, one occasion stands out above all the others. When Dad decided to divorce Mom, Chris called me. I shared with him that I had been thinking about moving away from the business. He stopped me in mid-sentence, something he had rarely done.

"No way! This business has been built by *you*. The customers' relationships are with *you*. They depend upon *you*. Right now, they need *you* more than ever."

Chris built me up when I felt let down. He built me up with words of affirmation. This was a pattern that I desired to implement in my own life. I am absolutely amazed at the power of words of affirmation. From children to business leaders, people rarely receive words that build them up. Consequently, when such words flow authentically from our mouths, they enter a person's ears and travel straight to their hearts, bringing restoration.

Jesus was known for building up others—so much so that the people that He built up into faith in Him, with the Spirit's power, literally changed the world after His ascension. The Apostle Paul was also the recipient of that building up, and he taught that we should do the same: "Do not let any unwholesome talk come out of your mouths, but only what is helpful for building others up according to their needs, that it may benefit those who listen" (Ephesians 4:29). Paul knew that there is something about encouragement that restores the heart.

What about you? Will you choose to encourage others by building them up with words of affirmation? You'll be amazed at what a few words directed toward building up another person can do for your relationship and for their encouragement.

Finally, Chris was a *comforter*. *Comfort* literally means "to call alongside." It comes from the Latin, *com* meaning "together" and *fortis* which is translated "strong." Consequently, comfort means that we come alongside someone in order to invite him to restoration; we strengthen together.

When I had shared with Chris my two-minute story including my Holy Spirit prompting to become a direct carrier of the message of restoration toward authenticity, I had expected him to say something similar to what he had said twenty-four months earlier. I was wrong. He encouraged me to move forward with the prompting. He comforted me in my most difficult business decision. In essence, he came alongside and strengthened me.

Jesus was not only aware of the needs of others and not only built them up with words of affirmation, but He also comforted them by meeting their needs through restoration. He called the Holy Spirit the "Comforter" (John 14:26 NASB). The psalmist said that God encourages the afflicted (Psalm 10:17). He comforts us in our times of trouble.

Paul described Christ as the source and the flow of comfort when he wrote, "Praise be to the God and Father of our Lord Jesus Christ, the Father of compassion and the God of all comfort, who comforts us in all our troubles, so that we can comfort those in trouble with the comfort we ourselves have received from God. For just as the sufferings of Christ flow over into our lives, so also through Christ our comfort overflows" (2 Corinthians 1:3-5). Christ is the inlet, the flow, and the passion for the outlet.

Paul equated encouragement with strengthening and comfort: "But everyone who prophesies speaks to men for their strengthening, encouragement and comfort" (1 Corinthians 14:3). There is something about Christ's encouragement that restores the heart.

What about you? Do you comfort others by coming along side them and inviting them to restoration?

When we were leasing a private jet to travel to and from auctions, I developed relationships with customers whom I would invite as passengers on the plane. If they would buy cars at the auction, that was great. If they did not, we still developed our friendships, which was the primary purpose of the invitation. Little did I know how one invitation would impact someone for eternity.

Sonny and Cathy Gandee were friends who had bought and sold hundreds of muscle cars at our auctions over the years. I had invited them to fly with us to an auction in the southern United States. Just before takeoff from Auburn, I asked Sonny where he got his name.

"My dad. He played for the World Champion Detroit Lions," He responded.

"I think that Chris Schenkel was the broadcaster for the game," I offered.

"I think he was. I never got to see my dad play. I would love to have watched a game," Sonny said wishfully.

"Do you want to relive a moment from the world championship?" I inquired as I dialed Chris' number on my cell phone. I knew Chris would remember, but I could not remember if he had actually been the commentator for the game.

"Chris."

"Mitchell!" Chris responded in his encouraging tone.

"I'm in a Citation II sitting at the end of the runway in Auburn ready to go wheels up to this weekend's auction. I'm sitting with Sonny Gandee, the son of Sonny Gandee who played for the world championship Detroit Lions. Did you call that game?"

"Yes I did!" Chris confirmed.

"Well, Sonny was not fortunate enough to see his dad play. Could you give him a little play-by-play from the world championship game so he can experience what it was like?" I knew Chris' memory was picture perfect.

"Sure!" Chris obliged.

I handed the telephone to Sonny and watched the expression on his face as he listened to Chris, the master ABC encourager. I've never seen that expression on another grown man's face. Chris had breathed life into yet another soul with his classic rewind of an actual play from the world championship.

There is something about encouragement that restores the heart.

You see, it was not merely Chris who encouraged me and others, it was Christ in Chris.

The writer of Hebrews summed up the power of frequent encouragement in this way, "But encourage one another daily, as long as it is called Today, so that none of you may be hardened by sin's deceitfulness" (Hebrews 3:13). Notice that hard hearts of sand and stone sinfully stop the flow of encouragement. They actually discourage, or drain the life, from others. However, encouragement flows from a soft heart of clay. The writer then went on to say, "Let us not give up meeting together, as some are in the habit of doing, but let us encourage one another—and all the more as you see the Day approaching" (Hebrews 10:25). As long as we are on this side of the grave, we should be ABC encouragers who bring the Restorer's strength to others.

Jesus, the Restorer, said, "Come to me, all you who are weary and burdened, and I will give you rest. Take my yoke upon you and learn from me, for I am gentle and humble in heart, and you will find rest for your souls" (Matthew 11:28-29). There's something about encouragement that restores our souls and our hearts.

When you encourage others with a clay heart, you will realize that it is not you, but Christ in you who renews others with encouragement that restores their hearts.

Chris' Legacy in My Business Life

A pivotal story for me that defined what a clay heart was occurred in 1998. After the events of this story, I began to make sense of the encouragement that I had received from Chris Schenkel.

After years of being in business, we had never been approached by a prospective buyer for Kruse International. Now we were presented with several unique options.

The first was one I had initiated. A few of our customers had taken their businesses public, and I thought that doing so was the ideal way for us to garner the funds we needed to grow beyond what we could accomplish through profits alone. It would also give us an opportunity to take a few chips off the table, providing some liquidity for our family. Since Dad and I traveled together in our leased private jet nearly every week, I thought it would be wise to draft a corporate and family survival plan in case of a catastrophic event. I also had another reason for making a deal like this work: I wanted to figure out a way to spend time with my daughters during that short season of life when they were living at home. Reluctantly, I had resolved that this value would have to be compromised.

I began the due diligence process with an investment banker who was enthusiastic about the prospect of taking our high-profile company public. He had me gather all of our prior years' financial reports and place them in a package that told our story. It included press clippings, auction marketing plans, and catalogues of renowned auctions that we had conducted. After reviewing the packet, the investment banker made it clear to me that my life-long commitment to the future of our company was paramount to the success of the IPO. I understood what that meant for my future.

After months of moving forward with the investment bank, I was prompted to pray a simple prayer, "God, please open the door so wide that I can fall through it or close it so tightly that I can't get it open." I applied what I had learned about a clay heart, surrendering my pursuit to take the company public. That week, the investment banker called me with news that our company needed to be twice its size to conduct an initial public offering. Otherwise we would experience the detriments of being public without the benefits of liquidity and stock appreciation. He thought I might be angry. I thought about my prayer. God had another plan, and I was finally willing to wait on Him.

Not long after this, a large corporation considered acquiring Kruse International in a way that would allow us to achieve all the growth strategies in my vision for the business. It would allow us to accomplish things that had been unaffordable on our own.

There were several parts to my plan for the business. I wanted to provide guarantees for private collections; this would remove the reluctance of prospective sellers to take their cars to auction due to perceived risk. I wanted to develop Kruse Auction Park into a first-class convention center where we could conduct other events. I planned to develop a 24/7 auction that would place buyers and sellers together via the internet, which at that time was a newly discovered technology. This would make my long-term goal of connecting buyers and sellers in uninterrupted fashion an affordable reality. I anticipated that we could purchase collections from sellers who wanted a quick, quiet sale and were willing to close the transaction at a knowingly discounted price for the convenience and limited risk. We would then resell the collections at auction. Additionally, I believed we could develop real-estate auctions that far surpassed any that we had previously done. This was the single greatest potential for increased sales volume. One property was typically worth more than most entire car auctions. To accomplish this, I planned to partner with a real estate brokerage firm who maintained a strong international presence.

The courting corporation's interest provided an opportunity for a quick, quiet, and convenient sale that would allow us to rock the auction world. It was a simpler avenue to growth than taking our company public. Consequently, we moved forward. As with the previous opportunity, I was told that in moving ahead I was committing my entire future to this endeavor because I was the key leader, the primary revenue generator, and basically the future of the business. Again I agreed, and again I prayed that simple prayer.

That same week as my prayer, the prospective purchaser's representative called me with news that the company was being sold to a wealthy investor who had placed all acquisitions on hold. He thought I might be angry. Again, I thought about my prayer. My heart of clay had become patient for what God had in store.

During both of these scenarios, I had a chance to think about what I would change about my quality of life if I had closed the transaction. We lived in our dream home. I enjoyed complete autonomy in my business life. I traveled in a private jet. I drove our corporate sponsor's new SUV. Outside a small modification to our property, there was only one thing I could think of that I might possibly change—although this one seemed impossible.

By this time our family had grown. In addition to our first daughter Megan, Kelsey Grace was born in May, 1994. We gave her Grace as her middle name to remember the grace I had received as well as carrying the legacy of her maternal grandmother's namesake. I wanted to spend more time with the girls and Susan instead of traveling nearly 45 weekends each year. In doing so, I also wanted to communicate the message of restoration to a culture filled with unrestored people. As a result, two questions lingered: (1) Would I continue to miss every event that the girls participated in during weekends? (2) Would I ever be able to invest my gifts, abilities, talents, and experiences into a movement that would evangelize and disciple others toward the Restorer in the same way I had evangelized people into the collector car auction arena?

I offered my questions to God. I had learned that this was the only way to discover the answers. I applied what I had learned about the four chambers of my heart, my desires, and three resources of life. I reflected on what I had witnessed in others with sand and stone hearts as they had chosen journeys toward restoration with hearts of clay. I yielded the outcome to God and waited. I was about to learn that what I had intended in the previous two negotiations was far short of what God had intended. His *vision* was about to be followed by His *provision*.

eBay

Wisdom would be my tool to resolve my overarching business conflict with Dad. It was time for me to separate the *valuable* from the *vulnerable*. What happened next made sense of my two-minute encounter.

Shortly after our Ft. Lauderdale conversation, Dad and I talked about me transitioning from the company for the first time. This meant that Dad would have to come up with a way to buy my position in the company. At that time, someone very close to him suggested that he look at a young internet auction company for help. That company was called "eBay."

Dad seemed to be motivated for me to exit, so he quickly made a call to San Jose, California, only to learn that eBay had been watching our efforts on the internet. We believed we were the first company that had conducted a live auction on the world wide web. Not long after this initial telephone call, a meeting was scheduled in Auburn with the company's top three executives, including its cofounder.

The cofounder was warm to what I had been prompted to do with my life. For the first time, someone was willing to acquire Kruse International and let me walk away to pursue the desires of my heart.

eBay's publicly traded stock had skyrocketed on to the market. Their unprecedented escalation stemmed from their 95 percent share in the internet auction business. In our meeting, I asked, "What keeps a company like Microsoft from flicking you off the map?" I made a gesture at our conference room table as if I were playing caroms. The cofounder answered with a story that I will never forget.

A woman who had frequently traded goods on eBay had gone through a bitter divorce that left her penniless. Those who had bought and sold with her noticed her absence from the auction site. They tracked her down, learned of her story, and each pitched in to buy her a computer so that she was trading on eBay again.

"In a word, *community*," he said in answer to my question. I thought back to the parable of the two sons and their father's longing to restore community between them. One of the Bible's deepest values, that of *loving* others as ourselves, was being lived out in one of the greatest success stories in the history of Wall Street.

eBay planned to merge with Kruse International; their objective was to convince the 400,000 names on our customer list to become eBay users. The live auction business would merely be a conduit to achieving that end. At the same time, Dad was eager for me to move on, so the "Dean of Auctioneering" sold himself to the eBay team.

The initial meeting was followed by another where we traveled to San Jose to meet with Meg Whitman and the leadership team of the eBay community. Shortly after this meeting, they agreed in principle to acquire Kruse International. I was still torn between whether or not I should remain in a sales capacity to leverage my relationships for the organization; however, eBay's policy at the time was to pay no sales commissions. With one conference call, we closed the transaction. At the end of the closing, I inquired whether eBay executives had decided to pay commissions to individuals. They replied, "No."

Their answer was a clear confirmation of my call to walk away from Kruse International and enroll in seminary. Susan was pregnant with our third child. If a girl, she would be given the name, Lillian Faith. *Faith* because we were about to take a leap of faith. In May, 1999, we took that leap of faith. In July, Lillian Faith took us.

My Career Shift

Restorative change places the value of the process over the results. When I was discerning what I had believed was God's prompting to become a direct carrier of His message of restoration, I became aware of the following change equation: Dissatisfaction with the present state (DPS) plus awareness of a better state (ABS) plus first steps (FS) equals change. I modified the equation by multiplying all three components by wisdom and leadership (WL) to produce restorative change (RC). Consequently, it looked like this: (DPS + ABS + FS) WL = RC.

Dissatisfaction implies that something is unmet in our desires. *Awareness* means that we *see* in our hearts a better way—which is truly the only way—to satisfy those desires. *First steps* communicates that in our hearts we are choosing, thinking, praying, and wanting to move forward in a God-honoring way with our *time*, *talent*, and *treasure*.

During this time of reflecting, I asked myself a revealing question, one that I would later use to prompt many who were discerning their own Holy Spirit promptings to make a career shifts. "What would I love to do, even if I failed?" In other words, "What process would I absolutely love doing, even if successful results never came?" I kept coming back to "connecting the culture with Christ the Restorer through communicating the Bible." This became a vision-mission combination for my life. *Connecting* is *leading*. My three expressions would be: (1) writing, (2) teaching, and (3) preaching. I planned to *communicate* in order to *connect*.

After my "two minutes" story, I had a sense that God was going to open the floodgates for me to share in His work of ministry. In reflecting on this, I have often categorized my thoughts using the acronym *GATE*:

G: Gifts
A: Abilities
T: Talents
E: Experience

Gifts include our spiritual gifts. *Abilities* are our learned skills. *Talent* is our unique identity and passions expressed in something that we can never remember *not* doing. *Experiences* are the complete package of our tragedies and triumphs in life. All four reside in our hearts. Was my GATE unlocked and open for ministry?

I reflected on my primary spiritual gifts. A few years earlier, my brother Stuart led a group of us at Kruse International through Willow Creek Community Church's *Network*, a simple curriculum to discover one's spiritual gifts. I was not surprised that I scored the highest possible points on leading. However, there was a second gift of the Holy Spirit that I also scored the highest points possible: teaching. This was a defining moment for me. I would never have guessed this prior to the test.

I thought back to how much I had loved coaching Stuart's elementary school basketball team to a championship while I attended high school and college. I thought about how I had taught our employees systems so I would not have to readdress the same problems more than once. I reflected on how I had produced educational materials for our prospects and customers, including videos, infomercials, pamphlets, and newsletters, all designed to evangelize others regarding the gospel of collector car auctions. It dawned on me that teaching was indeed a passion of mine. It was so interwoven into the fabric of my being that I could not remember ever not doing it. Perhaps all of the memory techniques that I had used to do well in school were tools given to me in order to teach others.

There are two types of gifts that most people have. The first are *primary*, those that point to a divinely built, genetic wiring in each of us. However, the Bible is clear that all gifts are working in each of us according to our *need* (1 Corinthians 12:6). The remaining gifts are *secondary* gifts. They are deployed through us whenever a need arises and we seek His guidance. At one point I asked myself a telling question regarding my two primary gifts, "Would I rather *teach leading* or *lead teaching*?" As I pondered the answer, I realized that I would give my life to one, but the other almost drained me at the question mark.

Before I share which way I went, consider this: I think that the verb in each of the two-letter phrases defines what could have been my mission (what I would desire to *do*). The noun defines what could have been my vision (where I would desire to *go*). Both flow from the heart (who I would desire to *be*). In the end, I decided that I would rather *teach leading*. I am passionate about developing wise leadership in others, and I have an embedded desire to communicate, or to teach, on that subject area. Consequently, in my giftedness I am designed to *communicate to connect*.

My *abilities*, or learned skills, were auctioneering, brokering, and leading a movement that included an intense focus in the 3 M's of business: *marketing*, *management*, and *money*. All of my abilities included *communication*.

My *talent* was *connecting*. I could never remember not connecting with another person's inner being. I guess you might call it my sensitive side. I had used this talent in connecting buyers and sellers for years. My passion for connecting always took place through communication.

My *experiences* were vast for a young, bald dude from Auburn, Indiana. I had traveled millions of miles throughout the world leading the auctioning and marketing of nearly 300,000 vehicles — as well as numerous real estate properties, collectibles, museums, and vintage aircraft. This meant developing relationships with many customers, vendors, employees, prospects, and even competitors.

I concluded that my GATE could not be used in the form of direct ministry…or could it? I thought about my *gifts* of leading and teaching. When combined, they sounded a great deal like preaching. They appeared to be ideal for forming a new, church-type ministry. When I rethought my abilities, I realized that they could be summed up in the phrase, "motivating others to a decision." That sounded like ministry. I examined my *talent* which was connecting—connecting with God and connecting with others so that they connect with God was similar to the function of a priest. Finally, I considered my *experiences*. I had conducted an almost infinite number of public communication engagements and managed conflict on a daily basis as I dealt with difficult people. Both were ideal experiences for ministry, but as I pondered where to begin I started to struggle with how God could use my relationships with people scattered all over the globe. I am still searching for that one. Top it all off with the fact that ministry is service, or the work of the people. I had been in a service business since I was a minor. Selling was evangelizing. Servicing the client was discipleship.

The bottom line was that my GATE for ministry had been unlocked and opened. However, the questioned remained, "Would I walk through it?"

There was just one more problem, my foolish sins. Would my past preclude me from being a direct messenger of the Restorer's grace and wisdom? Would I ever be allowed to teach the Bible? For some stone hearts I could not, but for every pastor I consulted I could. Many of them reminded me that the Bible records from cover to cover how God uses damaged people to minister to others with His gospel of restoration. In fact, I would like to take this opportunity now to encourage you that no matter what you have done, you are not beyond the reach of the Restorer using you to restore others (Isaiah 59:1; 2 Corinthians 4:1-12; Philippians 1:6; also see Numbers 11:23).

I was amazed to learn from firsthand experience that God's *vision* was indeed followed by His *provision* when He provided an exit strategy from Kruse International that I could never have crafted on my own. I found out that He had a bigger, better plan for my life.

Seven years after the IRS raid, I was beginning a new journey on Restoration Road. I thought back to the raid, and to the cassette tape that Derald had given me. I remember listening to it in my car, and sitting there riveted to the speaker's every word. After I had listened to the entire tape, I arrived at three conclusions. First, Derald was going to give me eleven more tapes—I had just listened to the *First Step* of the *Twelve Steps*. Second, I determined that I was a workaholic, a money addict, and a materialist. Third, the tape would forever change my perspective of church. The message was originally delivered at a weekly church service that had transformed thousands of lives. I not only listened to the remaining eleven tapes, but over the next fourteen years I continued to listen to sermons from both the church's weekend and midweek services. These messages had a tremendous impact on my life.

What Next?

Shortly after our sale to eBay, I suffered from post-Kruse-International LOST syndrome: *Lack Of Stressful Transactions*. After the first five consecutive stay-at-home weekends of my life, I began to feel like a failure. I thought there was something wrong with me. I realized that these feelings were the result of the absence of deal-making in my life. I felt *insignificant*, *discontent*, *out of control*, and *insecure* from the pace of my life slowing to what appeared to be a screeching halt. A constant need for the next deal had been removed from my time, talent, and treasure. Consequently, I determined that I had nothing to contribute to society. Did I get my spiritual signals crossed?

I examined the four chambers of my heart: my choices, my thoughts, my prayers, and my feelings. I kept asking God if I had misunderstood his promptings. It dawned on me one day, sitting at my desk, that my mom and dad were polar opposites. However, if I could uncover where they were alike, perhaps I would discover what caused this LOST syndrome in me.

I arrived at two similar parental traits: (1) high expectations and (2) hidden flaws. Both of my parents placed high expectations on me—Mom mainly from a character standpoint, Dad primarily from a performance standpoint. Don't get me wrong, Mom wanted to see superior performance both in athletics and academics. She did not have any obvious flaws, but believed that one did not air one's dirty laundry in public. She kept conflict in the smallest circle necessary (Matthew 18:15-20). Now, Dad was a politician. He merely accentuated the positive, placing an optimistic spin on any negative situation. Combined with my perfectionistic temperament, these two family environmental influencers helped me to be off-the-charts LOST. Like both sons in Jesus' trilogy, I needed to be FOUND: *Focus On Understanding New Direction.*

In order to be FOUND, the Restorer needed to change my focus. To borrow an illustration from Philip Yancey, life is like a magnifying glass that magnifies the centered object in focus while the surrounding objects remain fuzzy. We focus on either Christ or our circumstances. When we focus on Christ, He becomes magnified, and our circumstances become fuzzy. When we focus on our circumstances, they become magnified, and Christ becomes fuzzy. Unfortunately, I had been focusing on my circumstances and Christ had become fuzzy. Then a friend of mine whom I consider a spiritual giant told me that I was headed for the best place in life I could possibly be—sitting at the feet of the Master to learn wisdom and to be restored for a new direction.

The Restorer is always renewing clay hearts, even when we change directions down Restoration Road.

In June, 1999, I enrolled in seminary. I planned to earn my Masters and Doctorate degrees because I had been impacted by a Bible teacher, and local church leader, who talked openly about his liabilities. Since the raid, I had listened to his messages. He opened my heart, desires, and three resources of life to the idea of the continual process of restoration—that was *authenticity*. His words moved me from *perfectionism* to *excellence* and *encouraged* me to do the best with what I had as I yielded the outcomes to the Restorer.

Toward the end of 1992, I attended one of his conferences for Christian business owners, and we ended up eating dinner at the same table. As I listened to Bill Hybels speak, I thought back to my dirt-road walk as a child and the prayer I had offered to God while alone in the County Line sanctuary. I wondered if I had missed my calling.

I watched as Bill glanced at our name tags. Next to me sat John Bertrand, skipper of *Australia II*—the yacht that in 1983 competed for the America's Cup and won, ending 132 years of victories by the New York Yacht Club, the longest winning streak in sports. When Bill saw my name tag he noticed I was from Auburn, Indiana.

"That's where they have the biggest collector car auction in the world," Bill said.

I nodded.

Then he asked me, "Mitch, what is it that you do?"

He almost fell out of his chair when I responded, "I do that auction, and you just made my life!"

We both laughed together. We hit it off. Bill had left his family business to start a church. He had built a student ministry movement inside a church to almost ten times its adult attendance. When he had discerned his own Holy Spirit prompting to create a new movement, he and a group of like-minded friends walked door-to-door asking people if they attended church. If the answer was, "Yes," they thanked the people and moved on. However, when the answer was, "No," they asked, "Why?" The top three responses were that church was: (1) it's boring, (2) they're always asking for money, and (3) they always end later than scheduled.

In classic Bill Hybels fashion, he founded a church targeted toward those who did not attend. Each service would be engaging, its leaders would refrain from asking new attendees for money, and each gathering would start and end on time. The first services took place in the Willow Creek Movie Theatre (hence the name, Willow Creek Community Church). At the time of this writing,

Willow hosts 22,000 attendees each weekend and 5,000 during its mid-week services. These mid-week services are populated mostly by believers who fully surrendered their lives to Christ during the weekend gatherings.

Whenever I had an auction near Willow Creek Community Church, I stopped by to see Bill. He did church like I did business. It sparked a connection between us. Experiencing his wiring made me question if I had it all wrong years prior. Did I misunderstand my dirt-road calling? Did I misunderstand the altar at nine years of age? Was God actually telling me to be a ministry leader like Bill, or had I been destined to auction across the globe first? I can only assume the latter, because I had not been exposed to Willow or anything like it until 1992 when God unlocked my gate to Restoration Road.

My decision to walk away from the auction business was made clearer due to the investment in my life by Bill Hybels. Seven years later, now that I had put the responsibility of Kruse International behind me, I sensed God leading me in a new direction.

I continued to study full-time in seminary, completing my Masters degree and beginning the work on my Doctorate. During this time, I attended a leadership conference at Willow Creek where I was amazed at the sight of 4,000 pastors, church staff, and volunteers who attended from all over the world. I noticed one person in particular who looked familiar.

Kelly Byrd was much taller than he appeared on the *Bible Hour* broadcast on Fort Wayne television. He stood 6' 8" and was a member of the 1983 NIT-Champion Fresno State University basketball team. I stepped forward and reached up to introduce myself to Kelly, and surprisingly the next morning we ended up sitting next to each other. As we shared our stories, our numerous similarities became clear. Our fathers were a lot alike.

After our conversation, we agreed to get together after we returned home. I knew he would be busy with his church of 1,500 people, so I was not in a hurry to bother him with my questions about starting a new church. However, later that week, I received a voice message from Kelly who tracked me down through my pastor at County Line.

Kelly and I decided to meet for breakfast on Thursday morning—something we would do for the next year and a half. In our first meeting, Kelly asked me what I believed God was calling me to do. I told him about my vision to start a new church similar to Willow Creek. He surprised me by immediately inviting me to join him in teaching at Blackhawk Baptist Church, where he was senior pastor. He shared that Blackhawk was a clean canvas, ready for someone like me to paint with my colors. My study of personalities combined with my experiences with thousands of customers warned me that many times people over-promise and under-deliver. I struggled to determine whether an existing church structure would accept the entrepreneurial spirit that I would bring. Could the old contain the new? Consequently, I decided to finish my Doctorate before making my decision to accept his offer to volunteer as a teaching pastor at the church.

Restoration Road included a few speed bumps: stone and sand. The reactions of stone hearts, like the older brother in Jesus' trilogy, hampered me from continuing on my path toward connecting ministry and marketplace. The reactions of sand hearts, like the younger brother in Jesus' parable, saw my career change as crazy. I was at the pinnacle of my industry. Many collectors bought and sold solely on my advice. I have to admit, their argument made sense. However, my prompting had been clear to me. One customer and friend comforted me with these words, concluding a telephone call where we had discussed my transition, "Mitchell, everyone did business with you, not because of your position, but because of your person." In his own way, he was saying that who

I was designed to *be* determined what I was designed to *do* and ultimately determined where I was designed to *go*.

Looking back at Restoration Road, I realize that it has been filled with many defining moments that the Restorer pieced together to bring me to this point. It did not mean that He made me steal the metal box; rather He used it, in spite of myself, to shape me into who He wanted me to *be*. He used the events that unfolded when I auctioned the curio cabinet to fashion me into what He desired me to *do*. He used the meetings in Derald's storage room, especially his question about wisdom becoming the new target of my life, to take me where He wanted me to *go*. Since that day of full surrender when I was nine years old, my heart, desires, and three resources of life were being restored to authenticity to be like His.

March 10, 2002, was another defining marker for me on Restoration Road. Kelly Byrd had invited me to preach at Blackhawk on Sunday morning, since he would be traveling back to his California hometown for his birthday. I jumped at the chance to communicate what God had done with my life up to that point, and there was no better text to describe my journey than the parable of the father who had two sons. I still remember this like it was only yesterday.

A pastor had told me that when I preached, I should picture an audience of one in the balcony applauding his approval. That person is the Restorer who said, "There is rejoicing in the presence of the angels of God over one sinner who repents" (Luke 15:10). At the conclusion of the sermon, a young woman walked down the aisle to pray with me. She humbled all four chambers of her heart with the Master Key of full surrender to unlock her gate to Restoration Road where the vertical intersected with the horizontal, freeing her from the prison of pride and pretense. This was an indication to me that there was thunderous applause in heaven. God's vision had been followed by his provision. He was using me while on my own Restoration Road journey to bring His restoration to others.

The one thing that we are guaranteed on this journey down Restoration Road is change. I had been locked in pride's prison of pretense from separating the vertical from the horizontal. Sometimes it seemed like I had a stone heart on Sunday and a sand heart Monday through Saturday. The Master Key that unlocked the gate to Restoration Road had been inside me all along. It was cross-shaped. When I humbled all four chambers of my heart to the Restorer, I began life with a clay heart, one that was malleable in His hands of change. This led to a humility in horizontal relationships that transformed my life's desire from foolishness to wisdom.

The Restorer renewed me by working from the inside out so that those outside would come in. This was the ripple effect of His restoration. He restored my heart, my desires, and my three resources of life including my business. He restored my *communion* with Him, my *community* with others, and He was beginning to use me to restore my *culture*.

Chapter Fifteen

RESTORING OTHERS: EVERY ENCOUNTER IS A THREE-WAY CALL

In August 2002, I became a full-time volunteer in a newly established role of teaching pastor at what Kelly and I renamed Blackhawk Ministries. Soon afterwards, I proposed to Kelly that I start a Wednesday night gathering as a unique expression of the kingdom of heaven, where people could learn about Restoration Road. This replaced the mid-week service that had been a duplicate of Sunday morning. We called it Common Ground—the name was Kelly's idea. Leading this gathering became one of the most effective catalysts to move me further on Restoration Road.

Wednesday nights represented an opportunity for up to one hundred people to investigate God. Many of them who attended were in church for the first time in their lives. We enjoyed a great band who led us in worship, then we invited the audience to help us select the "Super Size Reprise:" a repeat of their favorite song from the set. I welcomed everyone, reminding them of the four hallmarks of our gathering. First, we had all sinned and desired life apart from God, yet He offered grace in Christ to restore us. Second, I shared that our format was relaxed. It was the biggest come-as-you-are party in the city. Third, I taught that the gathering was authentic. It was a safe place to say, "I got it wrong," or even, "I got it right." We were to check the pretense at the door. Fourth, I reminded everyone that we were going to have fun.

We laughed every night—sometimes to keep from crying, because we included a prayer time. I invited anyone to share a joy that could be multiplied or a burden that could be divided. The stories of death, divorce, disease, debt, and distress were gut-wrenching. Yet the stories of life, reunion, healing, freedom, and peace were invigorating. Sometimes a person shared a need only to have someone else provide for that need by the end of the service. Either an attendee or I would conclude the prayer time by communicating our joys and our burdens to God.

Next, I taught the Bible with my best effort to make the message relevant to the audience. Usually, I asked the question that the text answered and followed it with a real life story that introduced the topic. I read the selected verses from the Bible, and we walked through the passage line-by-line, as I explained, illustrated, and applied the main themes, often supporting them with other Bible passages. I always invited questions as I taught in an effort to keep the gathering open, free-flowing, and personal. I tried to get to know every person who attended. I discovered that the four desires were evident in each one. Common Ground provided an opportunity for them to realign their hearts, desires, and three resources of life in the Restorer.

One night, something amazing happened. It was the first in a chain reaction of events that taught me the ripple effect of a story that unfolded on Restoration Road.

A couple sitting next to me stared blankly as I asked them the same question I would ask countless others. During the remainder of the worship songs, I watched as they wrestled with the answer. After the music ended, they approached me and said, "We're ready."

I surprised myself when I asked if they would share their story with those who were in attendance. They agreed, and as everyone gathered, they spoke about their prodigal stories of sand and stone and their attempts at self-restoration, including their struggles with pride. They bravely confessed and humbly surrendered their lives to the Restorer as their Savior and Lord.

The week following this meeting, I thought about how my life had collided with so many who were now attending these Wednesday night meetings. I learned that traveling along Restoration Road was as much about listening as it was about speaking. Our unique stories add value to life as they become teaching parables. God has given each one of us a unique story so that we can share His story with others. When we listen to others' stories, they listen to ours. I had the opportunity to experience this firsthand.

One Wednesday night, I was sitting in my church office wrestling with the Holy Spirit prompting me that I was supposed to go to Common Ground and ask people to share the trials they had been experiencing. I interpreted this prompting as an indication that someone wanted to surrender his life to the Restorer. The only problem was that this meant that I would not be preaching a message—a radical idea for a church service. I decided to go for it. I shared my struggle with the group and was shocked at their response as many hands were raised throughout the room.

I listened to each person's story about tremendous burdens, needs, and the unmistakable longing to be restored to authenticity. At the close of the night, like an auctioneer, I asked once more if there was anyone who wanted to surrender his or her life to the Restorer.

No one else raised a hand.

I taught from a few Bible passages that were applicable to the stories that had been shared. I prayed for each person who spoke and dismissed the group. It had been an incredible night. I was thankful to God for placing me among those who were ministering in the midst of their brokenness. While the circumstances were unique, the stories had one common thread—no one can restore himself. It had been a decade since my late-night conversation with God, but since then I had experienced countless conversations with Him and others who were on this same dirt-road journey. Still I thought that my Holy Spirit prompting had been to listen for someone who desired to fully surrender his life to the Restorer.

On my way out, I was stopped by a young couple. They said to me, "I think we're the people you were talking about at the end."

The young man shared with me their roller-coaster life. He had been a criminal defense attorney who owned a prestigious firm. One day, a client paid him for his services with cocaine. It reignited a casual usage from his high school days and leveraged an addiction within a matter of months. Just like the younger son in Jesus' trilogy, he lost everything. He and his new bride were forced to return home to live with his mother.

I responded to their questions, sensing that they might be ready to surrender their lives to the Restorer. Perhaps my spiritual wires had not been crossed. She was ready; he was not. I saw how surrendering their lives to the Restorer was a difficult decision. They were still in the midst of their struggle to find satisfaction of their desires apart from God. As with all of us, their sins were many.

The darkest sins are the hardest for us to give up, because they are so embedded in our hearts. Yet, when we feel the heat of the Refiner's fire beginning to burn, we realize that we are on borrowed time. Soon we'll be due for a face-to-face, heart-to-heart encounter with the Restorer.

I prayed with them as she fully surrendered her heart to Christ as Savior and Lord. We chatted a little, and they were on their way.

I would later learn that her husband had asked her if she had felt differently as they exited the church. She replied, "All I can tell you is I feel a tremendous peace that I've never felt before."

The Refiner's fire must have been scorching because the following week her husband returned to our Wednesday meeting. After speaking with him, I realized that he was trying to clean himself up as part of his own self-restoration program instead of coming to the Restorer to get cleaned up. I shared with him pieces of my journey, hoping that he could learn from my mistakes. I let him know that all of my attempts at self-restoration always fell short of humbly receiving the grace of the Restorer. He was incarcerated in pride's prison of pretense, and he needed the Master Key of full surrender.

"You're right, Mitch," he replied. "And if that's the case, then I need to do this right now."

He fell to his knees and prayed to God in his broken words, "I can't. You can. I can't free myself from the penalty of my sin. You can. I can't free myself from the power of sin and be lord of my life. You can."

The Restorer was at work, and He was not finished.

The following week the wife returned alone to share with me that her husband had stolen $100, pawned their wedding rings, and went out to buy cocaine in a church parking lot. This time his binge was different. For the first time, he felt guilt and remorse for what he had done. I told her to have him come back the next week and not let this be the deal-breaker for his life. Sometimes, restoration involves taking two steps forward and one step back.

The couple returned a week later, and he shared the story of his binge with the rest of the group. It was the last time he ever used illegal drugs. He later went on to earn his degree in pastoral ministry and volunteered at a local church as a teaching pastor. He also decided to work on reinstating his license to practice law in order to provide legal services as a ministry to people in need.

Once again, the Restorer transformed a heart of sand into a heart of clay.

That morning at a restaurant, I had invited my waitress to the gathering. Now in attendance, she stood up while the man shared his story. She said, "I have a cocaine problem. I want what he has." I asked her if she was ready to fully surrender her life to the Restorer. She said, "Yes." In front of one hundred people, she prayed to God for forgiveness and restoration to authenticity. When the night was over, she had been flooded with names and telephone numbers of others who told her to call them if she was tempted to reuse drugs. With tears in her eyes and mine, we walked downstairs where her two daughters had been enjoying a Bible class to share the news with them. Both girls surrendered their lives to Christ that night.

A few weeks later, we baptized her. She had invited the entire staff from the restaurant to watch as she publicly responded to the Restorer's invitation to live with a clay heart where the vertical intersected with the horizontal.

I witnessed miracle after miracle, restoration after restoration. It was real, unadulterated, and authentic. I found more satisfaction in watching others share their stories than when I had shared my own. I discovered that when I became a carrier of the message of restoration to the unrestored, the Spirit of the Restorer had to accompany the message in order to connect with others. Paul described this to his audience when he wrote, "My message and my preaching were not with wise and persuasive words, but with a demonstration of the Spirit's power, so that your faith might not rest on men's wisdom, but on God's power" (1 Corinthians 2:4-5). At the same time, Paul advocated the necessity of wisdom in relating to the unrestored, "Be wise in the way you act toward outsiders; make the most of every opportunity. Let your conversation be always full of grace, seasoned with salt, so that you may know how to answer everyone" (Colossians 4:5-6). Paul was not contradicting himself; rather, he clarified that the Restorer was the source of his wisdom.

Every encounter in my life became a divine appointment for me to reveal the heart of the Restorer. I used His gracious words to connect with the hearts of others who became so thirsty for restoration that they asked me questions. The more convinced I became about the message of restoration, the more inspired I was to share it. The cross-shaped Master Key of humility provided wisdom that unlocked the hearts, desires, and lives of those who were ready to walk Restoration Road.

Have you ever struggled with how you should go to others with the gospel of full surrender to the Restorer?

When a person is caught in his sin, desiring life apart from God, we tend to go to him in one of two extremes: we are either *condemning* or *careless*. These responses are rooted in the two expressions of a proud heart: (1) stone (*condemning*) or (2) sand (*careless*). In the Sermon on the Mount, Jesus described the *be-do-go* of full surrender. Jesus taught that who we are to *be* (Matthew 5), determines what we are to *do* (Matthew 6), which determines where we are to *go* (Matthew 7).

The Master Communicator elaborated on the heart and mannerisms of an effective carrier of His gospel message. Jesus conveyed that we should not go to the world either *condemningly* or *carelessly*; rather, we should go *connectedly* with the Spirit of God in total humility, and with a heart of clay (Matthew 7:1-12). Consequently, every encounter with another person is a three-way call. When we are connected with God and connected with others, then they are connected with God. Whereas pride brings static on the line, humility offers a clear connection.

We are not to approach others condemningly with a hard heart of stone (Matthew 7:1-5). Jesus commanded, "Do not judge" (Matthew 7:1). Jesus was communicating that we should not *condemn* because we will be in turn condemned by God and others (Matthew 7:2; cf. Luke 6:37-38). Paul said that when we condemn others we pass judgment on ourselves because we do the same things (Romans 2:1). Jesus indicated that the judgment of God is predicated on how we flesh out His heart with others (Matthew 5:7). A hard heart of stone condemns out of judgment and legalism. A heart of stone often pretends to connect with God, while disconnecting with others. A heart of stone requires a severe tool to be shaped.

Are you condemning others? Jesus linked a condemning heart with the eyes, or one's perspective. Borrowing an illustration from His construction days, He said that the antidote to a condemning heart was to take the plank out of our own eye so that we can see clearly enough to help someone with the speck in his (Matthew 7:3-5). The plank in our own eye is our personal sin of pride, and it leaves a blind spot (Ephesians 4:18). Jesus referred to a person with this blind spot as a *hypocrite*—an actor, one with a mask, a pretender. Paul told the Galatians to go restore someone caught in sin with total humility as if they were capable of committing the same mistake—no acting, no masks, no pretending. (Galatians 6:1).

Someone who has truly received God's forgiving grace simply cannot condemn another person.

Jesus, the Author of grace, did not condemn the woman caught in adultery: "Jesus straightened up and asked her, 'Woman, where are they? Has no one condemned you?' 'No one, sir,' she said. 'Then neither do I condemn you,' Jesus declared. 'Go now and leave your life of sin.'" (John 8:10-11).

One of my mentors owned a landfill outside an upscale southeastern community. We traveled throughout the United States together searching for collector cars to add to his collection. On one trip, he was telling me how challenging it had been for him to receive zoning approval for his landfill—something that every community needs, but no community seems to want. I will never forget what he told me. He said, "Mitchell, everybody thinks garbage stinks, except his own." In many ways Jesus was saying the same thing, the plank in our eye is believing that our own sin garbage does not really stink.

One tool we can use to recognize and remove the plank in our own eye lies in two simple words: "Me too." Before we go to anyone caught in sin, we need to be able to look inside our hearts and say, "Me too." These two words free us from going to others with a condemning heart of stone. I know this to be true because Derald listened to my confessions in that unfinished storage room in 1992, and he looked me in the eyes and said, "Me too." He was aware enough of his sand and stone heart condition that although he had not committed mistakes identical to mine, he recognized that he had fallen short with similar sinful desires. I paid his authentic act forward by looking into the eyes of every unrestored person that I encountered in a confessing moment and saying, "Me too."

Recently, at the beginning of a school year, I received a call early in the morning from my daughter's teacher who was co-ordinating chapels for the school. She confided that she had lost her chapel speaker for the first four weeks of the school year and asked if I could teach one of the sessions. When I inquired what she wanted me to talk about, she replied, "Anything about Jesus." I said, "Praise the Lord."

I went on with my workout, continuing to think about the work-sheet I was preparing for my upcoming radio broadcast, "Wisdom Works." The topic was "The Parable of the Unforgiving Debtor." I am bald, and I am slow. Consequently, it took me a while to realize that I could teach on this parable at the school's chapel. So a couple of days later, I was standing in front of a group of elementary school students challenging them to "forgiveness," which means "to let go." I asked them to examine their hearts for any white knuckling, or holding on, of unforgiveness. With the music playing, heads bowed, eyes closed, and palms up, an electric impulse of conviction ran up my spine.

I am sensitive, and my wife is from Waterloo. Consequently, her occasional Waterloo tone of voice hurts my feelings. I realized right there in the chapel that I had been teaching about not withholding forgiveness, while at that very same time, I had been withholding forgiveness from my spouse. I rushed home that morning, stood in front of the elliptical machine while she was exercising, and fell on my knees pleading for forgiveness. She accepted.

This incident is just a husband and wife thing. However, it serves as a model of how we condemn others who have unrestored hearts. But we are called to look into the eyes of the unrestored and authentically say with our hearts and our mouths, "Me too."

We are also not to approach others carelessly with a loose heart of sand (Matthew 7:6). Jesus warned of the opposite kind of pride, one that is *careless* and loose with the gospel message, naively scattering it to cynics who would automatically reject what they hear. Jesus painted the image of wild, ravenous dogs and pigs who would not give any consideration to a pearl of wisdom (Matthew 7:6). Proverbs teaches of the same dilemma that occurs when one attempts to argue with a fool (Proverbs 26:4-5). A heart of sand *tells carelessly* because a sand heart is loose and licentious. A heart of sand often pretends to connect with others, while disconnecting with God. A heart of sand requires a storm to be malleable.

This is why Jesus taught in parables. Jesus was careful with his words. He discerned the wisdom appropriate for the level of hard-heartedness among his listeners. Jesus pointed out that cynical hearts were already hard, so if He merely presented truth, it would automatically be rejected. However, He knew that if He would share a story, then people would leave thinking about the details of the story, and from that could perhaps discover the truth of the story in an unthreatening fashion. The truth *concealed* could be the truth *revealed* by sharing a story. Two thousand years ago, a Rabbi would teach a parable and then explain it more fully to those who would call themselves his disciples.

Jesus warned the hard-hearted Pharisees of carelessly speaking against the Holy Spirit (Matthew 12:34-37). Contrastingly, Jesus was careful with his words with Nicodemus (John 3:1-21).

Jesus discerned the wisdom appropriate for the level of hard-heartedness with the rich young ruler. Solomon communicated that when attempting to connect with others, we must discern the wisdom appropriate for the level of hard-heartedness: "Whoever corrects a mocker invites insult; whoever rebukes a wicked man incurs abuse. Do not rebuke a mocker or he will hate you; rebuke a wise man and he will love you. Instruct a wise man and he will be wiser still; teach a righteous man and he will add to his learning" (Proverbs 9:7-9). The Apostle Paul agreed, teaching that we should be wise with outsiders, discerning the wisdom appropriate for their level of hard-heartedness (Colossians 4:5-6).

We often see careless words played out this way. A believing woman is married to an unbelieving husband. Over time, their marriage gets dinged and corroded, resulting from two people with totally different hearts being united in matrimony. The believing woman begins to seek counsel from her believing friends and their husbands. That group begins to go carelessly one after another, loosely handling the Gospel pearls of wisdom with her unbelieving husband. Not once do they attempt to discern the wisdom appropriate for the level of hard-heartedness in the unbelieving spouse. Going carelessly with a heart of sand often confuses the person we want to bring to Christ and leaves a disconnect with them.

We are to go connectedly with a soft heart of clay (Matthew 7:7-12). Jesus described the three connections in a way that resembles a three-way call today.

Connection one—ASK God.

Jesus said that we should go to others with a heart of humility that is first connected with God. Whereas a stone heart *tells condemningly*, and a sand heart *tells carelessly*, a clay heart *asks connectedly*. Jesus commanded us to ASK—Ask, Seek, and Knock. He described a progressive intensity of humility in prayer, one's heart connected with God's. He promised that if we ask humbly, we will receive; if we seek (making our muscles move with our prayers), we will find; and if we knock persistently, the door will be opened (Matthew 7:7-11).

You might ask, "Receive what? Find what? Open what door?" In Luke's parallel passage, we discover that the answer is not *what*, but *who*. "Your father in heaven (will) give the Holy Spirit to those who ask Him" (Luke 11:13 [parentheses mine]). The Holy Spirit removes the planks from our own eyes and gives us wisdom to discern, but not condemn. He keeps us from being careless with the pearls of the Gospel message, giving us wisdom to answer outsiders (Colossians 4:5-6). He offers us a clay heart that connects, one that is malleable in the hands of the Potter. A clay heart is the humble heart of Christ (Matthew 11:29). We must first ask the Holy Spirit into our lives and then ask Him for wisdom regarding each encounter.

Connection two—ask others.

Jesus summed up the Sermon on the Mount with the main horizontal theme, "So, in everything, do to others what you would have them do to you, for this sums up the Law and the Prophets" (Matthew 7:12). When we do to others what we would have them do to us, we connect with them. Jesus said that if we ask others about their needs, then we will be better equipped to meet them in order to *connect* others with God. We will never know how to serve them in the way that they need to be served unless we humbly ask and listen. Solomon said that anyone who answers before listening is foolish (Proverbs 18:13). A humble clay heart connects with both God and others.

I have developed a few simple questions to connect with others. To date, these have never resulted in push back from those who were unrestored.

First, I often ask, "What is your church or spiritual background?"

Next, I inquire, "Will you please tell me your story?"

After asking this question, which often generates descriptions of tragedy and triumph in another person's life, I ask, "Where is God in all that for you?"

Then I ask this penetrating, unthreatening question, "In terms of the God thing, would you describe yourself as skeptic, seeker, or surrendered?" Someone who is unrestored will usually attempt to choose between skeptic and seeker.

Connection three—others ask God into their lives.

When we ask God for guidance and ask questions of others, the Holy Spirit connects others with God. The Law and the Prophets (Matthew 7:12) were designed to connect others with God. Jesus described this humility toward God and others as the greatest commandments (Matthew 22:37-40), and Paul said that the entire law was summed up in one command, "Love your neighbor as yourself" (Galatians 5:14). He told the Romans that love fulfilled the law (Romans 13:9-10). Jesus' half-brother James agreed (James 2:8). The apostle Peter clarified the importance of others asking God into their lives: "But in your hearts set apart Christ as Lord. Always be prepared to give an answer to everyone who asks you to give the reason for the hope that you have. But do this with gentleness and respect" (1 Peter 3:15).

On a hot Middle Eastern day, Jesus provided the ultimate picture of a three-way call when He connected with the heart of the Father and with the woman at the well, who then also connected with God. He was not condemning. He was not careless. He was connected, and He asked. Consequently, she asked the Restorer into her life (John 4:1-54).

I have prayed with scores of people to surrender their lives to Christ. Every single one was asked. I usually phrase the question this way, "Would you like to draw a line in the sand, put a stake in the ground, and fully surrender your heart and life to Christ as Savior and Lord?" Then I ask each to pray a simple prayer to God, "I can't. You can. I can't free myself from the penalty of my sin.

In Christ, You can. I can't free myself from the power of my sin. In Christ, You can. I fully surrender my heart and life to You as Savior to free me from the penalty and Lord to free me from the power of my sin. Please forgive me and restore me."

Trade your condemning heart of stone or your careless heart of sand for a soft heart of clay that is connected with God and others. Ask the Holy Spirit to take the plank out of your own eye so that you can clearly see the speck in others' eyes. Ask Him for wisdom to answer outsiders. Ask others how you can serve them. Listen. In everything, act with Christ's heart of humility, and His Spirit will *connect* them with God. Every encounter is a three-way call. Whereas pride causes static on the line, humility offers a clear connection.

Chapter Sixteen

THE GATE, THE ROAD, THE DESTINATION

Susan and I were returning from our annual anniversary week of rejuvenating in the sun at Atlantis in the Bahamas. We sat and talked in the Nassau Airport awaiting the boarding announcement for our return flight home. When our flight number was called, we quickly grabbed our bags and merged into the line to enter a secured area leading to the tarmac. We followed the flow of foot traffic through the gate, down the jetway, and onto the plane where the only two vacancies on the small jet matched the seat assignments on our boarding passes. I wondered how everyone had boarded so quickly, because we had immediately responded to the first boarding call.

Then I noticed that something was not right.

Having traveled more than two million miles by air, I was sure that I was sensing a vibe of American Airlines blue rather than Delta Airlines blue. When I looked at the logo on the flight attendant's badge, I knew we had a problem. Instead of a letter from the Greek alphabet pinned to his shirt, I saw two adjoining A's flanked by wings. If my eyes were deceiving me, my ears were not. At that moment, I heard the final pre-takeoff announcement over the plane's tin-can public address system: "Ladies and gentlemen, please stow your luggage under your seats or in the overhead bins as we prepare for an on-time departure to Miami." We were going to Cincinnati.

Susan and I grabbed our bags, sprinted off the plane, up the jetway, and through the gate. We ran through the airport hallway like Usain "Lightning" Bolt, searching for our airplane's gate, worried that we would miss our flight. Suddenly, we were stopped by a team of uniformed, armed airport staffers. We learned that in a post-9/11 world, airport security guards do not appreciate two travelers who board a plane and then immediately run off it.

We were searched in more ways than I care to remember. The security personnel, apathetic to the fact that we might miss our flight, combed through every crevice in our carry-on bags. The more I pleaded that we were risking having our flight take off without us, the more they found a new zipper to open in our duffle bags. Finally the guards finished their search, and we were set free. We ran past several gates with our eyes scanning ahead. Finally, we entered through the correct gate, sprinted down the right jetway, and boarded the flight that would arrive at our scheduled destination. Two different gates led to two different roads which led to two different destinations.

Two Gates, Two Roads, Two Destinations

We approach life with God through one of two gates, traveling one of two roads, leading to one of two destinations. One is religious, traveling from the outside in. The other is relational, traveling from the inside out. In the Sermon on the Mount, Jesus described the two gates, the two roads, and the two destinations: "Enter through the narrow gate. For wide is the gate and broad is the road that leads to destruction, and many enter through it. But small is the gate and narrow the road that leads to life, and only a few find it" (Matthew 7:13-14).

The first gate is *wide* (Matthew 7:13). Jesus referenced the Pharisee's outside in righteousness, using an analogy of wide city gates typical of the day. They had taken God's covenant community through a wide gate of rules, adding 1,500 of them to the 613 Old Testament laws. Paul said that they had created a righteousness of their own, not one that came from God (Romans 10:1-3).

The road is *broad*. Two thousand years ago, the main road traveling in and out of city walls spanned about 24 feet wide, an image familiar to Jesus' audience. The broad road most likely referred to the sinful nature. When we trust in our own man-made righteousness, we end up trusting in our own sinful nature for success. We fluctuate between legalism and license, based on our personal preferences, leaving us disconnected from intimacy with God. Paul said that those who are controlled by the sinful nature cannot please God (Romans 8:5-8).

The destination is *destruction*. The wide gate and broad road lead to death. Jesus said that the Pharisees' outside in righteousness actually closed the gates to the kingdom of heaven to others and even themselves (Matthew 23:13-14). The result is no life abundant and no life eternal.

Many are entering through it. The many are the proud in heart, both the legalistic and the licentious (Matthew 7:1-5, 6). Our natural state, by birth and by choice, travels through the wide gate, down the wide road, and to the destination of destruction (Genesis 8:21). Pride is the lock on the human heart.

The second gate is *narrow* (Matthew 7:14). Narrow meant that only one gate led to life. Jesus described inside out righteousness, one that looks within to find His Spirit. Christ is that Gate (John 10:7-9). Jesus told the Pharisees that the kingdom of God was within them, or in their midst (Luke 17:21). Describing the two gates to the Israelites who were entering the Promised Land, God said through Moses that the narrow gate was in their mouths and in their hearts (Deuteronomy 30:14). Referencing this passage, Paul told the Romans that the narrow gate within is where they find Christ (Romans 10:4-13). He called this the mystery of the Gospel—Christ in you, the hope of glory (Colossians 1:27).

The road is also *narrow*. Jesus' hearers would have been very familiar with the images here. Two thousand years ago, cities had narrow roads to private entrances where people could enter and exit the city walls. These entrances spanned only six feet wide. Here Jesus was describing the personal relationship with His *Spirit*. Paul described this as the road that led to life (Romans 8:9-11*)*. Again, Christ is that Road (John 14:6).

The destination is *life*. The Greek word for "life" is *zoe*, which means abundant and eternal life. Jesus said that we find life with God when we enter His narrow gate (John 10:10). Christ is that Destination of Life (John 14:6).

Few find it. And the few who do are the humble in heart (Matthew 5:3; 18:3). The key to the narrow gate of Christ is humility. He holds the key (Revelation 3:7) because He is humble in heart (Matthew 11:29). His half-brother James said that we should humbly receive the word of God planted in us that can save us (James 1:21).

Choose life (Deuteronomy 30:19). Go through the narrow gate. It is a matter of the heart, and the only way to experience life with God.

Consider these scenarios. Two people read the Bible. One goes through the narrow gate, one through the wide gate. One softens his heart to Christ in order to build up others, while the other hardens his heart to be puffed up with knowledge.

Two people go to church. One goes through the narrow gate, one through the wide gate. One softens his heart to Christ's mercy while the other hardens his heart hoping that others will see his religiosity.

Two people pray. One goes through the narrow gate, one through the wide gate. One softens his heart to Christ's Lordship while the other hardens his heart in an attempt to manipulate the Savior.

Two people give. One goes through the narrow gate, one through the wide gate. One softens his heart to Christ's generosity while the other hardens his heart, desiring attention and recognition for his gift.

Choose life. Go through the narrow gate of Christ, not the wide gate of religion (legalism or license). Travel down the road led by the Spirit, not the road blinded by our sinful nature. Enjoy the destination of life abundant and life eternal with God over the destination of destruction. Pride is the lock on your heart. Humility is the key.

Luke chapter 15 offers eight insights into the *destination* of a fully surrendered heart of clay. First, a heart of clay lowers a life of pride to one of humility. Second, it seeks the *light* of God's vision for ministry and marketplace. Third, it *listens* as it prays and obeys. Fourth, it *learns* wisdom from God's heart and applies it with street smarts to relationships with others. Fifth, a clay heart *leans* on God through repentance and faith that bring others to Christ with humble hearts. Sixth, a humble heart of clay is led by God and *leads* others in authentic truth. Seventh, a humble heart *loves* God and others. Eighth, this fully surrendered heart offers us the liberty to *let go* of the prison of sin that is rooted in pride, through receiving and offering forgiveness, the hallmark of Restoration Road paved by the Restorer.

But how do we get there? As you travel Restoration Road and discover your unique design of the Designer, I want to leave you with a summary of the eight characteristics of an unrestored gate of the heart, the unrestored stone and sand road of the desires, and the unrestored destination of our three resources of life. To map the restoration journey, I will also summarize the eight characteristics of a restored gate, a restored clay road, and a restored destination so that you can connect others with the Restorer. Remember to bring your Master Key of full surrender and the lessons you've learned in this book to intersect the vertical with the horizontal -- your sweet spot to live a life restored to authenticity.

First, our unrestored wide gate (heart) is locked in position toward life apart from God. Our problem is a depraved heart, rooted in pride. Our broad road (desires) is closed. We live closed — either like the older son's self-imposed definition of eternal life, or the younger son's wild search for abundant life. Our destination (three resources of life) is death. The danger of pride, through sand and stone, is that it makes one closed to the Restorer and results in death, or separation from Him.

On Restoration Road, our narrow gate is unlocked with the key that lowers our pride to the Restorer. He unlocks our hearts with the Master Key of the fully surrendered, humble heart of the Restorer. Our narrow road is open. This lowering of our pride makes us open to the Restorer. Our destination is life. This is the life of humility. When we live restored to authenticity, we discover the clay heart of the father in Jesus' trilogy instead of the sand and stone heart of his two sons. Like the Restorer, the father embraced a life of humility and unlocked his sons' hearts, opening them to considering both eternal and abundant life.

Stone-hearted older sons surrender what is convenient to them for eternal life. They deem themselves worthy of eternal life by their efforts. They work hard at not doing wrong. They try to be flawless in their approach to God. Often times they see only heaven, but miss life today. Older sons are evidenced in the Pharisees of Jesus' day.

Sand-hearted younger sons surrender what is convenient to them for abundant life. They focus on life on this earth now, and do not spend much time thinking of heaven and hell. They have a natural bent toward living for the moment which is sand-hearted jargon for living for themselves. The result is that they see this earth as a great place on which to build their own kingdom. They know that they do not measure up to God's standards, so they hope for the best.

Each son partially surrenders that which is convenient for him to surrender. Each is locked from the eternal and abundant life that God intends. Left to himself, each son remains on a journey toward separation from God because his lock pins are only partially raised.

Both stone-hearted and sand-hearted sons' destination is death because they pursue life apart from the Father.

However, Jesus said that the kingdom of heaven is here (Mark1:15). Nearly every Bible scholar and every church denomination agrees that Jesus Christ demonstrated the kingdom of heaven in its ultimate clarity. It includes today as well as the future of heaven, but it is not limited to either.

The Father's gate is unlocked with His key of humility because His heart is humble and is passionate for full surrender to eternal and abundant life. His road is open with grace, as the Author of eternal and abundant life. He creates children in His image as spiritual beings, able to access His heart (Genesis 1:26; John 1:9). His destination is eternal and abundant life. He opens Himself gracefully to granting outrageous requests, even if it means a lower status in the eyes of others. He lets His children choose, even when it hurts Him, though He graciously continues to offer the key to abundant and eternal life that flows from His humble heart.

Second, our unrestored wide gate is locked in clouded vision of purpose apart from God. Consequently, we hide in our broad-road detour from the Restorer. We hide either in older-son ministry or younger-son marketplace. Our destination is darkness.

On Restoration Road, our narrow gate is unlocked with 20/20 gospel vision. God draws everyone to this 20/20 vision. Therefore, one with a heart of clay travels the narrow road that seeks the Restorer for His vision, that intersects ministry with marketplace, leading to the destination of light. This is the vision of humility, evidenced in the lives of those who were fully surrendered to God, whose stories are recorded in both the Old and New Testaments. The Restorer turns our detours of darkness into light and shows us how ministry and marketplace must be focused on humility.

Stone-hearted older sons partially surrender to their moralistic worldview, resulting in a false ministry that they cannot relate to the marketplace. Their broad road hides them from others, including the Father, in the safety of their own detoured vision of high moral standards, focusing on others' faults. Ironically, their detour leads to the destination of darkness. Their hearts are darkened because their moral bar is not high enough when compared to the Father's.

While morality is upheld in Scripture, it is not presented as man's inherent ability to make himself right with God. Morality flows from the life of God in each man (Leviticus 19:2), but man's fallen morality, or righteousness, is like filthy rags to a holy God (Isaiah 64:6).

Sand-hearted younger sons partially surrender to their relativistic worldview ample with marketplace contact, but void of ministry, clouding their vision and taking them far from the Father's ministry heart. Their wide road hides them in the marketplace in a detour from the Father. They live irresponsibly only for the moment darkened with low moral standards because they see God as only grading on a curve that allows them entrance into the kingdom. They often minimize everyone's faults by placing theirs in full view for others to see.

Lacking their Father's vision, both stone-hearted and sand-hearted sons arrive at a destination that is a detour from the Father's vision, hidden in darkness.

The Father's gate humbly draws all to His gospel vision, seeking full surrender to both a ministry and marketplace mission. His road is to seek those who have detoured, running to chase them down or stooping to pick them up, becoming light for their paths as He draws them to His vision that intersects ministry with the marketplace. He challenges His children to do the same. He says that the humble are "in" and the proud are "out." His destination is light. This is the ministry and marketplace vision of His humble heart.

Third, our unrestored wide gate is locked in hurried busyness, a disunity of the heart that searches for contentment apart from God. When we're too busy, our wills, intellects, spirits, and emotions travel in opposing directions affecting our desires and resources. Our broad road tells God and others our plans in disobedience void of heartfelt prayer. Consequently, we work offline from God in disobedience and non-heartfelt prayer. Our destination is deafness to God and to others.

On Restoration Road, our narrow gate is unlocked with peace, an alignment of our hearts with the Restorer. We are a work in progress in His hands that are constantly at work in our lives (Ephesians 2:10). Consequently, we receive a heart that is in peaceful alignment with the Restorer. Our narrow road asks in prayer intersecting with heartfelt obedience. We ask God, and we ask others. Thus, humility's transformed desire is to pray and be obedient. Obedience makes our muscles move with our prayers. Our destination is to listen. We listen to God, and we listen to others. Listening to God is exercising the risk of humility. This example of full surrender restores deaf ears into ones that pray to and obey the Restorer in order to listen—even in those moments when we're tempted to disobey.

Stone-hearted older sons partially surrender to mechanical obedience. They think that they will obey their way to contentment with the Father, but they miss a heartfelt prayer life. Though the

Father calls them to live online in the peace of their journey together, stone-hearted older sons remain offline. They protect their pride and blame others. Their disobedience is camouflaged in their heart because their perceived obedience is actually joyless and rigid, trapping them in the past or the future as they miss the present with the Father. They simply over-plan, and perceiving that they have everything to lose, they take no risks.

Sand-hearted younger sons partially surrender to prayer void of obedience. Because of their hurried hearts, they also protect their independence by continuing offline from the Father who offers an online call. They are full of shame because they openly disobey; thus, they do not measure up when comparing themselves to others. Perceiving that they have nothing to lose, they risk everything, nearly all of the time. Their disobedience leads to a great need for selfish prayer as they frequently plead with the Father to cover commitments they have made beyond their limits.

Both stone-hearted and sand-hearted sons' destination is deafness to the Father

The Father's gate is peace for hurried hearts as He aligns them with His. He is the Restorer who humbly completes His children's hearts, joining them on their journeys, calling them to full surrender. His road asks His children to approach Him in prayer and obedience on their journey, risking their response. His destination is to listen, offering His children peace from an online connection with Him. This is the risk of His humble heart.

Fourth, our unrestored wide gate is locked in competence for conflict management apart from God. In our hearts, our sinful nature and the Spirit of the Restorer are in conflict with each other (Galatians 5:17). This leads to the broad road of stubborn gratification of our desires in resolving conflict led by our sinful nature (Galatians 5:16-17). We separate God's righteousness from street smarts. Our destination is dense in foolishness as we dam the flow of wisdom in our lives.

On Restoration Road, our narrow gate is unlocked with wisdom. This begins with fully surrendering all four chambers of our hearts to God (Proverbs 1:7; 9:10) in humility toward the Restorer (Proverbs 11:2; 22:4). Our narrow road is God's righteousness intersecting with street smarts. This is the sweet spot where God's heart is lived out in our relationships with others. Our destination is to learn. God desires that we learn His character. Humility allows us to change and grow wise by learning from God and others. Learning wisdom comes through the application of humility by making God's heart apply to our relationships and tasks. Instead of living foolishly dense, we are able to learn the Restorer's wisdom in order to live restored with God's righteousness and street smarts applied to our lives.

Stone-hearted older sons partially surrender the task of attaining the Father's righteousness. They believe they have the Father's morality through their own self-righteousness, but they lack street smarts; thus, they rarely communicate wisdom. Because they fear loss of achievement, in conflict they fight for self-righteousness.

Sand-hearted younger sons partially surrender to street smarts with people at the expense of the Father's righteousness. They make deals that skirt morality in their unrighteousness. Fearing the loss of their loose relationships when conflict arises they often flee any resemblance of righteousness.

Both stone-hearted and sand-hearted sons' destination is damming the flow of their Father's wise heart into their lives. Both become dense, or foolish.

The Father's gate is wisdom, that His character of humility be revealed in conflict, so He offers a river of His Spirit of wisdom. His road requires full surrender to the intersection of His righteousness and street smarts. He collaborates, valuing people and task, producing win-win resolutions. His destination is to examine the heart and teach wisdom, so that we will learn the application of His humble heart.

Fifth, our unrestored wide gate is locked in control from broken communion with God and broken community with others. When community is broken, we attempt to become like god in our lives as we roll against the will of God and others. Our broad road is trusting in ourselves as we trust in our giftedness rather than our godliness, missing communion with God and community with others. Our destination is divided in slavery rather than sonship.

On Restoration Road, our narrow gate is unlocked with power in a relationship. God desires relationship rather than religion. This begins when we fully surrender our hearts to Him. Our narrow road is faith intersecting with repentance as we trust in God and others. Humility allows us to turn from trusting in ourselves in repentance and turn to trusting God in faith. This leads to trusting in others. Our destination is to lean on Him and others with faith and repentance. This is the commitment of humility. Living restored to authenticity takes a life divided and transforms it into one that leans into communion with the Restorer in faith and repentance and leans into community with others.

Stone-hearted older sons partially surrender to repentance, but waver in faith. They interpret the Father's faithful desire for a relationship with them as religion, seeing communion with the Father as being dependent on their own ritualistic activity. They live the life of a stone-hearted slave. When they do not sin and times are difficult, they blame God. When they perceive that they sin and times are rough, they blame themselves. They keep control in the name of religion. Consequently, they see the Father as a taskmaster, rather than a loving parent. They do not perceive that they have already received unmerited grace; thus, they do not issue it to others, resulting in broken community. They desire rules without relationship.

Sand-hearted younger sons partially surrender to faith, but not repentance. They trust themselves, willing to break communion with the Father because they see themselves as slaves needing to be set free to pursue their tainted version of sonship. They want control in the form of carte blanche authority to support their lifestyle. They take a random approach to relationship without rules.

Both stone-hearted and sand-hearted sons arrive at a destination that is divided from the Father.

The Father's gate is the power of a relationship that stems from humble communion with His children. His road is the intersection of repentance and faith in communion and community that He offers relationally to all. He is faithful, or trustworthy, in relationships. His destination is to lean into His children so that they can lean on Him in repentance and faith as two inseparable sides of the same coin. The result is trusting communion with Him. He offers the hope of sonship, rather than slave-like religion. This frees His children to enjoy community with each other. Rules support His relationships. This is the commitment of His humble heart.

Sixth, our unrestored wide gate is locked in hard-hearted security; we maintain a rigidity of heart that seeks security from the outside in. Our broad road is denial of truth. Our destination is deception, pretending from the outside in.

On Restoration Road, our narrow gate is unlocked with authenticity that reflects the design of the Designer from the inside out. Our narrow road is recognizing authentic truth that intersects evangelism with discipleship. We receive evangelism and discipleship from God. Rather than hoarding both with a focus on one, while hindering the release of the other in relationships, we authentically release both horizontally. This means that our connection with others will run both wide and deep from the inside out. When all four chambers of our hearts are led by the Restorer, then the Restorer in us leads others by connecting with all four chambers of their hearts (1 Corinthians 11:1). The Restorer takes a deceived life and transforms it into one that leads, to evangelize and disciple, with an outpouring of influence through humility found in hearts of clay. Consequently, our destination is to lead.

Stone-hearted older sons partially surrender to discipleship, ministering to other older sons, void of evangelism. They deny the breadth of truth from a hard heart of stone, ignoring the Father's heart of clay. Abusing objective truth, they do not surrender to authentic evangelism and serving younger sons. They see a heart condition as exclusively an outside in movement. They deny the truth by telling so much detail of it that what they say is actually untrue. They are critical of others. They are artificially deep, but not wide, robbing themselves of the influence that the Father desires.

Sand-hearted younger sons partially surrender to evangelism void of discipleship. They deny the depth of truth, pretending with their hard hearts of compacted sand. Abusing subjective truth, they are often a mile wide, but only an inch deep. They tell too little of the truth, frequently offering false compliments.

Stone-hearted and sand-hearted sons arrive at a destination of deception.

The Father's gate is an authentic heart condition, flowing from His humble heart with the breadth and depth of full surrender. His road is truth that leads with both evangelism and discipleship. His Lordship produces His destination, that His children will lead others to Him. This leadership is wide in that it is available to all (evangelism), and it is deep in that it never ends (discipleship). His desire is that His children will communicate the same contagious, authentic, clay heart, malleable in His hands. Leading is the connection of His humble heart.

Seventh, our unrestored wide gate is locked in self-centered significance, we carry an internal sign that says, "Hey, look at me!" Our broad road is rejection of God and others. Our destination is detachment from the Restorer and others because we build walls around ourselves, walling ourselves in and others out.

On Restoration Road, our narrow gate is unlocked with God-centered worship. This is bending the knees of our hearts to God.

We worship Him with our wills in service, with our intellects through the Word, with our spirits through symbols, and with our emotions through music and the arts. Each chamber is not limited to a particular worship style; however, each chamber leads the others in its aforementioned corresponding style. Our narrow road is acceptance of God and others. God desires that we be God-centered, which is fleshed out in our being others-centered. Humility accepts God and others (Romans 15:7). Our destination is love. Humility loves God and others, receiving the Restorer's gracious provision and protection and freely issuing the same to others. This is the action of humility, humbly loving God and worshiping and serving Him with our lives. This is impossible without serving others. When the Restorer moves hard hearts from being detached in either stone or sand by building walls to clay hearts who love and serve by building bridges, we provide for and protect those in need through the generous giving of our three resources of life: our time, talent, and treasure.

Stone-hearted older sons partially surrender to provision and protection of their love for the Father without provision and protection of love to others. Their wall is in the form of prejudice because their self-centered perspective is one of top-down superiority. What might have begun as legitimate provision and protection for themselves has escalated into self-indulgence.

Sand-hearted younger sons partially surrender to provision and protection of love to others, but not to provision and protection of their love for the Father. They reject others with a wall of jealousy because their self-centeredness comes from the bottom up, despite the Father's example of building bridges to others. What might have begun as appropriate provision and protection for others has escalated to younger sons becoming over-extended.

Stone-hearted and sand-hearted sons arrive at a destination that is detached from the Father.

The Father's gate is Christ-centered and anchored in humility. His road is accepting His children, whom He receives with vulnerability and without favoritism, so that they will do the same. His destination is love that serves. He provides and protects for others by building bridges rather than walls. From His children, He seeks full surrender to loving God and loving others. Love is the action of His humble heart.

Eighth, our unrestored wide gate is sin. We fall short of the goal. We twist misses in order to make them right. We miss on purpose; and we never shoot, leaving good undone. Our broad road is resisting and withholding forgiveness. We hold on and remain imprisoned by breaking apart the cross, the vertical from the horizontal, leaving four walls that we form into a prison for our offenders. The irony is that we, the withholders, are the ones incarcerated inside the four walls. Our destination is the dungeon of unforgiveness.

On Restoration Road, our narrow gate is unlocked with forgiveness. Our narrow road is the intersection of justice and mercy that is received from God and issued to others. Humility receives forgiveness by surrendering to God and offering forgiveness to others. God's passion is for us to live free in the Restorer who offers justice and mercy in forgiveness—which means "to let go." We owed a debt that we could not pay. The Restorer paid a debt that He could not owe, and we were set free. Our destination is to let go of sins against us because the Restorer has freed us from the penalty and power of sin in our lives. This is the transportation of humility. Being forgiven by Christ requires that we humbly transport forgiveness to others. The Restorer frees us from holding on to the dungeon of unforgiveness to let go with justice and mercy, to forgive and be forgiven.

Stone-hearted older sons partially surrender to justice void of mercy. They approach sin in a way that resists receiving and withholds offering forgiveness because they do not perceive that they need it, nor that others warrant it. Their distorted form of justice without mercy escalates to condemnation of others, missing the freedom the Father offers them through the white flag of full surrender.

Sand-hearted younger sons partially surrender to mercy without justice, desiring license from others. Their approach to sin is resisting and withholding true forgiveness because they do not perceive that they warrant it, nor that others need it. They withhold the white flag of full surrender to the Father by ignoring justice, missing the freedom their Father has in store for them. Their abuse of mercy void of justice slides into their desire for pity and licentiousness with others.

Misdirected and unable to find satisfaction of their accounts anywhere but in the father's forgiveness, both stone-hearted and sand-hearted sons find themselves arriving at the destination of the dungeon of unforgiveness.

The Father's gate is forgiveness. His road is surrendering payment for sin because He paid the price from His own account with justice and mercy. His destination is freedom for forgiveness which is the only concept that includes full surrender to both justice and mercy. He humbly invites all to His celebration of freedom. Forgiveness received vertically warrants forgiveness issued horizontally. The Father's clay heart allows Him to let go, and that's how He transfers his humble heart.

———————————

Who you are designed to *be* (a son) determines what you *do*, which determines where you *go*. Both stone- and sand-hearted sons confuse the *be-do-go* principle. Both believe that what they *do* and where they *go* will determine who they are designed to *be*. Both think that they can earn sonship. Stone-hearted older sons believe that staying home with the Father *(go)* and obeying His commands *(do)* makes them a good son *(be)*. Sand-hearted younger sons see liberty to leave *(go)* and friendship with the world *(do)* as the mark of a successful son *(be)*. However, with God, the alignment of life is *be-do-go*, authenticity that reflects the design of the Designer from the inside out.

The Father is relational with both stone- and sand-hearted sons. He offers both a chance to be restored when they sin—privately and publicly—against him. The Father relates to his sons. He is not loose, nor is he hard or legalistic. He is soft, yielding, and loving, relationally connecting grace to both stone and sand hearts.

God offers us restoration through the Restorer, in whom He humbles Himself to reach us and heal our problems. God's passion (*be*), perspective (*do*), and priorities (*go*) are perfectly aligned in the Restorer, who is Jesus Christ.

Eight characteristics of Christ demonstrate His sufficiency to restore us. First, Christ is gracious. He is the life of God (John 14:6). Second, Christ is the light of God (John 8:12). Third, Christ is the peace of God (Ephesians 2:14; Romans 5:10). Fourth, Christ is the wisdom of God (1 Corinthians 1:24). Fifth, Christ is the power of God in whom we find the hope of a relationship with the heavenly Father (1 Corinthians 1:24). Sixth, Christ is the truth of God (John 14:6). Seventh, Christ is the love of God (John 3:16; 15:13; 2 Corinthians 8:9). Eighth, Christ is the forgiveness of God (Matthew 9:6; John 8:11). He is our Savior and Lord.

Too often, sand hearts try to become stone hearts to regain their position with God. Much like the younger brother had tried to contrive a plan where he would work his way into the family business as a hired hand, thus earning his right to return, sand hearts often become stone hearts in their process of self-restoration. Sand hearts are weary from their license. Stone hearts are burdened with their legalism.

Jesus said, "Come to me, you who are weary and burdened, and I will give you rest. Take my yoke upon you and learn from me, for I am gentle and humble in heart, and you will find rest for your souls. For my yoke is easy and my burden is light" (Matthew

11:28-30). These three short verses offer the Master Key that unlocks the gate to Restoration Road.

"Rest" is synonymous with "restoration." In order to receive it, we must humbly come with a heart of clay, one that recognizes its journey through stone and sand, to the humble heart of the Restorer.

"Take my yoke" means that we become the Restorer's disciple (an idiomatic expression of Jesus' day). "Disciple" means "learner." Consequently, we begin a journey toward wisdom (remember Uncle Derald's new idea for my life?). This requires listening through prayer and obedience. The word "yoke" is often confused with the Greek word used for yoking two animals. However, Jesus' choice of "yoke" was the Greek word zugos. This word was used to describe the yoke used by person carrying buckets of milk or water. The yoke made the load lighter.

That the Restorer's "yoke is easy" means it is not filled with the heavy burden of legalism created by the stone-hearted Pharisees and teachers of the law who had added about 1,500 laws to God's 613 spoken in the first five books of the Old Testament.

That the Restorer's "burden is light" means that the invoice was paid in full. We are forgiven. On the cross, Jesus said, "It is finished" (John 19:30). The Greek word for the phrase, which was among Jesus' last, is teleo. This was the same word written at the top of a Bill of Sale meaning, "paid in full."

I took part in auctioning nearly 250,000 collector cars, each of which had begun life as a clay mold. When they traded hands, each car included a Bill of Sale that was marked "paid in full."

The design and payment for these cars resembles God's work in the world. God made man from the clay of the ground, and He breathed in life (Genesis 2:7; Job 10:9). Man's pride, in which he desired the satisfaction of his desires apart from God, was the first sin. This sin led to an immediate need for restoration. God promised it (Genesis 3:15), and the Restorer came.

Christ paid a world-record price for us (1 Corinthians 6:20). He offers His restorative forgiveness to all, freeing us from the *penalty* of self-restoration, the *power* of self-restoration, and on the other side from the *presence* of self-restoration (namely sin). He appropriates that forgiveness only to those who humble themselves to Him and come to Him with clay hearts—the authentic design of the Designer, the heart of the Restorer who restores us to authenticity from the inside out.

The Restorer has made and continues to make us new (Revelation 21:5). Whoever comes with a thirsty heart of clay, the Restorer gives him the free gift of the water of life (Revelation 22:17). That sounds a lot like that land where we built our house. We transformed the rolling hills into a pond nestled along a dirt road filled with stone and sand. That road led to County Line Church of God, where inside I found communion with God and community with others—the sweet spot where the vertical intersects with the horizontal.

My gate, or the "be" of my heart, shifted from me to the Restorer. I moved from fostering a desire for my position, to pursuing a passion for His grace for life. I transitioned from a desire for my purpose, to a passion for His vision, or light. I changed from a desire for my contentment, to a passion for His peace. I journeyed from a desire for my competence, to a passion for His character of wisdom. I traveled from a desire for my control, to a passion for trusting His power relationally manifested in my life. I left a desire for my security to pursue my passion for His authentic truth. I gave up a desire for my significance in exchange for a passion for His love. I let go of my desire for liberty to sin in lieu of a passion for His forgiving freedom in Christ. The Master Key of full surrender unlocked the gate of my heart to the Restorer.

My road, or the "*do*" of my desires, shifted from me to the Restorer. I moved from closed to open. I went from hiding to seeking. I traveled from protecting my pride and disobeying to praying and obeying. I changed from stubborn to becoming teachable. I ceased trusting myself and began trusting God. I transitioned from denying truth to recognizing and acknowledging truth. I left rejecting others for accepting others. I stopped resisting and withholding forgiveness to surrendering to receiving and offering forgiveness. Restoration Road intersected the vertical with the horizontal and satisfied my desires.

My destination, or my *"go"* of life, shifted from me to the Restorer. I moved from the lock of death to the key of life. I went from the darkness of detouring from God to the light of His vision for my life. I transitioned from living off-line, deaf to God, to living on-line, listening to Him. I traveled from damming His river of wisdom, dense in conflict, to the flow of His wisdom in my life, learning from Him. I no longer went through life as a slave, dividing myself from God, but now I lived as a son, leaning on Him. I gave up going through this journey with a heart of stone or sand that is deceived for a heart of clay that can lead others toward the Restorer. I stopped prioritizing walls in relationships where I was detached, and I built bridges through love. I no longer lived in the dungeon of unforgiveness for my wrongs and those of others, but now I lived waving the white flag of full surrender to freedom in Christ that allowed me to let go. My destination was authentic, life-giving restoration.

The Restorer holds the Master Key of full surrender to unlock the gate of your heart to Restoration Road. When He walked the earth, He clarified inside a Nazareth synagogue that His purpose was to restore: "The Spirit of the Lord is on me, because he has anointed me to preach good news to the poor. He has sent me to proclaim freedom for the prisoners and recovery of sight for the blind, to release the oppressed, to proclaim the year of the Lord's favor" (Luke 4:18-19; cf. Isaiah 61:1, 2).

Jesus was quoting the prophet Isaiah, who went on to record that God's restored ones would rebuild, restore, and renew His kingdom (Isaiah 61:4). They would be priests living at the crossroads of the vertical intersecting with the horizontal; they would be ministers of their God (Isaiah 61:6). With the gates of their hearts unlocked by the Master Key, they would walk Restoration Road to find the celebration of life as they brought that life to others.

When the Restorer unlocks the gate of your heart with His Master Key, He will rebuild your communion with God, restore your community with others, and use you to renew your culture with both. All you need to do is bend the knees of your heart to the Restorer and say, "I can't. You can."

EPILOGUE

I n the fall of 2003, our fourth daughter Haley Joy was born. We gave her the middle name "Joy" because our leap of faith led to joy.

In July 2006, I lost my earthly source of heavenly wisdom. Derald, in his late sixties, passed away after being diagnosed with colon cancer earlier that year. I lost the one who had generously introduced me to Restoration Road.

Less than a year later, I lost one of my greatest encouragers, Grandpa Russell. He lived to be 85, about the same age of his father when he died during my senior year of high school. I probably shared more stories back and forth with him than I did with any other human being.

About a year before Russell passed away, he traveled with Dad and me to the Brickyard for Carburetion Day. While he was entering Dad's Prevost bus, Russell was really proud.

"Mitchell, I just want you to know that I just finished planning my funeral arrangements yesterday, and I ordered a beautiful copper casket," Russell said.

"I know," I replied. "Derald called me." I was joking, setting the stage for him to walk into my funny moment. You see, Russell had suffered from a stroke a few years earlier. This had led to his short-term memory loss. I would always kid him about the benefits that he seemed to leverage from not recalling the past.

"He did?" Russell asked.

"He said you wanted me to use the word *saint* about you at your funeral," I answered.

"I did?" Russell replied. "I want you to use the word *saint* at my funeral?"

"Yeah, don't worry I already know how I'm going to use it," I said to Russell as I looked over at Dad. "I'm going to say, 'Russell appreciated the beauty of a woman; he told many racy stories, but compared to his son, Dean, he was a *saint*.'"

I loved hearing Russell burst out laughing, especially if it was at Dad's expense.

About ten months later, I received a telephone call from Russell asking me to meet him at Parkview Hospital in Fort Wayne where he would hear the results of his heart tests. I finished my appointment and met him at the heart center. We both waited patiently until the doctor entered the examination room.

"Well Russell, you have two problems," the doctor said.

"Only two?" Russell replied, referring optimistically as if he were to have only two flaws.

The first problem was congestive heart failure. The second was its affect on his kidneys. That was the beginning of the end.

Over the course of the next few months, we relived many years of stories. I received more joy from those conversations listening to Russell share his life and his legacy than anything else we discussed. Time after time, I observed how he had faced tragedies and triumphs, along with many moments where he had needed restoration. One tragedy in particular became a defining moment for him on Restoration Road.

In the 1940's, Russell, a farmer in his mid-twenties, was combining the fields of their family farm with his sixteen-year-old brother, Harold, at his side. They had planned to be business partners in a couple of years when Harold turned eighteen. As the two of them discussed their future, Harold, who was athletic, jumped off the combine to chase a rabbit that had caught his eye. After a couple of minutes, Russell felt his combine run into an obstacle in the field. He got out to look, only to encounter a scene that would be forever embedded in his mind: it was his brother, Harold, twisted in the blades of the combine.

Near death, Harold was whisked to the hospital where he underwent weeks of treatment that restored him to health. When his doctors finally told him that he would be released from the hospital the next day, Harold was excited. He had his softball glove in one hand and a softball in the other as he threw the ball repeatedly into his mitt. "I'm going home tomorrow, Rusty," he said enthusiastically to Russell as the glove popped.

That night, Harold went to sleep without being given his medication to assist in the prevention of blood clots.

Harold never returned home.

When I look back at Russell's life, I realize that he had for decades carried a major tragedy with him that required restoration. While Russell lived his next sixty years on this earth without Harold, there was only one way that he would be restored with his brother.

Jesus' half-brother James penned a picture of the brevity of life, "Why, you do not even know what will happen tomorrow. What is your life? You are a mist that appears for a little while and then vanishes" (James 4:14). When I think about that picture, I remember exhaling my moist breath on the cold glass of my elementary school bus window, then writing my name in it. God exhales our life into the clay of the ground as the Designer, and continues to inhale and exhale through us as the Restorer. We are God's mist. As we walk, He is writing His name in our hearts, our desires, and our lives: "Like water spilled on the ground, which cannot be recovered, so we must die. But God does not take life away; instead, he devises ways so that a banished person may not remain estranged from him" (2 Samuel 14:14).

When I think about my four beautiful daughters, my wife, and the lives of Derald and Russell, I realize that one day we are all going to return to the ground from which we came. The question remains, "What part of the ground will our hearts resemble: sand, stone, or clay?" The condition of our spiritual hearts at our departure will determine where our hearts travel into the next life: *north* or *south*. The time given to each of us on earth is a gift from the Restorer; our task is to leave a legacy to restore future generations. Keep that life and lose it. Give that life and keep it. Die once; live twice. Live once; die twice. While we travel, there is only one road that travels north. It is called "Restoration Road."

Imagine if we lived convinced that what God has in store for us is more authentic than anything we could ever achieve or acquire on our own. In the words of Russell, "If I can get you convinced, I can get them convinced." We can walk together on Restoration Road, restoring others to authenticity. It all begins when you say to Christ the Restorer, "I can't. You can."

I believe the father in the parable knew firsthand what his sons were going through. He knew because he had been there too. He had faced the same heart challenges as both of his sons, but he had always returned to live restored to authenticity. He chose to leave his legacy as a humble heart of clay.

I imagine Russell and Derald like the father in the parable—they understood my struggle of sand and stone because they had been there and failed. As I listened to the people on those Wednesday night meetings, I understood their struggles with sand and stone hearts because I had been there too.

Several months after Russell's memorial service, I boarded a plane to the Orient. A friend had invited me to speak about sand, stone, and clay in one of the most unexpected places. Fourteen hours later, I stepped off the plane into the humidity of the Philippines. Over the next seven days, I shared my journey on Restoration Road—from the times when I watched the teacher share a Bible story on the green felt board, to my prayer in County Line's chapel; from the rise, fall, and rise again of my auctioneering life, to the years when God restored me into a man who lived with a heart of clay.

I traveled with my friend through a gate, down a road, and to the destination of a city dump just outside Metro Manila where more than 14,000 families live in extreme poverty. It was difficult for me to comprehend the images that my eyes were burning on my heart as we met the children and their parents who literally lived hand-to-mouth, day-to-day. I had the opportunity to share what God had taught me as I journeyed from sand and stone to clay. I encountered even more stories of those who were traveling their own unique journeys on Restoration Road as they were being restored to authenticity.

From that experience, I was reminded that God had taken me from pursuing the rich for my benefit to pursuing the poor for theirs. I learned that both ends of the socioeconomic spectrum are in need of the Restoration Road: rich and poor, whether licentious or legalistic, whether sand or stone.

Restoration Road is a journey that we travel our entire lives. Our steps include continual choices, thoughts, prayers, and feelings about to whom or what we will surrender the four chambers of our hearts, our four primary desires, and our three resources of life. We will frequently approach speed bumps of sand or stone on our journeys fully surrendered to and fully aligned with the Restorer. Every encounter with another human being will offer yet another opportunity to reflect the design of the Designer, our Restorer.

As I continued to participate in the Restorer's transformational work in the lives of others, I discovered that He was leading me outside the four walls of Blackhawk Ministries. I clearly sensed His prompting for me to communicate a message that would connect both those in ministry and the marketplace with the Restorer. After witnessing His regeneration of all colors, backgrounds, ages, and socio-economic classes, I responded to the Restorer's perfectly timed fashioning in my clay heart that would transition me into this new part of my journey.

Regardless of where your life has taken you, whether a sand heart, a stone heart, or a clay heart, your story is not finished. In fact, the next step always provides a new beginning. There is one road that leads to a life that loves God and loves others. It is the road that you were designed to seek, the authenticity discovered only on Restoration Road.

As a fellow traveler who is still on the dirt road of being restored to authenticity, I leave you with this prayer.

When my heart is hard help me to sow
Where my heart is shallow help me to grow
Whatever my heart's thorns help me to let go
And the Restorer answers,
"Listen to Me speak, I knock at your door,
Seek Me, find Me, I will give you more.
Loosen your grip, return to Me, I will restore
When your heart is open, into your life holy rain I will pour."

THE LEGEND OF J-249

At a height of 5 feet 4 inches, John Factor may have been small in stature, but he was a man who lived large. The son of a Jewish Rabbi and half-brother to cosmetic giant Max Factor, John made a fortune during the height of the "Roaring 20's." When Duesenberg introduced their Model J in 1928, it was hailed as the finest motorcar in the world. And Factor knew he had to own a Duesenberg!

In 1929 he purchased J-143, a Murphy-bodied Convertible Coupe. Respected as one of the world's foremost builders of stylish custom bodied automobiles, Walter Murphy Coachbuilders was located in Pasadena, California.

According to the Auburn Cord Duesenberg Newsletter No. 9 (1977), Factor returned J-143 to the Duesenberg factory just a few months after its purchase. It was used as a down payment toward a second Duesenberg. Automobile Quarterly Volume 30 #4 reports that Factor then purchased J-249, one of only five short-wheelbase Torpedo Roadsters built by Murphy Coachbuilders. Featuring a stylish disappearing top and a short-raked back windshield, he must have been impressed with the unique boattail design and the highly polished aluminum accenting the top of the hood, doors, and upper rear deck. It was far and away more dramatic in appearance than the convertible coupe.

What would inspire a man of means to own such an automobile? A more thorough look into John Factor may reveal his motives.

Put simply, John Factor was one of the most charismatic and elusive criminals in history. Factor was also known as Jake "the Barber" Factor.

Having been raised in the US, in 1923 John Factor returned to England where, for four years ending in 1928, Factor sold stock in a nonexistent diamond mine in South Africa. He garnered more than £5 million from this scam, and his victim list read like a "who's who" of English society—including several members of the royal family and the chief of Scotland Yard. Facing prosecution in England, Jake "the Barber" fled to France and other parts of the world, including Monte Carlo, where he orchestrated a scheme that broke the bank using rigged tables.

Arnold Rothstein, an infamous New York con man, funded Factor's stock swindle. Rothstein is well known for rigging the 1919 World Series, paying members of the Chicago White Sox to throw the series. Rothstein was murdered in 1928 after refusing to pay a $320,000 gambling debt.

Now in Chicago, Factor became one of the Windy City's most colorful characters. A public relations genius, he secured favorable press for himself and Al Capone, with whom he was in league in exchange for protection. Touted as good Samaritans, the press reported stories of Factor passing out food packages to the poor from his Duesenberg, and Capone supplying food for local soup kitchens.

In 1933, despite his good deeds, the courts granted an extradition order to return Factor to the U.K. to face charges for his stock scam. However, rather than be extradited, Factor was allowed a stay after his son was abducted by a competitor of Capone's.

At this time in Chicago, kidnapping for ransom had become big business. Roger "the Terrible" Touhy used kidnapping as a means to control other gangs. In April of 1933, Factor's son Jerome was abducted. A ransom of $50,000 was paid and eight days later Jerome was returned. The sympathetic press earned Factor a delay in his deportation hearing.

Conspiring with Capone later in 1933, Factor staged his own kidnapping. As Jake "the Barber" left the Capone-owned Dell Roadhouse near Morton Grove, Illinois, in his Duesenberg, he was forced off the road by a band of six heavily-armed thugs (men on his own payroll). They yanked Factor out of the car and made off with him. As a result of the staged kidnapping, Jake was unable to make his next deportation hearing. He turned up weeks later, claiming to have escaped from the kidnappers, and he fingered Touhy for the crime.

Touhy was convicted and sentenced to 199 years in prison. In 1959, 25 years and nine months to the day after he entered prison, Touhy was granted parole. Just 23 days after his release from prison, Roger Touhy was gunned down by mob hitmen. While being rushed to the hospital, Touhy told a newsman, "I've been expecting it. The bastards never forget!" Touhy lived only an hour, dying of shock and loss of blood.

In 1955, Factor became the front man for the Chicago mob in Las Vegas, taking over the Stardust Casino after its creator, crime figure Tony Cornero, died mysteriously. About to be deported back to England in 1962, Jake gave the Kennedy administration $25,000 in cash to help fund the failed Bay of Pigs invasion. His generosity earned a Presidential pardon from John F. Kennedy. Factor then sold the Stardust Casino for $14 million and claimed bankruptcy.

Jake spent the last twenty years of his life as a benefactor to California's black ghettos, spending millions of dollars building churches, gyms, parks and low-cost housing in these poverty-stricken areas. Three U.S. senators, the mayor of Los Angeles and several hundred African-Americans attended his funeral.

What was John Factor's reason for owning a Duesenberg? Was it status? Was it "keeping up with the Capones"? Was it for outrunning his enemies or the law? We may never know. Before his death, Factor reminisced fondly of his exploits driving his Duesenberg.

The opportunity to own and drive the finest automobile of the coach-built era still compels collectors worldwide today. Simply stated, "It's a Doozy."

What happened to J-249?

Records indicate that J-249 was registered in London, England, by the Honorable John Douglas Berry on June 23, 1937. Surviving the Battle of Britain, and making it unscathed to the end of World War II, it changed hands several times through dealers throughout England. Sold March 4, 1946, to Osmond Philip Raphael, London, E.C., it was last taxed Dec. 2, 1949, and then went to breakers (a salvage yard) in Birmingham.

In 1950, the engine and panel gauges went to John Morris of SU Carburetors. In 1952, the engine and gauges went to Brian Morgan, Birmingham. The engine was later installed in a Bentley. The Bentley eventually came to America. Ray Wolff mentions in the 1988 No. 3 ACD NL, "the engine is in use in the U.S.A."

Leo Gephart located and purchased the original Bentley's engine and exchanged it for J-249. The now-loose engine was purchased by George Walther of Dayton, Ohio. Walther was in the process of restoring a Murphy Convertible Sedan, using engine J-249, when he passed away. The far-from-completed project was purchased by Richard Losee of Provo, Utah. Upon discovering J-249's unique origins, the rarity of the Murphy Torpedo Roadster body style, and with a strong desire to return a "lost" Duesenberg to the world, the decision was made to re-create J-249 as produced "in the day."

Using two factory photographs supplied by Jon Bill, the Archivist of the Auburn Cord Duesenberg Museum, and detailed photographs of an original Torpedo Roadster on display at the Museum, the body was faithfully re-created as originally produced. Body panels were formed from aluminum, and then attached to the hardwood frame. A distinguishing feature of Murphy-built bodies, and particularly the Torpedo Roadsters, was the polished upper body panels, as well as style-line divisions where paint meets polish. Hundreds of hours were required to polish the upper-body panels to a mirror finish.

The raked-back windshield was cast using a hand-formed plywood pattern to form the sand mold. The window frames and all the chrome trim on the body were produced from brass sheet or extrusions, and formed to match the originals. The trim strips on the running boards were formed using specially made rollers, and the rubber inserts were cast using an original sample as a mold. Outside door handles were replicated by enlarging the original photograph to reveal the unique details. The lower rumble-step plate was reproduced using the shadow evident in the original factory photograph.

Original and reproduction Duesenberg parts were found literally all over the world: gauges came from the UK and Canada, original Duesenberg fenders from Arizona. The search for the correct Stromberg wiper motors took a full four years. The accurate honeycomb radiator core came from New Zealand, and the exacting reproduction frame was sourced from Pennsylvania. Duesenberg expert Brian Joseph at Classic and Exotic Service supplied many of the original and reproduction parts, including the Leo Gephart/ Brian Joseph manufactured dual carburetor supercharger.

The engine was completely rebuilt. Much stronger than the original, Carrillo H-beam connecting rods were used as well as Aries racing pistons. The cylinder head received hardened seats and modern valves to accept modern fuels. To enhance performance, the camshafts were ground with a slightly higher profile. As was common during the era, a supercharger was installed to increase engine output from 265 horsepower to 320 horsepower. Today, the engine is strong and powerful.

An original Hi-Flex transmission was completely rebuilt using new gears and bearings. The Auto-Pulse fuel pumps were rebuilt and function properly. The original aluminum connecting rods, stamped "J-249," and stored in an original Duesenberg factory wooden case, remain with the vehicle.

Appearance options include a Winterfront radiator, a NOS Marshall Merks external exhaust with stainless conduit covers, fully covered side mount spare tires with rear view mirrors, dual trumpet horns, wing windows, and finally, dual Pilot Ray driving lights that turn with the steering to illuminate the road ahead. To our knowledge, J-249 was the only Duesenberg ordered with a front bumper installed on the rear of the car, and this detail was faithfully included in the restoration.

This magnificent Duesenberg is on display at the Kruse Automotive and Carriage Museum in Auburn, Indiana. The quality is evident after a painstaking, no-expense-spared, four-plus-year restoration recently completed by Kevin and Jason Marsh of Salt City Specialties, Utah. Every effort was made to assure concours quality attention to detail and correctness. This splendid automobile and restoration superbly reflects the power, beauty and authenticity that is truly Duesenberg.

Reprinted with the permission of Kevin Marsh,
historian and restorer of the mighty J-249 Duesenberg

RESTORATION ROAD

The Master Key to a New and Satisfied Life of Authenticity

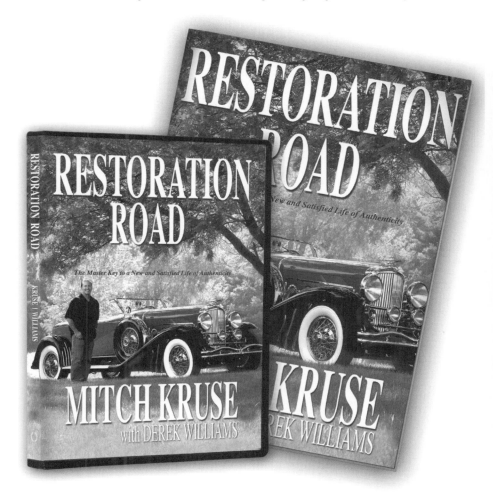

Discover your restoration journey through a 12-week experience

(DVD and Study Guide ideal for individuals or groups)

www.mitchkruse.com

forgotten stories

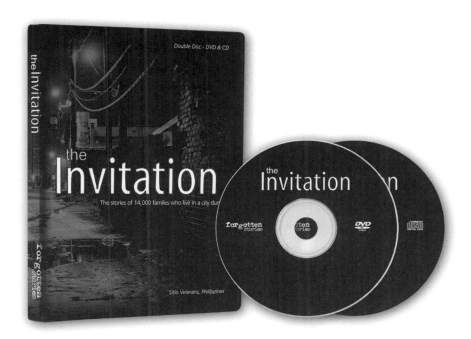

Mitch travels with his friends to the Philippines to capture on film the forgotten stories of the 14,000 families who live in a Manila garbage dump. While there, Mitch discovers children who are overcoming staggering obstacles because they have answered, "Yes," to the greatest invitation in history.

Set to original music, this project illuminates Christ's message and ministry to forgotten children, making it an unparalleled resource for any group desiring to serve those in need.

To order the DVD/CD visit:
www.forgottenstories.org

www.mitchkruse.com